Toute Allure

Falling in Love in Rural France

McArthur & Company
Toronto

First published in Canada in 2011 by
McArthur & Company
322 King Street West, Suite 402
Toronto, Ontario
M5V 1J2
www.mcarthur-co.com

First UK edition published in 2010 by Summersdale

Library and Archives Canada Cataloguing in Publication

Wheeler, Karen, 1967-
        Toute allure : falling in love in rural France / Karen Wheeler.

ISBN 978-1-55278-935-3

        1. Wheeler, Karen, 1967-. 2. Fashion editors--Great Britain--
Biography. 3. British--France--Biography. 4. Poitou-Charentes
(France)--Social life and customs. I. Title.

TT505.W46A3 2011   391.0092   C2010-907604-4

Cover Image © Andy Robert Davies
Printed in Canada by Webcom

10 9 8 7 6 5 4 3 2 1

To Frances and David with thanks for a wonderful gift

Karen Wheeler is a former fashion editor for the *Mail on Sunday* and currently writes for the *Financial Times' How to Spend It* magazine and the *Daily Mail*. Her work has appeared in *ES* and *You* magazines, *Sunday Times Style* and numerous international publications.

Contents

Note from the Author

There are several villages called Villiers in France, but my village is not one of them. I have changed names, places and details throughout the book in order to protect the innocent (and the not so innocent). I have also taken some liberties with the timing of events in order to make for a better narrative.

Chapter 1

May

I ROLL OFF the ferry to a moody spring morning in Le Havre. The sky is as many shades of grey as the Dior boutique in Paris (fifty-seven according to a recent press release) but a pale lemon sun is rising on the horizon. I'm back in the land of the illicit love affair and the *fosse septique* after a two-night trip to London for a work assignment.

On paper it was an opportunity I couldn't refuse: the chance to interview world-famous fashion designer Rick Dorff about his new perfume. In reality, I drove over 500 kilometres and spent a total of fourteen hours on a ferry for precisely thirty minutes of the iconic designer's time. Gallingly, he wasted five of those precious minutes discussing the highly camp decor of his hotel suite; another fifteen minutes on pedestrian observations on the fragrance market and ten minutes rattling off minutiae about his new scent, Of The Night – all of which I had just read in the glossy dossier of marketing material I was handed before the interview. And just when it got interesting –

he revealed that his favourite smell was cigarettes and Scotch on someone's breath – the American PR girl cleared her throat ostentatiously and called time on our meeting, declaring that Mr Dorff had to leave for his in-store appearance (despite the fact he wasn't scheduled to appear at the department store in question for at least five hours).

Later, as I watched the darkly handsome designer – also known as 'Mr Raunch' because of his provocative ad campaigns – signing scent bottles and smoothly greeting his public, I chatted to the store's creative director, who had spent eight months preparing for today's thirty-minute appearance. (The designer's life is obviously parcelled out in half-hour slots.) I shuddered as she recounted the instructions dispensed by 'Mr Dorff's people' in New York. They included a constant supply of sushi and San Pellegrino mineral water served at room temperature – so far so predictable – as well as purple carpet for the public to queue upon and flattering amber lighting overhead. It was a sobering reminder of my former life as a fashion editor, in a surreal world where a football squad of people would deliberate over the size of the teaspoons to be used at a designer launch. I know, *I know*, that the devil is in the detail and that there is a lot to be said for being a perfectionist, but no one ever went to their deathbed wishing they'd used a different sized teaspoon. In rural France, people worry about more basic things such as: 'Will I make it to the supermarket/DIY store/post office before it closes for two hours in the middle of the day?'; 'Will my roof hold up in the next vigorous Poitevin downpour?' and 'Should I open a bottle of red or white with dinner?'

Still, it was a coup to have landed an exclusive interview with Dorff and the trip also gave me a much needed shopping fix, culminating in a forty-five-minute trolley dash around

Sainsbury's in Portsmouth. As I accelerate past a Portuguese truck it gives me a warm glow to think of my car boot packed with cans of chopped organic tomatoes (very difficult to find in France and very expensive when you do), BRITA water filters (ditto), washing powder (also surprisingly expensive thanks to the dire exchange rate), as well as organic watercress, halloumi cheese, M&S chocolate ginger biscuits and several cans of Dulux undercoat.

Thankfully the paint is not for me but for Sarah Merryweather. My life in France no longer revolves around close encounters with toxic chemicals or waiting patiently for artisans. The house is finished – or as finished as it's ever going to be while I'm living there. There is a huge attic still waiting to be converted and a long list of minor jobs to complete, but they can wait for the next owner. Maison Coquelicot, or 'house of the wild poppy', is fully plumbed, tiled and floored and warm as the hug of a pashmina.

I'm delighted to be back. Driving towards the buttermilk sun, I think back to the moment when I arrived here in darkness (literally and metaphorically) over two years ago, accompanied only by a car full of designer clothes and the baggage of a painful break-up and wondering if I had made a terrible mistake. Back then, I had no family or friends waiting for me, just a dilapidated village house and a year of hard labour, mostly spent up a ladder with a paintbrush.

Now, I have friends, lots of them – some of whom I love enough to consider family – and I have plans. With typical bad timing, I arrived here two years ago on the cusp of winter but I'm returning from my latest trip on the doorstep of spring. It feels like everything is before me. Or that could just be the euphoria I always feel when driving off the overnight ferry, having spent a torturous night in the 'club' lounge – all cabins were booked – surrounded by people snoring so loudly that I'm sure it constituted a breach of health and safety.

Feeling energised by the early morning sun, I speed along the dual carriageway that leads out of Le Havre, past the Novotel and towards the autoroutes. There's just one small problem: I'm not exactly sure which motorway I should be on. There is a roundabout ahead of me and I circle it half a dozen times before taking a wild guess. Unfortunately, I choose the wrong one and rather than driving due south to Poitiers, I take a detour to St Malo, adding about an hour and over 100 kilometres to my journey.

As I fly along the grey autoroute, the sun bleaches out the surrounding countryside, making it look like an overexposed photograph, and I am momentarily blinded by a mass of diffused lemon light. But I'm always happy to be making the trip from the ferry port to Villiers. For large stretches, north of Tours, you have the autoroute entirely to yourself – no suicidal drivers suddenly appearing out of nowhere in your rear windscreen with a hand-held mobile clamped to their ear, tailgating you at 120 kilometres per hour; no truck drivers flashing their lights and leering down at your thighs as you overtake them. It's (almost) worth the €80 in tolls that the round trip costs, just for that.

There is so much to look forward to in the months ahead: lengthening evenings, bike rides through fields of sunflowers or wild meadows of bluebells and poppies (just like the 1970s Flake ad), and several months of *fêtes*, *vide-greniers* (car boot sales) and barbecues in friends' gardens. And I cannot wait to get back to see if Andy Lawton has called.

It is several weeks since the former member of Her Majesty's Armed Forces – who had just arrived in France to renovate a barn – stopped to provide roadside assistance when my car broke down on a quiet country road. The least I could do was give him my telephone number when he asked for it, before he (literally) drove off into the sunset. He hasn't called yet but I live in hope. And I know how things are when you first move to France; he is probably camping out in a hay bale, making use of his army survival skills while he waits for France Telecom to come and connect his phone line.

I am *so* hoping that he will call. For a start, we are pretty much neighbours. In the French countryside, distances shrink like cashmere in a hot wash, so that if you live 20 kilometres away from someone, it feels like you are close enough to pop round and borrow a cup of sugar or (more likely) an onion after the 7.00 p.m. watershed, when everything is closed for miles around. Secondly, I could give him the benefit of my superior knowledge regarding, amongst other things, woodburner placement and which roofer is most likely to turn up and do the job before you are shipped off to a retirement home.

Even if Andy Lawton doesn't call – it's possible he has lost my number in the hay bales, cement mixers and roof tiles – there is every chance I will bump into him at an expat event in the coming months. It probably won't be at the bird-watching group or Le Club Floral de Bléssy, where Vanessa Carter, 'a very gifted floral demonstrator', is soon to 'transform flowers and foliage into something truly exciting and exquisitely stunning', according to the latest newsletter from the Le Club de L'Entente Cordiale, or 'Club of the Cordial Understanding'. This expat-run association is designed to encourage interaction between expats and local French people (although why the locals would want to interact with us when they've probably got enough friends already is a mystery).

It is possible, given his military background, that Andy Lawton might sign up for 'The Line of Demarcation', a forthcoming bus tour that someone called Bob Beale is organising. 'Bob has it in mind to hire a coach and someone really knowledgeable to lead us round the line that marked the border between occupied and free France during the 1939–1945 war,' said the Entente Cordiale newsletter. 'Prepare to be surprised and amazed! It will be fascinating!' But even the possibility of climbing on board a coach with Andy Lawton is not quite enough to make it fascinating to me.

It's more likely that I'll bump into him at someone's barbecue. Or he might join the Entente Cordiale's 'Wining and Dining Club', in which case we could get to know each other better over a stuffed cabbage leaf – a Poitevin delicacy – or a brick of farmed salmon, pulled from the deep freeze and served up in an artery-clogging butter sauce. (I feel disloyal for saying so, but excellent goats' cheeses aside, my region is a little lacking on the gastronomy front and in many restaurants the food is borderline inedible.)

Although I only met Andy Lawton for ten minutes, and for most of that he was lying under my car, I have pinned a lot of hope on that one chance meeting. For, despite all the reasons I have to feel cheerful, there is still one thing very much missing from my life in France. In the two years that I've lived here, I've gone back and forth between Villiers and London dozens of times for work by plane, train and tatty Golf. And, particularly as I struggle off the Eurostar or the TGV, laden with M&S organic vegetables, I long to have someone to rush back to. Thankfully, I am no longer pining for Eric, my former French boyfriend and the man that I imagined I would marry. But despite a few promising encounters over the past two years, no one has arrived to take Eric's place. As I drive towards Villiers – having found the right autoroute – I think how much better my life in France could be, if only someone was waiting for me.

There is, however, a very big surprise waiting for me when I arrive back at Maison Coquelicot late on Saturday afternoon – a posse of dark-haired men hanging around outside the house next door. The small, narrow house – previously rented by a quiet, elderly man – has been unoccupied for many months but, in the few days that I have been away, it seems to have been taken over by a Hispanic football team. They are obviously having a house-warming party: the loud music emanating from an upstairs window can be heard as far away as the village square. They are smoking and laughing, drinking beer and looking very cheerful in the weak spring sunshine – all dark tans, taut muscles and deep masculine laughter. They are speaking, or rather shouting, in a language that is not French but possibly Spanish or Portuguese and they watch with interest as I get out of my car and open up the shutters of Maison Coquelicot.

A couple of them say 'Bonjour' and nod politely in my direction.

I say 'Bonjour' back, despite being very perturbed by the noise. I came to France for peace and quiet, not a street party. Goodness knows what my elderly French neighbours make of it. Rue St Benoit has probably never experienced anything like this – although no one seems to be complaining. Feeling self-conscious with so many pairs of eyes watching, I ferry the canned tomatoes, baked beans and other British delicacies into the house. How many of them, I wonder, have moved in next door? The house is small, with just two bedrooms and no outside space, which is probably why they have taken over the street outside.

I close the front door and unpack my bags, floorboards reverberating to the sound of Bruce Springsteen's 'Born to Run', and I try not to panic about this new development. The party going on outside my front door is probably a one-off. Why shouldn't my new neighbours have their friends around to celebrate the fact that they have just moved in?

The phone rings – I only just hear it above the music – and it's my friend Mathilde to ask if I'm going to the night market in Villiers next week.

'What's that noise? Are you having a party?' she asks.

'Not exactly,' I say. 'I've got new neighbours.'

'Well, it sounds like they're having a party in your house,' she says.

In a way, they sort of are. I remember reading in my purchase documents that the two houses used to be one many decades ago, before a family dispute led to the house being spliced down the middle. This means that my bathroom effectively juts into the house next door and, as I am now discovering, we are separated by the thinnest plasterboard partition and no sound insulation. The loud, macho voices and music sound like they are coming from inside my house.

I was looking forward to a quiet evening, chatting to friends on the phone and catching up with emails. Instead, I shove some airline earplugs into my ears and hope the party will end soon. But it doesn't. It continues until the early hours of the morning. I don't complain. Live and let live, I tell myself. After all, it's not like my new neighbours are going to be doing this every night.

Chapter 2

Darling

ON SUNDAY MORNING, I drive over to Romagne, to drop off Sarah Merryweather's paint. I haven't seen her for a while and she has a new little black dog called Biff. He hurls himself on and off the sofa when I arrive in her charming farmhouse kitchen, and runs around in little circles of excitement. Sarah and Steve's other dog, Milou, a snowy white terrier with a black patch over one eye, is also very cute. How do they do it? They always seem to find rescue dogs with superior genes, no psychological problems and all eyes, ears and limbs intact.

By contrast, when I went to Battersea Dogs' Home in London several years ago to find a dog to rescue, I filled in a long questionnaire about myself – likes, dislikes, favourite pastimes, colour of my hair, etc. – and was matched with a large, depressed greyhound called Alan.

'You've got to be kidding me,' I said. 'I live in a top floor flat. He's enormous.'

While I felt genuinely sorry for Alan – he'd been waiting for a new home for a long time – I'd been hoping that my canine soulmate would be a sleek viszla or something small and cute like a cocker spaniel.

'It's a myth that greyhounds need a lot of exercise and outdoor space,' said Alan's handler. 'The most important thing is human company. He'd be very happy lying at your feet or under your desk all day.' She pointed to a sign on the wall entitled 'Common Myths About Greyhounds'. But with Alan in my flat, there wouldn't actually have been any room for me, let alone a desk for him to lie under.

Eventually, we compromised on a stocky Staffordshire bull terrier called Delia. Delia had dominance issues but the Battersea rehoming section seemed to think I could handle her because I'd had an English bull terrier as a childhood pet. I went home to think about it, armed with a set of instructions designed to establish myself as the dominant female. I would, for example, have to confiscate Delia's toys from time to time, pretend to eat from her bowl to show her who was boss, and vary my routine, so that Delia wouldn't know I was going out. I got cold feet. The truth was that I hadn't felt a real visceral connection with Delia and she wasn't blessed with winning looks or a friendly demeanour. People would probably cross the road when they saw us coming and, at the end of the day, there was only room for one diva in my household – and it wasn't Delia. But had I been presented with a darling little terrier like Biff, I would have installed him under my desk faster than you can say 'Bonio', with or without dominance issues.

Biff, it transpires, came from a privately run animal shelter near Bergerac called The Phoenix Rescue. I've met several Phoenix alumni before – many of my friends' dogs seem to come from there – and they all seem to be blessed with lovely temperaments and superior canine genes.

'The name really suits him,' I say, as he nudges his wet nose against my ankles.

'Yes, he's a cheeky little fella,' says Sarah, a former IT lecturer from Wales. Although she is in her fifties, and has three grown-up children, she could pass for a generation younger thanks to her elfin face and impish smile. In her teaching days it must have been difficult to tell her apart from her students, as she dresses in such a youthful, laid-back style – skinny-cut jeans and layered tops with Ugg boots and a hooded parka in winter; flip-flops and floaty chiffon tops in summer. Her passions in life are many and include dancing the tango, reflexology, aromatherapy, playing the flute, and dogs – her now deceased spaniel Charlie, was, I think, the great love of her life. She is also a fantastic cook, specialising in lavish roasts, old-fashioned puddings and traditional farmhouse fare. She entertains frequently and on a large scale, and her annual New Year's Day party – which is where I first met her, having tagged along with another guest – is one of the most hotly anticipated social events in the region, not least because it entails a fantastic feast of home-cooked Indian food.

Sarah, as far as I can tell, has never been short of a man in her life – she met her current boyfriend Steve in France when he came to build her some kitchen cabinets – and by her own admission, plans to whizz into her grave at the very last moment with a bottle of Bombay Sapphire in one hand and a chocolate bar in the other, 'having thoroughly enjoyed the ride'. Our outlooks are not dissimilar. The two of us are always talking about going on a diet – she really doesn't need to – or giving up alcohol for a month, although in reality neither of us ever manages more than a week.

'He seems very happy,' I say, nodding at Biff. 'He doesn't look like he was mistreated?'

'No, apparently he was thrown out of a van. But now that we know him, Steve and I think he probably jumped out of his own volition. He's very curious.'

'Yes, I can see that,' I say, as he stands on his hind legs and starts to rummage in my bag, which I've left on a chair. He seems to have a lot of self-esteem.

'But he did have mange,' says Sarah. 'It's possible that his former owners couldn't afford to treat it.'

'Mange?'

'It's a skin infection. He was a real mess when we got him. Bald patches and tufts of hair missing everywhere. To be honest it was embarrassing taking him out in public.'

'Oh the poor thing,' I say, removing my shiny black Chanel wallet from between his dazzlingly white teeth. 'He's such a darling.'

He sits down in front of me, his bobbed tail twitching with excitement, and flashes me a big doggy smile. He's as black as a YSL *smoking* ensemble, all shaggy hair and eager expression, with eyes like jet beads and big, gorilla-like paws that seem out of proportion to the rest of his body. He's really adorable. I can't help thinking he would be the perfect size for my home: a little smaller than a cocker spaniel, but big enough to be a real dog rather than something that could be carried around in a handbag.

'If ever you need someone to look after him while you're away, I'd be happy to do it,' I find myself saying.

Biff pitches his head to one side, and fixes me with his button eyes, as if considering my offer.

'Would you?' says Sarah. 'I might well take you up on it when Steve and I go back to the UK in July. Shall we go upstairs and start?' Sarah is giving me a free session of reflexology as a thank you for bringing the paint back from the UK. 'The dogs can stay down here.'

Milou is curled up on the sofa, but Biff has other plans. As Sarah opens the door into the main sitting room, Biff is through it in a flash of shaggy fur. He rushes up the staircase and then dashes back and forth along the corridor before following us into the room where Sarah does her reflexology.

Sarah just smiles. 'Are you OK with him staying up here?' she asks.

'Of course,' I say, pulling off my riding boots and sitting in the big white reclining chair. Sarah sits on a stool at the end and takes one of my feet on her knee. Biff gives a small bark and leaps up onto my knees.

Sarah laughs indulgently. 'He doesn't want to be left out,' she says, as he starts to lick my toes. 'No Biff, you *can't* help.'

He's so cute. I've only known this little creature for a quarter of an hour and already I feel a massive spark of affection.

'So have you seen Jon yet?' Sarah asks as she starts to work the pressure points on my toes.

'Jon who?'

'Jon Wakeman. He's back.'

'He is?' I say, sitting upright in the reclining chair. 'Since when?'

'Last week. He's left his girlfriend.'

This is surprising news. I haven't heard from Jon since January. It all looked so promising when, after Sarah's party on New Year's Day, and after many weeks of friendship and attending expat Christmas gatherings together, he declared that he was in love with me. At the time I thought it was too good to be true – and it was. He went back to the UK a week or so later to finish with his girlfriend – a relationship that had been floundering for some time – and didn't return.

'So what brings him back now?' I ask, trying to hide the fact that I am very pleased and extremely excited by this news.

'Well, I think that's really obvious,' says Sarah. 'Steve and I bumped into him in the Intermarché last week and he was asking about you.'

'But why did he stay in the UK when he was supposed to come back to me?'

'It's probably better if you hear it from him.'

'I'm looking forward to that,' I say, feeling angry as I remember the phone call he made to tell me that he had decided to stay in the UK indefinitely.

'Right,' I had said. 'So no wedding in a field in November as promised. No flowers in my hair. No *steak frites* or lashings of pink Laurent Perrier.'

'I'm afraid not,' he replied. 'In fact, it looks like I'm going to have to sell the house in France.'

'Can you at least tell me why or what made you change your mind?' I asked.

'It's probably best if I don't,' he replied. 'I'm really, really sorry. But please don't wait for me.'

And now, four months later, he is back. 'So has he returned to sell his house?' I ask Sarah.

'No, I think he's back to stay,' she replies, as Biff puts his paws on my shoulders and starts to lick my face. 'He said he was planning to get it finished as soon as possible and open it up as a B & B. *Biff, get down!*'

'It's all right. I think he likes me,' I say, kissing his button nose.

'I think he does,' says Sarah. 'And he's not the only one.'

I drive home along narrow back roads, past fields sprouting new green shoots and thinly spaced blades of grass, thinking of Jon. To be honest, I'm not sure how I feel about him coming back. I'd sort of erased him from my mind – we were, after all, only together for a matter of weeks – but I think that, deep down, I always knew that he would return. And now that he is back in the same country and a 15 kilometre drive from me, I wonder if it is possible to pick up where we left off in January? I have thought of him frequently since then, wondering what happened to keep him in the UK. I guess a lot hinges on the quality of his explanation.

As I drive into rue St Benoit, the sound of the samba played at very high volume greets me. The Portuguese neighbours are really going for it. The blue sky and early spring sunshine have brought them out of their house – all bright colours, board shorts and T-shirts. A couple of them are sitting on the curb drinking beer. I go straight into my house, ignoring their *'Bonjours'* – which are starting to seem like harassment – and avoiding eye contact. Once inside, I put in my earplugs and wish to God they'd go and party in someone else's house.

I don't have to wait long for Jon to arrive. On Monday morning I'm enjoying the peace and silence – the Portuguese neighbours are at work – when the doorbell rings. I throw open the bedroom window and see him standing below. He looks sheepish and is carrying a box of Ferrero Rocher, a fact I try to ignore. (They might impress at the ambassador's reception but they are not the way to woo me.) His hair is as unruly as ever and his face looks healthy and weatherbeaten. He must have been spending a lot of time outdoors in the UK, probably with his father who is a gamekeeper.

I go downstairs to let him in.

'I'm sorry,' he says.

'You should be.'

'Can I come in?'

'I suppose so,' I say, feigning reluctance, when in fact I am delighted to see him and cannot wait to hear what he has to say. I invite him into *le petit salon* – the small, book-lined room always looks full to capacity, even with just one guest sitting on the worn leather sofa – and gesture for him to sit down.

'So what brings you here after four months of no news?' I ask.

'I had to see you,' he says. 'I've thought about you non-stop since January. I wanted to see you so badly.'

'But not so badly to come back? Or even phone?'

'I've come to explain,' he says, looking suitably penitent.

'I'm all ears.'

'Jenny was ill,' he says. 'I went back to tell her it was over and before I could say a word, she told me she might have to go into hospital because of a problem with her heart.'

'Oh my God!'

'It's a hereditary thing that's been in her family for generations. She had to have loads of tests. I just couldn't leave her.'

'Is she OK now?' I ask, feeling immediately mollified. As excuses go, this is pretty good. It doesn't explain why he cut off all contact with me, but it takes the edge off my anger. And I'm actually pleased that he did the decent thing in the circumstances and stayed with Jenny.

'Yeah, she's in the clear but for a few months she was really worried.'

'But why couldn't you tell me that over the phone?'

'I dunno. I thought you'd be really cross and upset. And I didn't know how things would turn out or how long I'd have to stay with her.' Hmm. I'm not entirely convinced by this – he could have given me at least an inkling of what was going on – but the male mind works in strange ways.

'So you waited for her to get better and then dumped her?' I say.

'We came to a joint agreement to end it but remain friends,' he says. 'Anyway, I want to live in France and she doesn't, so that made things easier.'

He shifts in his seat, still clutching the box of Ferrero Rocher.

'So have you found someone else?' he asks.

I shake my head. 'No. But you can't just waltz back into my life and pick up where you left off.'

His face breaks into a broad smile. 'My darling minx, you've no idea how happy that makes me. I've had so many sleepless nights wondering if you'd met someone else.'

I soften at the word 'minx', his nickname for me. But I am determined to make him suffer a bit. He deserves it for building up my hopes and then dashing them so suddenly, leaving me for four months to wonder what I'd said or done to make him change his mind.

'So what else have you been up to in the UK?' I ask.

'I managed to get quite a bit of work, which means I won't have to go back for a while.' (Jon is an IT consultant and, like me, self-employed.)

'So how long are you back for exactly?'

'Indefinitely. The plan is to finish the work on my house and get the B & B up and running as quickly as possible.' He pauses for a moment. 'I've missed you so badly,' he says, getting up from the sofa and coming towards me. 'I'll make it up to you, I promise.'

'Look,' I say. 'I really can't talk now. I've got to get on and write a piece on anti-ageing serums.'

'Well, can we go for a cycle ride one night this week?' he asks. He knows that I will never say no to an early evening bike ride through the French countryside.

'Maybe,' I say. 'I'll have to think about it. This is all very sudden.'

'You don't know how happy that makes me, just to hear

you'll consider it,' he says, throwing his arms around me. 'What about tomorrow night?'

'Maybe later in the week,' I say, leading him to the front door. I watch him drive off and go back to the anti-ageing serums, very pleased that he is back.

'So what do you think about it?' asks Mathilde. 'I think it is good for you that he is back, *non*? He seems like a very nice, very kind person.'

This is what I was hoping she would say, when I told her that Jon had returned. We are sitting, along with Sebastian, her other half, and Albert, her young son, at a long trestle table covered by a white paper tablecloth – one of many set up in long lines in the middle of the covered market in Villiers. The evening air is laced with the aroma of frying onions and barbecue smoke, and all around us people are tucking into sausage baguettes or *steak frites* on paper plates.

'So why is he not here this evening?' asks Mathilde.

'Well, I think it's best to take things slowly,' I say. 'Given what happened. I said I'd go out cycling with him one evening this week.'

'*Bonne idée*,' says Mathilde. 'It is good to make him work a little. This is the French way. You must not give in immediately.'

Over the crackly PA system, Cyril, the master of ceremonies who's always shipped in from a nearby village for these events, exhorts us 'not to hesitate' to buy the merchandise of the local producers who have set up stands around the square. Punctuated by painful static, he roams around in his leather cowboy hat with his microphone, maintaining an enthusiastic running commentary on the 'delicious cheeses', the 'artisanal breads of very high quality' and the '*saucisson exceptionnel*' which are all available in the night market.

The procedure, as with most of these outdoor events, is that you buy your food from one of the market stalls – there are also local producers selling steak, sausages and pork – and then take it to be cooked at the enormous barbecue, where several local men, including Gérard, the owner of the wine shop, have selflessly offered their services. Red faced in the heat and haze of the barbecue, one or two of them look like they have themselves been cooked '*à point*', or medium-rare.

I spot Delphine, the newly elected mayor of a nearby village, coming towards our table. A passionate Anglophile, she is a very loyal customer of the Liberty Bookshop – the British-run bookshop and Internet cafe on the square, which is where we met. In addition to her new mayoral duties, looking after a small commune of 300 inhabitants, Delphine teaches English at an agricultural college in Clussay, some 30 kilometres away. As always, she is wearing high heels and scarlet lipstick. Several of the older ladies in her village, she says, only voted her in as mayor because she always wears red lipstick, even in the morning. Her other signature accessory is a brightly coloured necklace – she has dozens of them, one to match every outfit – dangling in her voluptuous cleavage. Delphine is forty-seven but with that cleavage (always with a glimpse of satin bra-strap showing), the luxuriant raven hair (always slightly tousled) and her jolly personality, she has many male admirers. Unfortunately, her husband is not one of them; he is currently suing for divorce, claiming that she neglected him during the mayoral campaign.

'*Bonjour, tout le monde! Ça va?*' she says, kissing each person at our table in turn. 'May I join you?' She sits down next to me in a gentle puff of J'adore by Christian Dior, her signature summer fragrance (in winter she always wears Chanel No. 5). As Sebastian pours her a glass of wine, there is a sudden burst of ear-splitting feedback from the antiquated PA system and Cyril announces that the evening's entertainment is about to begin.

A procession of men and women in cowboy hats, black jeans and black-and-red Western shirts, with red bandannas tied jauntily around their necks, file confidently into the space in front of the *mairie*, positioning themselves in perfect straight lines.

'*Mesdames, mesdemoiselles, messieurs,*' shouts Cyril. '*Voici les Adnaks!*'

'*Adnaks?*' I ask Delphine, mystified as this is not a word I've encountered before.

'It's the name of the dance group,' she explains. 'They have come from Brettes, about sixty kilometres away and are very famous in the region for *la danse country.*'

'Country dancing?'

'I think in English you would say dancing in a line,' she says.

'Oh, you mean line dancing.'

I have never encountered line dancing before and I'm not exactly sure what it is. Obviously I've heard of it and I also know that it is not very cool and mostly practised by old people. Its perceived image is of depressed pensioners with hunched shoulders shuffling around a church hall in shapeless jumpers and slacks. But here in France, if the Adnaks are anything to go by, it's tight jeans, cleavage and lipstick (not the men obviously) – an altogether more dynamic and youthful pastime than its counterpart across the channel. These people – several of the women especially – are in their thirties and forties and rather glamorous. As Shania Twain crackles over the loudspeakers, I watch as the Adnaks, heads up, shoulders back, fixed grins on their faces, perform a complex sequence of heel struts, hip sways, kicks, spins, shuffles and little hops.

It's hypnotic. How on earth do they remember all that? I'm mesmerised. And it seems I'm not the only one. Everyone claps furiously as they come to the end of the first dance (with the exception of Sebastian, who looks nonplussed). The Adnaks toss their cowboy hats into the air and then resume their lines for the next dance – a raunchy little routine involving hip bumps and grinds – to 'All Shook Up' by Elvis Presley.

'Eh, they're bloody good, aren't they?' says Jocelyn, one half of a lovely couple from Yorkshire, poking me in the ribs from the table behind. She and her partner Jill live in a little hamlet twenty minutes away from Villiers and are affectionately known as 'the railway girls' as they met over thirty years ago working as signalwomen. 'I wouldn't mind 'aving a go at that myself,' she says.

'Me too,' I'm horrified to hear myself saying. I know I should be sneering at this kind of activity, or at best saving it for my retirement years. My friends in London would be appalled that I'm even watching it, let alone thinking of participating, but I am inexplicably drawn to it. I love the small but fast steps, the nonchalant way that the men tuck their hands into their belt loops and the hilariously camp music. I want to know all those steps, stand in a line wearing cowboy boots and kick my heels in perfect unison with thirty other people.

'Well,' says Delphine, after they have been dancing for about half an hour, 'it looks like we are all going to be invited to have a little try.'

Normally I loathe audience participation of any kind, but as the Adnaks move among the trestle tables, picking dance partners out of the audience, I have to refrain from waving my hand in the air and crying, 'Me, me, me!' I secretly hope that I will be chosen. In fact, the Adnaks seem to zero in on our table and we are all picked – me, Mathilde, Delphine and little Albert.

My dance partner is in his forties, tall, with his spine ramrod straight. I had picked him out as one of the best dancers. We all line up. In front of me there is Mathilde, who is very petite, partnered with an Adnak twice her size; Delphine, behind me, with a man whose cowboy hat barely reaches her cleavage. We are talked through the steps – some shuffles, some twirls, some hops and some kicks – which we practise in slow motion without music. Then the music cranks up (a song I recognise, called 'Cotton-Eyed Joe') and we are off at a fast pace, each couple dancing a curious *pas de deux* around the outside of the *mairie*.

Embarrassingly, I find that I am absolutely no good at *la danse country*. I have two very uncoordinated feet and I've forgotten the short sequence of steps. As I mix them up and twirl and kick at the wrong moment, I sense that my dance partner is very disappointed. Mathilde, in front of me, gets the hang of it immediately, as does Jocelyn, strutting and hopping along with a glamorous blonde Adnak woman, and even little Albert. As we go once more round the *mairie*, I am hot, bothered and doing different steps to everyone else. Just as I am thinking that the song seems to be going on forever, I somehow manage to shuffle forward when I should be going backwards. I crash into Mathilde and her dance partner, causing a pile-up. Fortunately, it is only me that ends up on the floor. As my cowboy partner graciously helps me up, I look over to the bar area and see – oh, the horror – none other than Andy Lawton. He is standing with a group of male friends, beer in hand, smirking in my direction.

Dragged back on to my feet by my dance partner, I skip pink-faced several more times around the *mairie*, and when the dance is finally over, I hurry back to my table, feeling mortified. The obvious thing to do is to stroll over casually and ask him how the renovation is going, has he got hot water yet, electricity? Instead, I avoid looking in his direction for the rest of the evening.

'Is everything OK, *Ka-renne*?' asks Delphine at one point (pronouncing my name the way that all French people do, which I much prefer to the English version.) 'You look a little… stressed.'

I explain about Andy Lawton and the fact that he is standing at the bar.

'Which one is he?'

'The one with longish blonde hair.'

'Oh yes, he is very 'andsome,' she says, taking a discreet look over at the bar. 'Are you sure you don't want to go over and talk to him?'

I shake my head. 'I'm too embarrassed.'

'Yes, maybe you are right,' she says. 'If he has seen you, he can always come over and talk to you.'

'Oh, he definitely saw me.'

But unfortunately, he doesn't come over to talk to me.

Chapter 3

Neighbours

THE SOUNDS OF a spring evening in rural France: birds singing, pigeons cooing... and the heavy metal classic 'All Night Long', by Rainbow, being pumped out of the house next door. The Portuguese neighbours have shattered the peace of my rural idyll. At weekends they turn the narrow cobbled street outside our respective houses into a party space, sitting on the pavement or leaning against the wall outside or the house opposite, drinking beer, smoking, laughing, sometimes looking moody, but mostly having a good time, usually to a soundtrack of loud rock music. I'm still not sure how many of them are living next door (possibly just three) but on Sundays particularly there is usually a crowd of single, dark-haired men in their thirties hanging around outside.

I don't know what that they do for a living, but during the week they seem to work very long hours, leaving at 5.00 a.m. and often returning after midnight, before getting up again a few hours later. Even when they are getting ready for work, they sound like a carnival – shouting, laughing, banging around and generally making the sort of noise that, in London, would result in a noise abatement order or possibly an ASBO. Each morning a big white van, with the company name 'Supodal' written on it, draws up outside. The driver keeps the engine running while a colleague jumps out and bangs loudly on the door. Then, accompanied by much shouting and door slamming, they all pile into the van and roar away, leaving me and my elderly French neighbours to breathe a collective sigh of relief and go back to sleep. At weekends, however, there is little respite. There is nowhere for a bunch of single thirtysomething men to go apart from the bar on the corner of the square, which closes at 7.00 p.m. every night and at midday on Sunday, so they stay at home and party there instead.

It's especially bad news for me as I do a lot of my work at weekends, particularly on Sundays when everywhere is closed and there aren't many other diversions. Unfortunately, that's when my neighbours seem to have the most energy to spare. In London I would probably just go to a cafe with my laptop and work but, in rural France, nothing is open on a Sunday afternoon. I am trapped. Peter Mayle might have had to put up with wily French farmers, but I'd take them over my exuberant Portuguese neighbours any day. How ironic that I came to France for a quiet life only to find myself in the middle of a non-stop party.

On the third consecutive Sunday of loud rock music, I hear shouting in the street outside. I go to the bedroom window and see Monsieur Moreau, a genial chap in a flat-cap who lives several streets away, shaking his fist at them angrily. Surveying the scene from above, I am surprised to see that they are polite to him. They appear to apologise and respond by turning the music down. *Hallelujah!* But, after a boisterous lunch of burgers barbecued in the street outside, the volume slowly creeps up again. Their voices, meanwhile, are louder than ever – laughing, shouting and sometimes, it seems, arguing. A couple of times I have been worried by the raised voices and table banging, fearing that a fight was about to break out. But this, I have realised, is just how they emphasise a point. I don't think they are even aware of how much noise they are making.

'Christ,' says Jon when he arrives, as arranged, late on Sunday afternoon to go for a bike ride – the first step in his rehabilitation – a process that's had to be delayed by a couple of weeks as he had to make an unexpected work trip back to the UK. 'What's going on next door?

'I've got new neighbours.'

'I can see that. Has no one complained about the noise?'

'Yes. Someone did earlier today. But it doesn't make any difference.'

'There were loads of them watching as I rang the doorbell,' says Jon.

'Yeah, they're always there,' I say. 'But I guess there isn't a lot else going on.'

We get the bikes out of the garage – I have a spare bike for guests – under the scrutiny of half a dozen brooding macho men. I try to avoid eye contact as I'm miffed at the noise they are making but, as always, my neighbours nod politely and say *'Bonjour'*.

We cycle up to the square under their watchful gaze, with me praying that I don't do anything embarrassing like fall off my bike. Within five minutes we are cycling through calm, flower-sprinkled countryside. Pale yellow butterflies flirt with the bluebells in the grass verges; the only sounds are of sheep grazing, insects buzzing, and occasionally, leaves rustling as a bird or rabbit hops about in the hedgerow. It's a wonderful antidote to the disco on my doorstep at home.

Jon is good company. We seem to have reverted to the easy friendship that we had in the run-up to Christmas.

'So what do you think you'll do about the neighbours?' he asks, as we sit on a grassy bank, appliquéd with bluebells and daisies, overlooking a river.

'There doesn't seem like there's a lot I can do.' I shrug.

'They probably don't realise that they are living next door to a minx,' says Jon, with a wink. 'And that when provoked, a minx can be very dangerous.'

When we return an hour later, the noisy neighbours are still there. They nod and say *'Bonjour'* again and fall momentarily silent as they watch us put the bikes back into the garage. One of them – the most macho and muscular of all – is firing up the barbecue, a pair of tongs in one large brown hand, a cigarette in the other. He scowls and inclines his head in my direction and then his dark eyes flash Jon a contemptuous look.

'The one doing the barbecue looks like he might once have been a boxer,' says Jon, once we are back inside the house.

'How can you tell?'

'I just can. In fact they all look a bit rough. Isn't it a bit intimidating, having to walk past them every time you come out of the front door?'

'It's the noise they make that bothers me more,' I say. 'Listen, let's just leave now and spend the rest of the evening at yours.' I wasn't planning to let Jon back into my good books so quickly, but I honestly don't think I can stand another evening of my neighbours. Plus, Jon did have a passable excuse for his disappearance; he has grovelled extensively, calling me every night for the past week to ask me if he can come over; and he has been making an effort – this evening he arrived with another box of chocolates. (All these chocolates could be a clever ploy to make me pile on the pounds so that I don't attract anyone else ever but, fortunately, I'm not keen on either Ferrero Rocher or After Eights.)

'Back to mine? Seriously?' says Jon.

'Yes, but I'm not staying the night. You'll need to drop me back later,' I say.

We leave the house and get into his car. As Jon revs the engine unnecessarily and accelerates away from the street, I look in the wing mirror and see my neighbours watching.

On Monday morning I walk up to the *boulangerie* on the square, only to find that the hessian curtains are drawn. René Matout, the baker, has put a board outside, saying 'Closed Due To Exceptional Circumstances'. I wonder if he too has been bothered by the noise over the weekend. Walking back down rue St Benoit, I spot Monsieur Moreau coming towards me. He raises his cap and, after enquiring about my health as he always does, points towards my neighbours' house. 'You should go to the *mairie* and complain,' he says.

'Maybe they won't stay long,' I say.

'They will,' he replies, looking grave. 'I checked with the owner of the house. They are builders. They work for a company called Supodal and they're in the process of building a very big building in the industrial park outside St Maurice. They are planning on staying for a very long time. The owner of the enterprise is married to the blonde woman who owns the new shoe shop on the square.'

He has done his homework.

'That's not good news,' I say.

Monsieur Moreau shakes his head gravely. 'It's very bad news for you especially,' he says. 'The owner of the company has taken out a two-year lease on the house.'

'Do you know how many of them are living there?' I ask.

'Three,' says Monsieur Moreau. 'But they have a lot of friends. You should go to the *mairie* and register a complaint about the noise immediately. It is for you to do it as you are the nearest neighbour.'

I get the message, but I don't go as I don't want to be seen as causing trouble in my village. I'm a relative newcomer myself and so it seems wrong to be complaining about others. I'm hoping that one of my French neighbours will do it instead. Anyway, a week of blissful silence ensues, during which the builders don't return home at all for several nights. But early on Saturday morning I am jolted awake by salsa music and macho laughter. This is getting too much. I drag myself out of bed, throw on my clothes and go to the Café du Commerce on the square in order to escape the commotion. I sit outside in the sunshine for an hour, wondering what to do about the problem and dreading going home. Just as I get up to leave, my three Portuguese neighbours arrive. It's hard to ignore their presence. Dressed in jeans and bright T-shirts they are like a mobile party – laughing, smoking and making lots of noise as usual. They fill the cafe with their larger-than-life presence. Annoyingly, several of the old men drinking thimble-sized glasses of rosé greet them warmly, while the one who looks, according to Jon, like a boxer – he has luxuriant black hair and a big nose – eyes me up and down and says *'Bonjour'*. I don't respond. I dislike him more than the others as he has the loudest laugh and seems to be responsible for most of the noise. He is the one with the biggest presence – his personality alone could fill an aircraft hangar – and he wears the brightest colours (on this occasion, an orange T-shirt layered over a violet one with long sleeves). He also seems to be the leader of the pack, the alpha male of his group, and for that reason, along with his abundant hair, I have nicknamed him 'The Lion'.

His sidekick, who also appears to be in his mid thirties, is marginally more sympathetic. Quieter and more contemplative, he reminds me of a youthful, better-looking version of the actor Nicholas Cage, though that's not anywhere near enough to redeem him in my eyes. The third of their number is barely out of his teens, has blondish hair and looks like a stocky version of Brad Pitt.

Back home I manage 400 words of a feature on the return of the chain handbag in the hour of silence that ensues. Then, just before lunch, I hear them coming down rue St Benoit en masse, having obviously joined forces with other friends in the cafe. Even before they reach their front door it's obvious that the party has started. It continues all day. They have even acquired some children, a small boy and girl, who I later discover belong to their boss – a handsome, well-dressed man in his thirties who wears snakeskin boots. The children are also very noisy as they play hopscotch and then throw a ball around outside my window. It's all very stressful.

That evening, Jon picks me up to go over to dinner with Mathilde and Sebastian and, when he drops me back early on Sunday afternoon – he didn't have to try too hard to persuade me to stay the night, given the circumstances at home – the party is still going on next door. I go up to my bedroom, stuff the airline earplugs in my ears and stare at my computer screen for well over an hour but it's no good. I can't concentrate. I throw open the windows and shout in French, 'Be quiet and think of your neighbours!' My French always lets me down when I'm angry, but they seem to get the message. The handsome, quieter one, who is leaning against the wall of the house opposite, nods and goes into the house to turn the music down. But five minutes later a loud argument ensues between him and another housemate and the music starts up again, louder than ever. There doesn't seem to be much point in reasoning with them. Driven mad by several weekends of noise, I finally snap, storming down the stairs and out of the house, slamming the front door behind me. 'You're making too much noise. I'm going to the police!' I shout at them.

They seem to find this amusing. The neighbour whom I really dislike – the macho one whom I have nicknamed The Lion – is grinning as I march with purpose towards the *gendarmerie*. It's a white bunker-like building on the outskirts of the village, but (surprise!) it is closed. I walk back to my house shaking with adrenaline and anger, only to find that the music has stopped. My threat seems to have worked. All is suddenly calm in rue St Benoit.

The Lion is leaning out of the upstairs window, smoking, with a languid expression on his face. He is naked from the waist up. I look away from his tanned torso, which looks as hard and brown as a chestnut floor. I don't think I have ever encountered such an overt display of muscle and dark masculinity. In London, this breed of man is practically extinct. When he sees me, he narrows his eyes, exhales slowly and scowls. I narrow my eyes and scowl back. I think we both know that this is war.

Later that afternoon, desperate to get out of the house, I drive to the nearby market town of Vivonne and walk by the river for an hour, passing dogwalkers and couples of all ages. So *this* is where people come on a Sunday afternoon. The June sunshine and the sound of the water rushing over the weir makes me feel calmer, and as always, I enjoy the drive home through golden countryside. When I arrive back in rue St Benoit, I park the car in front of my usual audience and go inside. No sooner have I closed the door, than there is a huge commotion outside. I hear the sound of my neighbours shouting and running past my house. '*ATTENTION!*' cries one of them. What on earth are they doing now? I look out of the window just in time to see three muscle-bound men running towards my car which – oh God – is slowly rolling down the hill, towards a small van.

'The keys!' shouts the neighbour I really dislike, in my direction. 'Give me the keys!' I grab them from the side table, rush back outside and throw them at him. He catches them easily. In a swift, assertive move he opens the door and, with those smooth brown arms, yanks the handbrake up. His quick actions have stopped my car from smashing into a Renault van, used by one of my neighbours for hunting. '*Merde*,' says the Nicholas Cage lookalike, wiping the sweat off his brow.

Brad Pitt says something in Portuguese, which I imagine is along the lines of '****, that was close'. Macho-man simply hands me back the keys, without saying a word.

'*Merci*,' I say, feeling like the village idiot.

'*De rien*,' he replies (meaning 'it's nothing'), as he walks towards their open kitchen door. He turns his head with a slow grin, fixes me with his dark, charismatic eyes and says in French, 'Be careful! Otherwise you are going to worry the neighbours.'

'Touché,' I think to myself. 'Round one to The Lion.'

Chapter 4

Besotted

THE GREAT LOVE affair of my life begins on a Friday afternoon in July. Confident in his charms but not too cocky, he waltzes into my kitchen with a bottle of pink champagne and his kit bag packed for a week-long stay. I've been expecting him.

'Here are his Bonios,' says Sarah, placing a straw basket on the table. 'His brush and toys are in there too. He heard that you like pink champagne. And Steve is just bringing in the rest of his stuff from the car.'

Right on cue, Steve appears, tall and gangly and carrying an enormous wire cage.

'Where do you want it then?' he asks cheerfully.

'Oh,' I say. 'What's that for?

'Don't worry, he loves it,' says Sarah. 'He often goes in there of his own accord and just curls up on his beanbag. We put him in there at night so he can't do any damage.'

'What kind of damage?' I ask, alarmed, looking down at *le petit* Biff. He has a stuffed toy rabbit between his teeth and is trying to shake it to death. For the first time, it occurs to me that I might have invited the canine equivalent of Hurricane Katrina into my home. He is, after all, only seven months old – still a puppy. Who knows what devastation he could do?

'Did I not mention that he's a bit of a chewer?' says Sarah. 'He's gnawed through my dining room table legs at home.'

'And have you warned her about the clothes?' says Steve.

Sarah laughs. 'He's always stealing socks and T-shirts,' she says. 'And shoes.'

This is unwelcome news. I'm pretty laid-back about him chewing furniture legs – it can only add to the rustic ambiance of the house – but I've got some Prada shoes in the bedroom upstairs in leopard and zebra print that he might mistake for exotic prey. I don't want him cutting his puppy teeth on those.

'But don't worry, I've brought one of my old cardigans,' says Sarah, noting the look of anxiety that flashes across my face. 'That should stop him stealing your stuff.' I'm not reassured.

The shoe thief has climbed up onto the refectory bench, standing on his hind legs with his oversized paws on the table. It's as if he is demanding to be fed.

'*Biff, get down!*' shouts Steve, but Biff totally ignores him. He hops on top of the kitchen table and stands in the middle of it looking at us defiantly.

'Right, I think that's everything,' says Sarah. 'He's yours for the next seven days, so enjoy him.'

'Is that it?' I ask. I've been expecting a great long list of care instructions, of dos and don'ts, but Sarah is very laid-back. I am touched by her confidence in me. I am about to be entrusted with the care of a living creature – one that belongs to someone else – for seven whole days. I don't think anyone has ever shown this level of faith in me before, certainly not my parents, who never even trusted me with a front door key; nor my brother, who was always reluctant to let me take my small nieces out for the day, describing me only half jokingly as 'the dangerous auntie' – a slur, I think, on my driving.

'Oh, hang on, you haven't told me what he eats or anything,' I say, suddenly feeling a little panicked at the lack of instruction.

'Just a couple of handfuls of dried food in the morning,' says Sarah. 'And he'll have whatever you're having in the evening.'

'What, *anything*?' I say, imagining him tucking into a goat's cheese salad.

'Pretty much. He's not fussy.'

'He even likes curry, don't you Biff?' says Steve, jangling his car keys and eager to get going. 'He's a canine dustbin, don't you worry. He'll scarf anything down.'

'Give me a call on my mobile if there are any problems,' says Sarah. 'And Vanessa Keeling will give you a call next Friday as she'll take him for the second week.'

I look down at *le petit* Biff, his shaggy coat and his eager-to-please expression, and somehow I just know that, when Friday comes, I won't be handing him over to Vanessa Keeling.

'Have fun with him,' says Sarah, kneeling down to give Biff a hug before she leaves. 'I'm going to miss him,' she says. 'You're such a good little fella. Aren't you?' I wonder if all this talk about how good he is, might, in fact, be a smokescreen. Sarah seems to be protesting too much. Biff looks at her with his dark eyes, gives her a quick lick on the ear and then reverts to sniffing the kitchen floor.

He already looks very at home as he pads around the sitting room and kitchen, an eager expression on his black hairy face. We follow Sarah and Steve to the door, Biff looking a little confused as they leave without him.

'Come on, let's go for a walk,' I say to distract him, and immediately he starts jumping up and down and running round my ankles in excitement. He looks like he's going to be an easy house guest to entertain, which is good news as I want him to enjoy every single minute of his time with me.

We walk across the village square, past the people sitting in the sunshine outside the Café du Commerce, cross the main road and cut through the covered area, where men in flat-caps and blue overalls are playing boules, and then head down to the river on the outskirts of the village. We cross the old stone bridge and within ten minutes we are walking through the hot countryside – all vivid shades of blue, green and the yellow of those famous Poitevin sunflowers – with not a soul in sight. We walk at a fast pace, Biff straining on his lead, darting sideways into hedgerows, pulling me with him. I'm not sure which of the two of us is the happiest. It's a route I've taken dozens of times, on foot and by bike, under black, grey, blue, pink, orange and violet skies, alone or with Jon, Mathilde and Sebastian, or various other friends at my side. But never have I been so happy as with my little black companion dragging me through the countryside.

We walk for well over an hour, past sun-coloured fields of rapeseed, green meadows dotted with dandelions, ramshackle allotments and dilapidated barns. We cross the little wooden bridge by the secluded, tightly shuttered chateau, where Biff pauses to contemplate the water rushing below; then we walk up the steep gravel incline and along a narrow track with thick hedgerows on either side.

Back at home he sits cat-like, head cocked to one side, watching with interest as I open the fridge, wondering what you give a dog for dinner if you want to impress him. In the end, I decide on chicken casserole with brown basmati rice.

His nostrils twitch expectantly as he sits sphinx-like by the kitchen door, his large paws parked in front of him, watching me slice up celery. He remains there, watching the entire cooking process with interest until finally I dish up a bowl for him and another for me. I watch half appalled, half pleased, as he gobbles it down at speed. He is just so... animal. It must, I tell myself, be the legacy of his time at the animal shelter. No doubt he was always looking over his shoulder for a giant Dobermann or overbearing pit bull to shove him aside and gobble up his croquettes in two shakes of a tail.

Later I sit on the sofa in the sitting room watching *A Place in the Sun* and Biff climbs up next to me, uninvited, wedging his body alongside mine, resting his head on my knee. Already, I feel like we belong to each other, him and me. This, I realise, is what I've been looking for all of my life – a good-looking, adoring male with whom to go on long walks in the country, cook a delicious dinner and curl up on the sofa at the end of the day.

I take him for one last walk around the square before bedtime, waiting patiently as he stops at least half a dozen times to lift his leg against my neighbours' front doors. Back home, I look at the cage in the kitchen and think, he can't sleep down here on his own. *He's only a puppy and I don't want him to be lonely.*

Suspiciously, he hasn't put a paw wrong all afternoon – he hasn't sneakily chewed any table legs or marked out his territory anywhere that he shouldn't – but perhaps he is lulling me into a false sense of security. The possibilities for disaster are considerable in my bedroom. There is the very expensive Turkish silk Hereke rug that I haggled for in Bodrum on a sailing holiday many summers ago and my animal print shoes lined up against the wall like exotic pets. Who knows what he could get up to in the night? He follows me up the stairs, tail wagging, and I wonder for whose benefit I am doing this. If

I'm truthful, it is me that wants to be near him rather than the other way round.

I place his cage within sight of my bed and put his little green beanbag, printed with bones and the word 'woof', inside it. He does not, as Sarah suggested, go in willingly. Instead, he drags his paws and looks at me beseechingly. I feel guilty as I gently push him in and close the door. I climb into bed and start to read (appropriately enough, *Marley & Me*) just as he starts to cry. A plaintive, heart-wrenching wail fills my bedroom, ruining my enjoyment of the scenes of domestic devastation in my book. I tell myself that my house guest will eventually settle down, but the wails get progressively louder. He is not happy in his cage. He is crying his eyes out and I cannot bear the sound of his distressed doggy sobbing. I hop out of bed and open the cage door. He slinks out, tail wagging sheepishly. I take his little beanbag and place it next to my bed – where we can both see each other – and he climbs gratefully onto it.

'Now you be good,' I say, as I turn off the light. 'I'm trusting you. *Bonne nuit.*'

As I look at him curled up on his beanbag, the spark that I felt when I first saw him at Sarah's house has, in one afternoon, become a big roaring bonfire. Suddenly, I am a bottomless pit of molten love. It is difficult to remember when a human being had this effect on me.

Early the next morning, I am woken by the sight and sound of a breathless black creature manically dive-bombing and hurling himself at my bed, head nodding with excitement, pink tongue hanging out. He reminds me of the 'Animal' character, the one with the wildly nodding head in *The Muppet Show*.

I am still half asleep, but Biff's enthusiasm for the new day is hard to ignore. Before I know it, I am dragging myself out of bed at least an hour earlier than I normally would, pulling on my clothes ready to take him for a walk. I look around the room nervously for evidence of nocturnal misdemeanours but there are no little puddles on the floor, no damaged shoes and the Turkish Hereke rug is still intact. No signs of naughtiness whatsoever. What's going on? He is, after all, still a puppy. It's as if he thinks he is here on approval and must be on his best behaviour. The love I already feel for the black shaggy beast currently running amok in my bedroom ratchets up yet another level.

And so, without even stopping for breakfast, we set off through the countryside again. This time I walk him for two hours and even at the end of that he shows no sign of tiring. It's still only 10.00 a.m. when we arrive back in the square and I decide to take him to the Liberty Bookshop for a coffee. 'Come on! Good boy,' I say soothingly, as we enter the cafe. *'Very good boy!'* This is another test. Will he, I wonder, lift his leg against the 'local author' section, disgracing us both and ensuring that we are not welcome again?

He does neither. Instead, he lies patiently under the table while I chat to Dylan, the hippy owner. He behaves so well and is so adorable that I am almost bursting with pride and love for him. I also discover something else about dogs: everyone loves you when you have one.

'Oh, isn't he gorgeous,' says Deborah, a glamorous Irish woman in her fifties, entering the bookshop with her husband Sam. 'Look at him! He's absolutely adorable. I saw you crossing the square with him. You look really good together.'

Biff lies smugly at my feet and bats his eyelids as Deborah bends down to pat him.

Dylan also seems very taken by him and brings him some water in a gold-coloured bowl. 'He's very well behaved,' he says.

'I think he's exhausted. We've just walked about ten kilometres,' I say.

But really, it seems to me that Biff and I have already reached an understanding. I will walk him for several hours every day; in return, he must indulge me and sit quietly under a cafe table as and when necessary. It is a very promising start. This dog, I realise, is slotting into my life perfectly. I've found my doggy soulmate. Unfortunately, he isn't mine.

Chapter 5

Jenson and Button

THE DAY BEFORE I'm supposed to hand over Biff to Vanessa Keeling, I phone her and suggest that I keep him for the second week as he seems very settled here.

'Really?' Vanessa says, sounding surprised. 'Are you sure?'

'Yes,' I reply. 'Unless you were really looking forward to having him…'

'Actually, you would be doing me the most enormous favour,' she says. 'Biff's a bit of a handful and I've got another friend's dog here at the moment.'

I wonder if we are talking about the same dog – Biff, a bit of a handful? But I put the phone down, delighted to have engineered seven more days with my hairy friend. I scoop him up in my arms and dance around my bedroom with him. He's mine for another week. Another week of being woken by an enthusiastic little creature, dragging my clothes across the bedroom floor to tell me it's time to get moving. Another week of early morning walks, sunny evening bike rides and days spent with a little dog curled up at my feet while I work.

In the two weeks that we spend together, I take Biff everywhere – to the Café du Commerce or the Liberty Bookshop for a coffee in the morning, to the treasury to pay utility bills, to the *mairie* to collect the yellow plastic recycling bags (I'm really showing him the high life), and to the post office, where he just sits quietly by my ankles, looking up with adoring eyes. He loves running errands and I notice that if I'm dressed up or wearing heels – recently I've started making more of an effort just for the hell of it – then he dances along with an extra bounce to his step, as if really proud to be with me.

It's not long before our progress round the village is punctuated by cries of *'Bonjour Beef!'* (as my French neighbours pronounce his name) or *'Ça va, Beef?'* Small children point and shout *'Toutou!'* (doggy) or *'Regarde le petit chien!'* when they see him. Compliments such as *'Il est beau'* or *'Il est magnifique'* follow us wherever we go. And each time someone praises Biff, it's as if they've told me that I'm cute, magnificent or clever – or have a beautiful coat.

Life takes on a new rhythm, a new shine. I feel energised by his presence and my heart soars as I watch him run across fields in fruitless pursuit of birds, bounding along as if he has springs in his paws. At other times, running full pelt after a deer, he looks like a miniature black racehorse. I take vicarious pleasure in all of this, as if it is me that is running and bunny-hopping through the fields. And when I take him to friends' houses for dinner in the evening, I am hugely proud of him as he lies quietly at my feet, or chases the little ball I have bought him around the garden on his own, like an only child used to entertaining itself.

One morning, I leave him home alone as a test, while I nip round to the Liberty Bookshop for a coffee with Delphine.

When Dylan asks where he is, I explain that I've left him alone deliberately, to see if he can be trusted. 'He might be eating your curtains or chewing your soft furnishings even as we speak,' says a friendly expat lady sitting at the next table. I think this might be wishful thinking on her behalf, given that she makes curtains and sofa covers for a living. Nonetheless, I rush back down rue St Benoit in a panic, only to find his eager black face waiting for me in the window. My soft furnishings – unfortunately for the curtain lady – are intact.

Gradually, I get to know Biff's likes and dislikes. He's very keen on broccoli, walnuts, and toast soldiers dipped in egg. He also loves stealing my shoes and socks – he's particularly partial to my cashmere ballet slippers – and he's very curious. If not curled up under my desk, he likes to sit on top of the antique radiator in *le petit salon* watching what the neighbours are up to (exciting stuff like buying baguettes, if the bakery is open). The extra week just flies by, and as Sarah and Steve's return date approaches, a feeling of gloom descends.

Sarah calls the day before. 'So I hear you've still got Biffy?' she says, and I sense that she is smiling at the other end of the phone.

'Yes. I've been showing him the bright lights of Villiers and he seemed to be having such a good time, I figured he might as well just stay with me for the second week.'

'Well, I'm really pleased you've enjoyed having him,' she laughs. 'Steve and I should be arriving back at about nine o'clock tomorrow evening, so we could come straight over and pick him up.'

'Oh, you won't want to drive over here at that time,' I say. 'You'll be exhausted. Why don't you let him stay here tomorrow night and collect him the next morning?'

'OK,' says Sarah, still laughing. 'But you are going to give him back to us aren't you? Steve and I are starting to get a bit worried.'

I laugh too, thinking, 'My God, I've been rumbled already.' Is it that obvious that I'm having devious thoughts about absconding to the south of France with someone else's pet? Still, the important thing is that I have wangled one more evening with *le petit* Biff. The following morning, a Saturday, I get up at 7.00 a.m. and take my little friend for a final run through the sunflower fields. It's as if they are smiling at him too. But as I watch him running in and out of the flowers or sprinting along the dusty track in front of me, I feel quite sad.

To cheer myself up, I stop off at the bakery to buy myself *un petit gâteau*, only to find that it is closed again 'due to exceptional circumstances'. What is going on with René Matout, the baker, I wonder? And what are these 'exceptional circumstances' that are depriving the good citizens of Villiers of his pert choux pastries and *petits gâteaux*, each created with as much colour, and attention to detail as a couture dress. I can't be the only one suffering withdrawal symptoms from my daily fix of sugar and friendly banter with the handsome baker who has brought such pleasure to the village.

Sarah and Steve are waiting outside Maison Coquelicot when we get back. With them is their other dog Milou who, like Biff, is blessed with stunning good looks. (Unlike Biff, she is fully vaccinated against rabies and was able travel back to the UK). Milou has white curly fur with a black patch over her eye, and together, they look like yin and yang.

'Biffy!' shouts Sarah, when she sees us and Biff immediately starts straining on his lead, his little docked tail bobbing with excitement. 'How's the little fella been?' she asks, bending down to make a fuss of him.

'Oh, he's been *so* good,' I say, opening the door. 'It's been such pleasure having him.'

'Have you lost weight?' asks Sarah.

'Lost weight? Possibly,' I say, for in the two weeks of walking Biff for two hours a day, there does seem to be a lot of extra space between me and my clothes.

'So he's had a good time then?' says Steve.

'I think so. He's had lots of really long walks and I've made him a nice dinner every evening.'

'We really appreciate you looking after him,' says Sarah smiling, as I gather up his bowls. 'Thank you.'

'Oh no, *thank you*,' I say. 'Any time at all that you need someone to look after him, just give me a call. He was no trouble whatsoever.'

'That's really good to know,' says Sarah, as Steve carries his beanbag and cage out to the car. 'So how's it going with Jon?'

'Oh, he's been back in the UK for work for the past fortnight. But it's going pretty well. I've almost forgiven him.'

'That's good,' says Sarah. 'I like Jon.'

'So do you think you might be going away again any time soon?' I ask, as casually as possible.

'Well, we only just got back.'

'But the weather's so gorgeous at the moment. If you and Steve fancy a weekend away and need someone to look after Biff…'

'Well, if we go away in France, we'll probably take him with us,' says Sarah.

'Oh.'

'But perhaps if we're going to Poitiers for the day we can leave him with you,' she adds kindly.

'I'd *love* that. And perhaps, occasionally, I could come over and walk him?'

'Of course,' says Sarah, looking bemused. 'Whenever you like.'

Biff is sitting between the two of us, looking up at Sarah and then at me. He seems confused. I give him a final hug, burying my face in his neck, breathing in his lovely furry scent, to hide the fact that tears are welling up. I watch as Sarah clips on his lead and he trots out of the house, and climbs into the back of the car. I follow them out, unable to stop the tears rolling down my cheeks. 'Oh dear,' says Steve, looking alarmed. 'Well, I think that's everything. Better be going.'

I notice that my Portuguese neighbour, The Lion, is standing on his doorstep watching Biff's departure with a scowl. Sarah gives me a hug. 'Remember, you can come over and see him any time.'

'What about Tuesday?' I say.

'That's three days away,' she says, with a smile. 'But just give me a call and let me know what time.'

I watch the car go down the hill taking my new *amour* away from me, and head back into the house, before my neighbour has time to say anything. Suddenly, Maison Coquelicot seems like a much lonelier place.

It's not long, however, before I'm presented with another dog-walking opportunity. The following morning, feeling like I've lost a close relative, I head round to the Liberty Bookshop. I've arranged to meet Delphine for a coffee before she heads off to teach 'The Mad Ones' as she has nicknamed a particularly troublesome group of students at the agricultural college in Clussay, where she works.

I notice that the tiny shop adjacent to the bookshop, previously shuttered up and empty, appears to be in the throes of a makeover. The old-fashioned, panelled facade has been decorated in a cake-icing blue and a workman is painting contrasting white borders on the panels under the window, and around the door frame. It looks charming and I am intrigued as to what it might be. Surely not another clothes shop? We are already blessed with three boutiques in the village (two of them specialising in polyester and a ploughed-field colour palette; the third, which opened more recently, is aimed at a younger clientele, but is conspicuously lacking in customers).

But by the standards of many French villages, which boast little more than a bakery, Villiers is a thriving commericial hub. In addition to two *boulangeries* (the second, on the main road out of the village, is very lacklustre in comparison to the delights to be had at René's) we also have two beauty salons, two pharmacies, a wine shop, a funeral parlour and a florist – albeit one that specialises in potted plants, novelty vases and funeral arrangements rather than freshly cut flowers. There is also a hunting shop selling the latest must-have rifles and camouflage clothing to the hunting fraternity.

The new shop (previously a nondescript office space) will be a welcome addition to what has become the bohemian corner of the square, thanks to local artist Félix Bouquin who lives and works in a vibrantly coloured atelier there. Félix, who moved to Villiers a few years ago from Poitiers, is famous in the region not just for his psychedelic artwork but for having spent most of his childhood locked in a dark cupboard. (I thought this was just a local rumour, until a local TV station ran a documentary on the artist and his tragic past.)

Poignantly, his years in darkness have resulted in a pent-up passion for colour – manifested in the naive flowers, fruits, polka dots and fantastical-looking creatures that he has painted on his shutters, front door, window panes and exterior walls. It's a flagrant breach of local building regulations – any shopkeeper overlooking the square who wishes to paint their shutters for example, must choose from the half a dozen shades of blue which are officially permitted – but no one seems to mind that Félix has gone so dramatically off-message.

The mayor also turns a blind eye to the fact that he often appropriates the parking spaces outside his atelier as his personal shopfront, displaying his giant canvases on easels there when the weather permits. Félix does not restrict himself to canvas or buildings: he is happy to paint almost anything in his signature style, including flower pots, furniture and old milk churns. (When looking after Biff, I worried that if we stood for too long outside Félix's atelier, Biff too would be painted with strawberries and flowers.) Recently, I spotted a young musician carrying away a large string instrument – it was, I think a viola – that bore all the bright hallmarks of Félix's paintbrush. It was certainly set to create a stir in the orchestra pit.

Félix, who has a haystack of thick grey hair and a matching beard, spends most of his life outdoors. If it's sunny he is usually to be found sitting at a small painted table outside his atelier, moodily dragging on a cigarette and surveying the square. When it is really hot, or on summer market days, he arranges deckchairs – also painted with his signature leitmotifs – on his patch. *'La plage de Villiers,'* (the Villiers beach) he once joked when I stopped to admire them.

This morning he is standing in front of the blue door that leads to his studio, smoking. He nods *'Bonjour'* and asks where my little dog is. I explain that Biff is not mine. 'Not yet,' he says knowingly, in French. After some small talk about the weather, I ask him about the new shop, but he just shrugs his shoulders. 'Shoo-pah,' he says, which is the local dialect for *'Je ne sais pas'*.

Delphine is waiting for me in the bookshop, chatting to a rather posh English couple at a nearby table. It seems that they have to go back to the UK for a wedding in a couple of days time but have been let down by their dogsitter at the last moment.

'That's terrible. What happened?' I ask.

'We've no idea-yah,' says the woman, who is called Annabel. She pronounces many words with 'yah' on the end and speaks in a high-pitched, compellingly girlish voice, even though she must be in her fifties. I think she may have had elocution lessons at some point. She has bobbed blonde hair and a slender frame and looks wealthier than your average expat in the Poitou, dressed in a kiwi-coloured dress, with chunky gold cocktail rings on her freckled brown hands. Her husband Charles is wearing shorts and sandals (without socks, so he passes my expat style test) and seems a little bit more down-to-earth.

'We-yah rally stuck,' says Annabel. 'Our dogs are *quite* lovely and they will go quite *mad* without human company.'

I ask what kind of dogs they are, thinking that if they are not Rottweilers or Dobermanns, then I will offer to help.

'Well, Jenson is a wolfhound and Button is a Labrador cross,' says Annabel. 'Rather energetic. But they're both rally *delightful,* aren't they darling?'

Charles shifts uneasily in his seat. 'They're both *very* friendly,' he says.

'We won't be away long,' says Annabel. 'Four nights in total. We just [she pronounces 'just' as 'jarst'] need someone to go in and walk them each day.'

It turns out that Annabel and Charles live in a small hamlet close to St Hilaire, a village about ten kilometres away from Villiers. And St Hilaire, I recall with a frisson, is also the village where Andy Lawton lives. Not that I am thinking about that – well not much – now that Jon is back in my life. 'If you're really stuck, I could probably go in and walk them for you,' I say.

'Oh Corinne *would* you? *Could* you?' says Annabel, clasping her hands together and causing her freckled brown cleavage to crease; while I marvel at the fact that she manages to make even my name sound super-posh. 'Our neighbour Don has agreed to feed them once a day but he won't be able to walk them too. That would be *rally* kind of you.'

'Maybe you should come and meet them first?' says Charles, looking wary.

'What about later today, Corinne?' says Annabel.

And so that evening, I drive to St Hilaire to meet Jenson and Button. Following Charles's instructions, I arrive in a small hamlet which consists of half a dozen stone cottages, a big dilapidated barn and a semi-dismantled tractor. Charles and Annabel live in the third house along – a converted stone barn – which is by far the biggest and most impressive. I park in front of large, pale-green iron gates and am confronted by a sight (and sound) that makes me want to jump back in my car and drive away at speed. Button, the black 'Labrador', has the head of a pit bull and the body of an ox and looks, frankly, terrifying. By way of a greeting, he is hurling his black bulk around the courtyard, barking and yodelling.

Fortunately, he is, as Charles promised, very friendly. So friendly that I am nearly knocked off my feet as he powers towards me, like a bus with a Formula One engine. I brace myself just in time as he thumps to a halt in front of me, stands on his hind legs and puts his paws on my shoulders by way of a welcome. He throws back his enormous head, opens his mouth to reveal a set of teeth the size of the Pyrenees, and lets forth a blood-curdling yowl. Jenson, who is as big as Charles's Range Rover, is a little more reserved. He eyes me up and down from a distance, in a very superior way. He's probably learned that trick from Annabel.

Charles drags Button off me. 'Down Button! *DOWN*!'

Oh God, I think. Too late to back out now.

'Come on in and have a drink,' says Charles.

'Thanks,' I say, wondering if it would be OK to ask for a large brandy.

Charles leads me across the gravel – all the time trying to pull Button away from me – and through some patio doors. I follow him across a wide hallway and into a cool white room with a terracotta floor, expensive white sofas, and modern art on the walls. Sliding doors lead onto a large stone terrace with steps down to a swimming pool. Dressed in a zebra-print kaftan, Annabel is lying on a sofa, flicking through an interior design magazine. 'Come through, Corinne, come through,' she commands, as if I'm the new domestic help and she's about to tell me where to find the Cillit Bang. She motions for me to sit down on one of the sofas. I do as I'm told, closely followed by Button, who jumps up alongside me and then trys to sit, all 65 kilograms of him (I'm guessing) on my lap. '*BUTTON, GET DOWN,*' screams Annabel, producing a cardboard tube with what sounds like pebbles rattling inside. She slams it down next to Button, but the dog is totally unfazed by it. Instead, it is me that nearly jumps off the sofa in fright.

'I think he's rather taken to you, Corinne,' Annabel says.

'A bit too much,' I reply, as Button launches an aerial attack and Charles drags him off me again. It's probably not helping that I'm wearing a new musk scent by Tom Ford. I really hope it doesn't give Button any ideas.

'Would you like a cocktail?' Charles asks, as Button heaves his bulk back up onto the white linen sofa. 'I'm just about to make Martinis.'

'I'm driving, so maybe just a glass of wine.'

'*GET HIM OFF THE FUCKING SOFA,*' screeches Annabel suddenly, making me jump for a second time. This woman, I'm beginning to think, is almost as terrifying as her dog.

'Jolly good,' says Charles, calmly dragging Button out of the room. 'What about a nice Bordeaux? Or I could open a bottle of Chablis if you prefer?'

'There's a bottle of Merlot from Lidl already open,' says Annabel sharply.

Charles serves the drinks at a table by the pool. As I sip my wine, I discover that Annabel is an interior designer and travels back to London once or twice a month to meet clients and oversee work projects. Charles has been many things including a tennis instructor and the manager of a golf club. After a little small talk, Annabel turns the conversation round to my dog-walking duties. Jenson and Button, I discover, don't have normal leads. Instead, Charles is instructed to fetch the apparatus – huge plaited ropes, harnesses and muzzles – that I must fit over their heads in order to walk them.

'Wow,' I say. 'That looks a bit complicated.'

'It's terribly easy, Corinne,' says Annabel breathlessly. *'BUTTON, COME HERE-YAH!'*

I watch, with mounting anxiety, as she attempts to demonstrate how to attach these ropes and harnesses to a beast that is having none of it.

'Why do they need muzzles?' I ask.

'Oh, just to stop them eating other animals,' says Annabel.

'She means dead animals,' says Charles, seeing the colour drain from my face. 'Jenson recently ate a dead rabbit in its entirety. He's a greedy beast.'

'He had the squits for days afterwards,' adds Annabel. 'Dreadful.'

As I watch the two of them trying to get the rope and muzzle around Button's head, I try to think of reasons why I might suddenly be otherwise engaged. But I'm too scared of Annabel to duck out now – though I can see why the other dogsitter did. Charles explains that there is a track leading out of the hamlet that will take me into open fields, where it is safe to walk them. 'Jarst one other thing,' says Annabel. 'The last house, the terribly scruffy one, is owned by a family of French peasants and they have a rather ferocious guard dog. That's why it's so important to keep Jenson and Button on their leads. We don't want a bloodbath.'

This will teach me, I think, not to make hasty offers of help.

'Don't worry,' says Charles. 'The gate is usually closed so that their dog can't get out.'

'But still, there will be the most enormous fracas when you walk past,' says Annabel. 'I don't suppose you've got anyone who can come over to help you?'

'Not that I can think of,' I reply, fighting the urge to add, 'no one I know is that reckless with their personal safety.'

'Right, you'll have to excuse us, Corinne, but we have to go oat now,' says Annabel, getting up suddenly. It takes me a minute or so to realise that she means they are going *out* now, and I am being dismissed.

'I'll see you to your car,' says Charles.

I follow him back through the house, across the gravel entrance and through the metal gates. Jenson watches from under the shade of a cherry tree, a snooty expression on his face. At least he seems easier to control, I think. As we approach the boiling furnace that is my car, I look over the stone wall of the house (or rather barn conversion in progress) opposite, and see – I can't quite believe it – Andy Lawton. He's wearing baggy shorts and a faded T-shirt and is carrying a large piece of wood on his shoulder.

Charles waves at him. 'Hello old chap.'

'You know him?' I ask.

'Yes, he just moved here a couple of months ago. Used to be in the forces, I think. Seems like a nice fellow. He's on his own out here.'

'Oh,' I say, as Andy leans the plank of wood against the wall of the barn and walks towards us, dusting down his hands.

'Know him do you?' asks Charles.

I shake my head. 'Er... Not exactly...'

'You'd like to know him?' says Charles, perceptively, probably seeing the sudden wash of pink over my cheeks. 'Well, I'm sure we can do something about that.'

'Well, actually I have a boyf—' I'm about to say, but Charles is already striding over to the neighbouring house.

'How's it going, old chap?' he says.

'Yeah, not bad,' says Andy, from the other side of the low stone wall. His long blonde hair and T-shirt are damp with sweat.

'This is our our new friend, Karen,' says Charles, at least getting my name right. 'She lives in Villiers.'

'Actually, we have already met,' says Andy, shaking my hand.

'Well, I'll leave you to it then shall I?' says Charles. 'Thought you two ought to know each other since you're practically neighbours. But I must go and get ready for dinner.'

After the not-so-subtle introduction, Charles heads back to his house, leaving me alone with his neighbour.

'The last time I saw you, it was at the night market in Villiers,' he says, with a boyish grin. 'You were dancing in the village square.'

'You were there?' I say, feigning surprise. 'Why didn't you come over and say hello?'

'I was going to, but you looked very busy with your friends.'

'So how's it all going?'

'Slowly,' he replies. 'It's a good thing that it's summer, as I haven't got any hot water or heating yet.'

For a second I think about inviting him over to Villiers for a bath, but it seems a little forward. And Jon might not like it.

'So what brings you over here?' he asks.

'Annabel and Charles are going to the UK the day after tomorrow and they've asked me to walk their dogs while they're away.'

Andy looks at me as if I'm mad. 'They've asked you to walk those dogs?' he says, nodding towards their gates with a raised eyebrow.

'Yes.'

'On your own?'

'Yes.'

'And you agreed to it?'

'Yes, but before I'd actually seen the dogs.'

'Well, good luck with that,' he says. 'Seriously, be careful as they're quite a handful. I'd give you a hand with them but I'm driving down to Bordeaux tomorrow to visit a friend for a few days.'

Damn, I think to myself. What terrible timing. 'Well, I'd better get going,' I say.

'Well, great to see you,' says Andy. 'And be careful with those dogs.'

'I'm sure it'll be fine.' I turn to walk away. 'Have a good time in Bordeaux.'

'Thanks,' he says. 'You take care and I'll see you soon.'

I hope so, I think. And I know I shouldn't: as my conscience reminds me, I have a boyfriend.

Or do I? Firstly, Jon is back in the UK, even though he was supposed to be back in France for what he called 'a good long stretch', making it sound like a prison sentence. Secondly, although I've decided to give him a second chance, I can't get it out of my head that he left me on my own for many months with no explanation. But if I was single (which I am not) what bloody unlucky timing: I'll be visiting Andy's hamlet for four nights in a row – the perfect opportunity to wangle a tour of his renovations and admire his joinery – but he won't be there. Most unlucky of all however, is the fact that for four nights in a row I've agreed to walk Jenson and Button.

Two days later I drive over to Charles and Annabel's house in the early evening with a sense of deep foreboding. Instead of looking forward to a relaxing stroll through fields of sunflowers, barley and lush green beets, I'm wondering if I'll end the evening in casualty. I've taken the precaution of telling Delphine that if she doesn't see me for a few days it's probably because I'm lying unconscious somewhere in St Hilaire. If it wasn't for the fact that it's 40 degrees inside my car – I so wish I had air conditioning – I'd be breaking into a cold sweat as I drive slowly and reluctantly into the small hamlet. I hear Jenson and Button barking before I see them, and sit in the car for a few minutes hoping they'll calm down. They don't. I look over at Andy's barn and think how annoying it is that he has gone to Bordeaux, as I'm sure he would have fearlessly gone through the gates first and used his military training and survival skills to bring them under control.

I take a deep breath and inch open the gate. Button immediately storms towards it, then turns around and rushes in the opposite direction, while Jenson canters towards me wearing a haughty expression. I manage to slide my body through the narrow gap and close the gate – just in time to see Button turn again and come hurtling back towards me. At the very last moment, just before he hits my knees with the full force of his terrifying bulk, I step aside and take refuge against the woodpile to my right. (Even Button's tail, which swishes like a whip, could potentially put a limb in plaster.)

'*CALM DOWN, BOYS!*' I shout, for Jenson has now joined in and is slobbering all over my face with his tongue. 'Come on! Be good! Stop that now. *STOP IT!*' I don't dare risk walking across the open space between the gates and front door as this would allow them to knock me off my feet from any angle. Instead, I edge along with my back to the woodpile, and then the stone wall of Annabel's gîte, and make my way into the house, all the time defending myself from paws, tongues and wagging tails. Fighting the urge to bolt back towards the gate and run for it, I look for the ropes, leads and muzzles, which Charles said they would leave hanging on a hook in the hallway. Just as I spot them, Jenson and Button both start barking in a terrifying manner and run back out of the house. I follow them through the door, and see a grey-haired man, whom I assume must be Don, their neighbour, edging through the gates with what looks like a sack of dog food.

'*GET DOWN!*' he yells and even the dogs can tell that he means business as they (almost) do as he says.

'Those bloody dogs,' he mutters, as he sees me. 'Are you OK? You must be Corinne.'

'Karen, actually,' I say, holding out my hand. (Although I much prefer Corinne and am beginning to wonder if I should stick with it.)

'Annabel said that you'd foolishly – sorry, bravely – volunteered to walk them.' His eyes aren't smiling behind his spectacles, which makes me think he didn't mean to crack a joke.

'I'm Don,' he continues. 'I'm supposed to be feeding them but Annabel didn't leave any food. When I came in this morning there was only a cupful left so I had to go down to Intermarché in Clussay and buy several kilos.' He doesn't look too pleased about it. *'GET DOWN, BUTTON!'*

He brusquely pushes the dog away. 'These animals are out of control,' he says, wiping his brow with the sleeve of his blue chambray shirt. I watch as he shovels a hillock of food into each of their bowls and then edges away. While they are wolfing down their victuals, I seize the moment and somehow, wrestle both dogs into their harnesses and clip on the ropes.

'Well, you look like you know what you're doing. I'll leave you to it,' says Don. 'I would offer to help get you past the house on the corner but I had an operation on my knee a few years ago and I don't want to take any unnecessary risks.'

During our brief conversation, I gather that Don is reluctantly feeding the dogs as Charles looks after his goats when he and his wife are away. It seems like a poor trade-off to me. I was hoping he might hang around for moral support – or to call an ambulance if necessary – but while Jenson and Button still have their noses in the trough, he slips back out through the gate, leaving me alone with them. After they've suctioned up every last croquette, I manage to strap the muzzles round their noses. I then pick up the thick plaited ropes, one in each hand, and I set off, one dog on either side: Button straining and snorting at the end of his leash, Jenson more sedate and regal.

Don watches our departure from safely behind his garden wall. 'Good luck!' he shouts, as I am pulled past his house by my charges. I imagine that we make quite a picture. Only this morning I was writing a feature on oversized handbags and how they fool the eye into making the wearer look smaller. But who needs a giant handbag, I think to myself, when you're swinging two oversized hounds from your wrist?

As we approach the cottage on the corner, I start to feel anxious. Right on cue a dog barks behind the gate and all hell breaks loose. Jenson and Button rear up like horses. There is no way I can restrain them. And I don't try. I let go of the ropes, unleash the beasts and keep walking. If, as Annabel predicted, there is going to be a bloodbath, I don't want to be part of it. Secondly, I know that I've got no chance of catching either of them: my best hope is to keep walking away from the scene of mayhem and hope that eventually Jenson and Button will follow.

Fortunately, the dog that's triggered this frenzy is locked behind a gate and, sure enough, within a few minutes I am treated to the sound of Jenson and Button galloping down the earthen track behind me. It's a terrifying sight but one that I'm going to have to get used to. At the last minute, I step aside, averting the need for several months of physiotherapy and possibly a knee replacement. I walk them for several kilometres, hoping to dissipate some of Button's energy. The only other soul that we see is a solitary farmer, going up and down his field in a tractor. Even he stops for a double take as the three of us proceed down the narrow track between rolling fields, bathed in the molten gold light of a midsummer evening. When we return an hour or so later, there is, fortunately, no sign of the dog in the corner cottage. Don, who breaks from watering his hydrangeas to watch our arrival back in the hamlet, looks surprised that we have returned without incident. 'Well done,' he says.

I lure Jenson and Button back behind the iron gates and, pleased that all bones, tendons and bodily parts are still intact, I drive home thinking of Biff and what a dear little dog he is by comparison. I had arranged with Sarah to walk him this evening and considered – for all of a nanosecond – bringing him along with Jenson and Button. Then common sense prevailed and I realised that meeting these two could scar a little dog for life, if not kill it.

The following two evenings I drive over to St Hilaire and repeat the procedure. I almost grow fond of Jenson and Button, who are essentially good-natured animals, despite their out-of-control manner. It's quite a nice feeling to know that they are waiting for me, and that with the exception of Don, who brings their food, I am probably the highlight of their day.

But by the fourth and final night, I am a little too self-confident, having convinced myself that I am practically the Dog Whisperer, such is my empathy with the canine world. Rather than easing myself in through the gates slowly and throwing them a few treats to divert them as I break for the woodpile – from where I usually inch my way to the front door, always with my back to a wall – I boldly make straight for the house. Big mistake. The next thing I know, I am lying on the gravel in the courtyard, with my Prada sunglasses crushed into the ground beside me. I'm not quite sure what happened but it involved Button, whose carpet-sized pink tongue I am now staring up at. He cannot believe his luck to find me there, playing an interesting new game, and starts to paw my hair in excitement.

'*STOP THAT! NOW!*' I hear a male voice shouting. I look towards the gates and see Andy Lawton running towards me. Damn. Bugger. Why must I always be knocked off my feet when I see him? Worse, he's looking quite dressed up (for the French countryside at least), in jeans and a loose white shirt. 'Are you all right?' he asks, pulling Button away from me and helping me up. 'Are you hurt?'

'No, no, I'm fine,' I mumble, trying to look unfazed as I pick gravel out of my palms, where it leaves painful imprints.

'I saw him flying at you from behind,' he says. 'It was so quick there wasn't time to warn you.'

'You all right?' shouts Don, who is standing at the gate. 'What happened in there?'

'It's OK,' I say, picking up the remains of my sunglasses, while Andy restrains Button, and Jenson watches with a disdainful expression on his face.

'I knew it,' says Don, shaking his head. 'I knew those dogs would injure someone. You were mad to take them on.'

'It's fine. No drama,' says Andy, and then, turning to me, 'are you sure you're OK?'

'Honestly, I'll be fine,' I say. 'He just took me by surprise, that's all.'

'Well, I hope you're not planning to walk them now.'

'No. I think I'll just quietly take myself off to casualty instead.'

'You've still got some gravel in your hair.'

'Oh, thanks,' I say, wondering if this could be any more embarrassing. At least I don't appear to have broken anything.

'While you're in there,' shouts Don, still on the other side of the gate, 'perhaps one of you could chuck some food into their bowls. I haven't managed to get in to feed them today.'

'Where is the food kept?' Andy shouts back.

'I know where it is,' I say. In the kitchen, Andy restrains the dogs, while I pour the food into their bowls.

'I thought you were in Bordeaux?' I say.

'Yeah, I was. But I decided to come back early. I was actually just on my way out to a friend's barbecue when I saw you hit the deck.'

'Yeah, I seem to be making a habit of that lately. Look, I don't want to hold you up if you're on your way out.'

'No problem,' he says, pushing his rose-gold hair away from his handsome face. 'I'll hold the dogs until you're through the gate.'

'Nothing broken then?' says Don, when I emerge. He sounds disappointed.

'I don't think so,' I say.

'Oh well, Annabel and Charles will be back tomorrow,' he says, heading back towards his house. Andy comes crunching across the gravel, followed by the dogs. He pushes them down in a masterful way as he lets himself through the gate.

'Right. Job done,' he says. 'Are you sure you're OK to drive home?'

'I'll be fine.'

'Well I'd better be off then,' he says. 'Take it easy.'

'Yeah, thanks,' I say. 'Have a good evening.' I slide my bruised self into my car, which is hot enough to glaze pots, and remove the gravel that's still embedded in my elbows. Given that he's only been out here a few months, Andy Lawton certainly seems to have a very busy social life.

A couple of days later Annabel drops by unannounced – she got my address from Dylan in the Liberty Bookshop – with a pot of home-made jam and a peach-scented candle (minus its cellophane and with well-thumbed packaging) to thank me for looking after Jenson and Button. I do my best to look thrilled but I am astonished by Annabel's reaction when Biff – who I am dogsitting for the day as Sarah and Steve have gone into Poitiers – jumps up to greet her with a friendly lick.

'*DOWN!*' she cries, looking horrified. '*GET DOWN!*'

'Don't worry. He won't hurt you.'

'That's not the point,' she snaps. 'I'm worried that he'll ruin my new linen trousers. They're by Nicole Farhi. *DOWN!*'

I pull Biff away from Annabel's parsley-coloured pants, but she's still not satisfied. 'The thing is, Corinne, you ought to teach him not to jump up at people like that. No one likes a dog that can't be controlled and he'll just make himself – and you – terribly unpopular,' she says.

I am too stunned to protest that, never mind her Nicole Farhi trousers, her out-of-control hound knocked me to the ground a couple of evenings ago and destroyed my Prada sunglasses.

'Now, Corinne, Charles and I would like to invite you round to dinner. We thought it might be fun for you to meet our friend Travis. He's a TV producer in London, about your age, but he's got a *maison secondaire* out here.'

'Oh, that's very nice of you but…'

'Although, you should know that Travis is a homosexual.' She says this in the same way that you might say, 'Travis is a bank robber' or 'Travis has just been convicted for major fraud'.

'Great, well, it would be nice to meet him.'

'Charles is also working on getting our neighbour Andy along.'

'He is?'

'Oh yes, he's been over several times to tell him how delightful you are and to say that you should get to know each other better.'

'That's very nice of Charles,' I say, horrified. 'But what did your neighbour say?'

'He said that he'd love to meet you properly but that he's not really free for the foreseeable future.'

'Oh God,' I say. 'That's terrible.'

'He's a terribly busy man,' says Annabel. 'Friends everywhere. Always off visiting people. But don't you worry. Charles has got the bit between his teeth. He won't let the matter go until he's arm-wrestled this chap into agreeing a date soon. And when he has, we'll be in touch.'

'That would be lovely,' I say, as she flaps to the door in her pristine linen, haughty as a wolfhound. 'I can't wait.'

Chapter 6

Yee-hah!

ON A VERY hot Tuesday evening in July, Sarah and I arrive at the primary school in Clussay, where the weekly *danse country* class organised by the Entente Cordiale takes place. Steve has also come along under duress. In a yellow-painted classroom with a beige speckle-tile floor, desks have been pushed back against the wall and there are about twenty women, all Brits – don't ask me how but I can tell – and one tall, thin man, who looks like John Cleese moving, in what might loosely be described as lines, to a song called 'One Step Forward, Two Steps Back'. Immediately, I have second thoughts. This is nowhere near as glamorous or dynamic as the Adnaks' performance in Villiers. This is the sort of thing pensioners do in draughty church halls to avoid osteoporosis.

The teacher, a fiftysomething *Anglaise*, wearing tight indigo jeans and cuban-heeled boots, tells us to stand in the middle and 'just join in'. She's clearly an optimist. The dance sounds simple, and it would be, if it weren't for the various turns, which frequently leave us facing an entirely different direction to everyone else. 'Don't worry, you'll pick it up soon,' shouts the teacher.

In pole position in the centre of the front row, I spot the 'railway girls': Jocelyn, dressed in her usual utilitarian outfit of jeans and a polo shirt – worn as always with the collar standing – and Jill, her partner of nearly thirty years, in cropped chinos and a fitted white shirt. They both look very proficient in *la danse country*. Jocelyn, short and sturdily built, keeps her hands casually tucked into her trouser pockets as she moves, which gives her a look of tough but casual insouciance; Jill, tall and slender, performs the steps more elegantly. She reminds me of the veteran tennis player Virginia Wade, with a little dash of Vita Sackville-West thrown in. Although I can't quite imagine Jill slogging tennis balls across a net, I do know that she is a passionate gardener and loves painting watercolours when she and Jocelyn are not out walking their dog, Tess, a grumpy Staffordshire bull terrier.

'Right,' says the teacher. 'That was "One Step Forward". Now for the "Cowgirl Charleston".' A ripple of approval runs through the room. Obviously a crowd-pleaser, this one. Jocelyn turns and gives us one of her twinkle-eyed grins and the thumbs-up. 'I'll just run through the steps for the benefit of the newcomers,' says the teacher, who hurries over and positions herself in front of us. She is very sweet, very jolly and very patient but after ten minutes of little progress, she says, 'Shall we just try it with the music?'

If I had to sum up the evening in one word, I'd say 'humiliating', but I haven't laughed so much in ages (mostly at myself but I also enjoy a discreet snigger at the expense of the John Cleese lookalike, performing the moves in a very exaggerated way). The tall, thin figure of Steve hopping around cluelessly, but gamely, in the middle also makes me giggle. At the end of the class, Jocelyn and Jill come over to talk to us.

'Isn't it wonderful?' says Jill, who is almost never not smiling.

'You were pretty good,' I say. 'How long have you been doing it?'

'Don't worry,' says Jocelyn, with a cheeky grin and a hearty slap on the back that almost knocks me over. 'We were as rubbish as you when we first started.'

'Gee, thanks,' I say. 'That's really encouraging to know.' Perhaps because I am also a northerner by birth, I really appreciate Jocelyn's sense of humour and her no-frills, tell-it-as-it-is approach. Her forthright manner is reinforced by her blunt northern vowels – like me, she says 'grass' so that it rhymes with 'lass' – but underpinned by a real kindness and warmth.

'Speak for yourself, you cheeky bugger,' says Jill to Jocelyn in her good-natured way. '*You* were rubbish but I wasn't.'

'Anyway, you'll pick it up eventually,' Jocelyn says with another grin.

'What, like swine flu?' says Steve.

'*Très drôle,*' says Jocelyn, blue eyes twinkling. 'You're good at one-liners, just not dancing in a line.'

'Don't listen to her, Steve,' says Jill, who can usually be relied upon to mitigate Jocelyn's more impertinent comments – often with a dry put-down of her own. 'You did much better than she did when we first started coming to the class.'

Several other women from the Entente Cordiale come over to tell us that we didn't do too badly and must come back again next week. Steve doesn't look too enthusiastic and I doubt that I'll be going back either.

'So have you seen Jon?' asks Sarah, as we head outside to the car park.

'Yes, he had an OK explanation for his absence, so I'm slowly restoring him to former privileges,' I reply. 'Though he's had to go back to the UK again for work.'

'Good,' says Sarah. 'We like Jon. He's a nice guy. Now, are you coming over to walk Biff at the weekend? He's expecting you.'

'Oh yes, please. How is he?' I ask, eager for an update on any events, large or small, in the life of my little furry friend.

'He's been a naughty boy recently. Keeps escaping. Even though Steve has reinforced the garden fence, he got out again yesterday. We found him taunting the donkey and the Great Dane next door.'

'Oh, he's such a feisty little dog,' I say, suddenly spotting the potential opportunity in this. 'You know, I could collect him on Friday afternoon, take him for a really long walk and then – if you don't mind me keeping him overnight – I could walk him again on Saturday morning and bring him back exhausted. Hopefully, after that he won't have the energy to escape for a few days.' I look at Sarah to see if she has rumbled my devious attempt to get an overnight pass. But Steve has already bitten.

'That's not a bad idea,' he says, turning to Sarah. 'We could do with a break from him. What do you think darling?'

'Yes, fine by me,' says Sarah, with an impish smile, as if she knows what I'm up to but is going to indulge me anyway.

On Saturday morning I make an exciting discovery. En route to the market with Biff to buy a fluffy white goat's cheese from the 'goat lady' – a jolly woman with a face as round as the products that she sells – I notice that the mystery shop has finally opened. *'L'Épicerie'* has been painted in old-fashioned white letters on a lavender-blue panel above the door. But this is no ordinary grocery store: the vibrant window display includes brightly coloured tins of tea, patchwork cloth bags and apothecary-style bottles of bath oil. Small cafe tables in pale-pistachio and hyacinth-blue have been arranged outside, creating a *petite terrasse* which blends seamlessly with the brightly coloured artworks outside Félix's atelier. It's charming, this colourful, impromptu cafe, and Félix himself is sitting at a brightly painted table, looking very pleased with it all. He looks even more pleased when he sees Biff and comes over to chat.

'He's your dog now?' he asks.

'No,' I say. 'He just came to stay for the night.'

'He looks very happy with you,' says Félix, which is true. Biff really appears to be enjoying his mini-break, not least because I let him swim in a stagnant river this morning. (Well, actually I had no choice as before I could stop him, his head was bobbing up and down in Shrek-coloured slime; but at least he had the good grace to stand patiently in the shower while I hosed him down afterwards.)

While Félix crouches down to stroke Biff, my eye is drawn to the willow baskets, each piled high with fruit and vegetables, displayed on an antique handcart outside L'Épicerie. One panier is overflowing with shiny red peppers, another with plump, unwaxed lemons. There are also velvety-green courgettes, frilly green lettuces in paper bags that look like they have been freshly plucked and densely red vine tomatoes. And none of the produce, I note, has the standardised look of supermarket fare – much of it speed-grown in polytunnels in Spain. L'Épicerie's fruit and vegetables look like they have been grown in a nearby allotment or *potager* and left to ripen slowly in the sun.

Just as I'm approaching the willow baskets for a closer look, my French friend Mathilde exits the shop with a big smile on her face and a straw basket swinging on her slender brown arm. Dressed in a tiered gypsy skirt, espadrilles and a cloth hat, she couldn't look more French if she tried.

'*Eh, bonjour Ka-renne*,' she cries, before we embark on the usual kiss-fest. 'I think you are going to like this shop,' she says. '*C'est tout bio.*'

All organic? This is fabulous news – exactly what I was hoping for when I noticed the produce in the willow baskets. Since moving to France, much of my daily life has been dominated by the search for organic fruit and vegetables, which ironically, given that I live in an agricultural region, are very hard to find.

In the summer, I am lucky enough to be given surplus produce from friends' gardens (last year for example, brought a deluge of courgettes, green bell peppers and the most delicious beetroots I've ever encountered). On my work trips to London, I invariably come back with a big, black nylon Mulberry bag filled with organic vegetables (to the amusement of the security staff in the Eurostar terminal, who once searched my bag only to find it full of M&S food). Otherwise, if I want to buy produce that hasn't been sprayed with chemicals, I have to make a 52 kilometre round trip to Le Pois Tout Vert, an organic shop on the outskirts of Poitiers.

Despite his plans for a smallholding alongside his B & B, Jon doesn't understand my fixation with organic produce. Instead, he jokes that the misshapen fruit and vegetables in Le Pois Tout Vert – which literally means 'the green pea' but is also a play on the words *Poitou Vert* or 'green Poitou' – are actually just the rejects from normal crops. He also points out that the carbon emissions generated by my weekly shopping trip are not very 'green'. In my defence, if it was possible to cycle down the N10 into Poitiers to buy my organic carrots, I would. Having witnessed at first hand the worrying cloud of pesticides dispersed onto food crops during the spraying season, I've become even more of an organic zealot since moving to France. And if I needed any more convincing as to the potency of the chemicals used, Delphine once told me that her brother, who uses the minimum amount of chemicals necessary to make a living, is invariably ill with headaches, nausea and dizziness for two days after spraying his crops.

So the arrival of L'Épicerie feels like someone has answered my prayers and dropped a big lavender-blue wrapped gift into the village. 'But there is no sign that says it is organic,' I say to Mathilde, not quite able to believe the good news.

'No, but it is,' she says, giving Biff a piece of baguette. 'Céline, the owner, used to be a journalist for a newspaper in Poitiers but she is very into all things *bio*. She is very nice. And so is her husband. Go in and see for yourself.'

I ask Félix if he would mind looking after Biff for a few minutes – '*Pas du tout!*' he says, looking delighted – and venture into the cool, dark shop. The interior is just as charming as the exterior, with a striking tiled floor featuring old red, white and brown tiles. The produce is displayed on red lacquered shelves – everything from mung beans to miso soup, all of it *bio* – while the far wall is devoted to aromatherapy oils and beauty products. In the fridge there are locally produced yoghurts in unusual flavours (almond, lavender and rose) and cheeses wrapped in white paper. Behind the cash desk there is a pleasant-looking woman with abundant dark hair and the sort of radiant skin that comes from a lifetime of clean living and keeping off the E-numbers. She is dressed in a pink top with a green muslin scarf draped around her neck. This must be Céline. She is chatting to a customer, or possibly a friend, with dreadlocks, dressed in flowing, brightly coloured layers. From now on, I think to myself, I will nickname this little corner of the square the 'hippy quarter'. I'm sure Céline will fit in perfectly with Lola and Dylan, the vegetarian, carbon-neutral owners of the Liberty Bookshop nearby. As for me, thanks to L'Épicerie, I will no longer need to drive 26 kilometres when I run out of rice. Life in France, I think to myself, just got a whole lot better.

Inexplicably, and against my better instincts, on Tuesday evening I find myself once again driving the 25 kilometres to Clussay and the Entente Cordiale class. I know it's very uncool and that I'm several decades too young to be doing country dancing, and that taking up bingo or morris dancing would be marginally more acceptable, but I desperately need the exercise. With the exception of the occasional country hike with Biff, the only exercise I get is the daily 100-metre walk to the *boulangerie*. And since that's currently closed for a week, I'm not even doing that. Plus there is the fact that I hate to be defeated by anything, as my physics O level proves. Admittedly, it was a long time ago, but I can still remember sitting in Mr Mayo's class in double physics, not having a clue what was going on. Then one day, fed up with spending two hours doodling pictures of Adam Ant in the back of my exercise book, I took decisive action. With the help of an enormous tome called *The Definitive Guide to Physics* I taught myself the laws of force and gravity and pressure and motion and angles of light refraction and reflection – the whole boring, bloody lot. Night after night, I sat in the local reference library memorising the formulas and the laws that I knew I would never, ever need to use in real life. In the process, I went from hating physics to almost loving it and eventually walked away with a grade A in what had been my worst O level subject.

And so it is with line dancing. I'm damned if I'll be beaten by a few dance steps and a Tammy Wynette track. Grimly determined, I take my place next to Sarah in the middle of the assembled ranks (Steve said he'd rather clean out the *fosse septique* with his bare hands than come back). The problem is that, just as I'm congratulating myself on facing the same way as everyone else, the rest of the class is several steps into a new sequence and by the time I've caught up, they've all changed direction again. My brain just doesn't work this quickly. But honestly, I can see why line dancing is a hit with the elderly: if you can remember these steps, you don't need to worry about Alzheimer's.

I leave the second lesson having learned that all the steps to all the dances can be found on a website called www.kickit.com. I get Jocelyn to write down the names of the dances that have been taught so far and then, like a true nerd, I go home and look them up on my computer, print out the steps and practise them in my courtyard. Yes, I am officially a country dancing geek. My working day takes on a new rhythm: I spend an hour writing (at the moment: 'The Return of the Negligee') then rush downstairs to *le petit jardin* and spend half an hour practising the 'Cowboy Stomp' or 'God Blessed Texas', clapping and stomping and shimmying my hips *toute seule*. Thank God, the neighbours can't see me. Or at least I hope they can't. There is a small opaque window in the side of the Portuguese house, that overlooks my courtyard, and I very much hope that they can't see through it.

I even stop to practise the steps every so often while walking Biff down a deserted country track at the weekend, performing a little jig and repeating the steps out loud – 'Kick, step, shuffle back; kick, step, shuffle forward' – and then continuing on my way. They say that talking to yourself is the first sign of madness. But I think dancing alone down a country track is a close second. Fortunately, it's July, so there are no hunters lurking behind the hedgerows with binoculars to witness the strange spectacle of the crazy, dancing *Anglaise*. Biff meanwhile, stops snuffling down rabbit holes to watch and then tries to join in, darting around my ankles.

Even more worryingly, in the week before the next line dancing class, I find myself scanning the Internet for cowboy boots, Stetsons and – oh God, I can't believe I'm admitting this – checked shirts. Jon is appalled when I tell him. 'Line dancing?' he says, sounding horrified, on the other end of the phone. It's as if I've just told him that I've bought a season ticket for Bolton Wanderers. 'For God's sake, keep that to yourself. And definitely don't tell any of your London friends, particularly not the ones who work in fashion.'

'But what's so wrong with line dancing?' I ask.

'Trust me. It's just wrong,' he says. 'It's something that people of retirement age do. Like golf, only less cool.'

'Well, I don't care what anyone thinks. It's really fun and actually, I quite like cowboy boots. I think they're long overdue a revival,' I say, wondering if I can convince one of my editors to let me write a feature about them.

'Hmm,' says Jon.

'When are you coming back?' I ask.

'I'm not sure. I've just had another couple of weeks' work come through.'

'Well, you should be careful,' I say, only half joking. 'If you leave a minx on its own for too long, who knows what it might get up to…'

He laughs. 'I love you, minx. I'll be back soon, I promise.'

By the time that the next week's class comes around, I am proficient in the full beginners' repertoire, which includes the

'Cowgirl Charleston', the 'Cowboy Stomp' and a highly camp number called 'Matador', about a bullfighter who is gored to death, which always goes down well with the vegetarians. We all ad-lib and shout *'Olé!'* a lot to this one. At the end of the session, Jocelyn comes over to tell Sarah and me about an informal line dancing session that she is planning to start on Wednesday mornings in L'Auberge de Claviers, a bar-restaurant in the little village of Claviers where she and Jill live.

'What do you think, girls?' she says. 'It'll be fun. We'll practise any new dances that we've learned here, so it will give anyone who's a bit behind or slow to learn' – she nods in my direction – 'a chance to catch up.'

'Don't be mean,' says Jill with a kind smile. 'Karen wasn't at all bad this week.'

'Yeah, why not?' says Sarah. 'It sounds like fun.'

'I'm not sure,' I say. 'I'm supposed to be working on weekday mornings – or at least pretending to.'

'Well, if you change your mind,' says Jocelyn, 'we're starting at ten.'

L'Auberge de Claviers is run by an expat from Yorkshire called Barbara, whose husband died of a heart attack shortly after moving to France to open the restaurant. Jocelyn has negotiated with Barbara that for a euro each, we will be allowed to stomp, kick and shuffle for two hours on the beautiful sprung wooden floor of her spacious ballroom. Sarah, who knows Jocelyn and Jill quite well, later tells me that the 'railway girls' are motivated not just by their new-found passion for line dancing, but by a more altruistic reason – they are hoping to drive some regular custom into Barbara's quiet, backwater bar.

Obviously, I'm not planning to go. And obviously, I do, having persuaded myself that line dancing is just like step aerobics but with Stetsons and more sequences to remember. And so the following morning, I don my jeans and flip-flops (Sarah and I are the only ones who have yet to track down a pair of cowboy boots on eBay) and drive to Claviers, a picturesque little village about twenty kilometres away. L'Auberge de Claviers, which takes up one side of the little square, is very pretty, and very French, with pastel-green shutters and lilac wisteria climbing up the walls. Outside, green plastic tables and chairs are set up in the shade of lime blossom trees. Inside, the bar is sunny and cheerful and refreshingly free of brown wallpaper. (In London, they say you are never more than a couple of metres away from a rat; in a French village, it's brown wallpaper.)

Behind the bar, a doughty Yorkshire woman in her fifties dressed in a white chef's jacket is wrestling with the coffee machine. She has curly blonde hair and big startled eyes and her face is a little pink and blotchy. She looks terrified – as if taken completely by surprise by the two dozen or so women who have descended on the bar in cowboy boots and hats this morning – but I immediately like the look of her.

'Bluddy machine,' she says.

'What's the matter?'

'Summat's wrong with it,' she says, in a broad Yorkshire accent. 'It wurn't switch on.'

'Are you Barbara?'

'I am, pet,' she says, holding out a swollen, pink hand.

I introduce myself. 'Have you got an instruction manual?'

'I think there wuh one but I've no idea where me 'usband kept it,' she says, blinking her big, child-like eyes. 'Are you 'ere for the dancin' luv? Cos they're all in there.'

She signals towards a door at the end of the bar. Behind it, I can hear the stirring sounds of 'Matador' and enthusiastic shouts of '*Olé!*'

Barbara looks a little taken aback by it all. 'Listen t'that. I dun't dare look at wot's going on in there,' she says, rolling her eyes sideways and upwards as if to suggest some kind of madness is taking place in the room next door.

I roll my eyes too, as if to agree, and head for the ballroom. It's a large, bright room, with a beautiful old wooden floor, and it smells of beeswax and coffee beans. Two dozen women are moving in wavy, undisciplined lines towards the far wall, robustly led by Jocelyn. There is a comb jauntily poking out of her jeans back pocket and I notice that her short brown hair now features blondish highlights. 'Point, step, point, step. 'Urry up Karen, yer late!' she shouts. 'Point, step, cross and kick. Point, step, point, step, shuffle back…'

I take my place at the back. As we work our way through the various routines it becomes obvious that Jocelyn was born to do this. Her voice carries natural authority as she calls out the steps and orders us around – 'Move forward, yer'all squashed up at the back' – in a good-natured way. As I watch her bumping and wiggling her hips at the front of the class, and cracking jokes – most at her own expense – I feel a huge wave of affection towards her. In fact, I feel a huge wave of affection for all of my fellow dancers. These women in their late forties, fifties, sixties and beyond, some of them trim, some of them not, are transformed when they dance. Strutting their stuff to Dolly Parton and jiggling bits of their body they haven't moved in years (or maybe that's just me), they look empowered, alluring, more youthful.

'Right, shall we have a break then?' says Jocelyn. 'Or shall we do one more?'

'One more, one more! The "Texas Waltz"!' yells one of our number. Unfortunately, it's me. It's deeply worrying.

'All right then, the "Texas Waltz" it is,' says Jocelyn, finding the music. 'That's one of the new dances we learned last night. And then we'll stop for a break.'

After the 'Texas Waltz', the sequence of which – 'Forward, two, three; back, two, three; turn, two, three' – is firmly etched in my mind (I woke up chanting it this morning), we head through to the bar. As we all line up along the counter, Barbara looks panic stricken, like a rabbit caught in full beam headlights and seconds from death. As she pulls levers and prods the coffee machine ineffectually, I really feel her pain.

After ten minutes standing in a line that doesn't move, Jocelyn pushes her way through to the bar. 'What's going on there, Barb?' she asks. 'It'll be Christmas before we get a coffee at this rate.'

'It's completely dead,' says Barbara, eyes blinking and looking half bewildered, half indignant at the machine's audacity. She is staring at it as if it were a stubborn child. We all gather round now, staring at the dormant piece of equipment as if willing it into life. It looks too new, too state-of-the-art, to have broken down. After a few more minutes of standing around and staring, Jill bends down, retrieves a lead, waves it triumphantly in the air and plugs it in. A red light comes on and the machine powers up. There are a few shouts of 'Yee-hah!' and someone throws their Stetson in the air.

Jill and Jocelyn to the rescue again, I think to myself, for I've also heard they come to the bar in the evening to give Barbara a bit of moral support. Despite their epithet of the 'railway girls', privately I've nicknamed them the 'Land Girls', thanks to their indomitable, 'good-in-a-crisis' British spirit. Had they been around during World War Two, I'm absolutely sure they would have excelled in the Women's Land Army, tilling the land and helping to keep the country on its feet. (Although earlier, *Dad's Army* and Captain Mainwaring also sprang to mind as

I watched the bossy but good-natured way in which Jocelyn marshalled us all into lines for the 'Cowgirl Charleston'.)

'It weren't switched on,' says Jocelyn, stating the obvious and looking at Barbara accusingly.

'I don't bluddy believe it,' Barbara replies. Incredibly, rather than looking sheepish or embarrassed, as might be expected, her face is a picture of defiance, as if the machine has somehow deceived her. You've got to admire her attitude. We form back into a queue, which, even with the machine working, moves very slowly, particularly when someone asks for a coffee. I get the impression that this is the first time Barbara has actually used the machine. It occurs to me that Barbara, like many Brits who move to France and open a restaurant – there are an astonishingly high number of them – has never even worked in a cafe before. Fortunately, quite a few ask for orange juice, otherwise we'd still have been there for dinner.

At a table overlooking the deserted square outside, I sit down next to Sarah and Jill, who are chatting about their gardens. 'Who among us,' I wonder out loud, 'could have guessed that when they moved to France, they would take up line dancing? Certainly not me.'

'Well it's hugely popular in France,' says Jill. 'Here, take a look at this.' She rummages in a small rucksack and hands me a flyer with details of a line dancing festival in early August, in a place called Brettes, about eighty kilometres away. It is a whole weekend of *la danse country*, with demonstrations, beginners' classes, barbecues, a best-dressed cowboy competition and various other Western-inspired activities. The top billing, I notice, is the Adnaks.

The flyer is passed around under the linden trees and pretty soon everyone is so excited that Jocelyn is talking of hiring a minibus and going en masse. Then, after compiling a list of those who would like to go – not me, I hasten to add, as I have to draw the line (sorry!) somewhere – we head back into the ballroom for the second half. And before we know it, the bells of the church across the square signal noon and the end of our dance session. As we file out, Barbara is polishing glasses behind the bar. There's one thing I've got to know: 'Barbara,' I ask. 'Did you have a cafe back in Yorkshire?'

'Oooh no, luvvie, I wuh a legal clerk,' she replies.

No wonder, I think to myself, that she looks a bit dazed by what she's taken on. But at least she now knows how to work the coffee machine.

The informal Wednesday morning session soon becomes the highlight of my week. I guess this is what happens with crack addicts: they dabble with it once thinking that it will be harmless and before they know it, they're sitting in a group therapy circle talking about their childhood (and those are the lucky ones). Me, I'm worried that I'll end up in a rhinestone shirt. I've got to get a grip. I'm a former fashion editor; in London I had cool friends; I'm definitely more rock 'n' roll than country. I shouldn't, in short, be doing this. But I justify my new habit in many ways, including the fact that it gives my sometimes too formless life in France a little structure.

Also, by strange coincidence, both the countryside and cowgirls seem to have found favour with the fashion world. 'GO COWGIRL!' was the recent cover line on one of the few fashion magazines that I still read. Inside, there were six pages devoted to fringing, frilly denim skirts, cowboy boots, neckerchiefs and plaid shirts – all deemed to be the look of the season and just what the good ladies of Claviers have been wearing for some time. 'Fashion's gone wild in the country for spring,' declared the magazine. 'So giddy-up girls and jump on our style stallion.' Hmm. Maybe my clandestine dancing activities are not so embarrassing after all.

Before I know it, I find myself singing along to Johnny Cash as I drive through the brilliant blue, green and yellow landscape of high summer to Claviers on Wednesday mornings. (Jocelyn has very kindly made me a CD of 'line dancing classics'.) Sometimes, if I'm early, I'll sit at the bar and have a quick coffee with Barbara before the session begins. I love her no-nonsense approach to life, and the fact that, despite losing her husband within months of arriving in France, and being left to run this place on her own – not 'living the dream' but the 'bluddy nightmare' – it's impossible to detect even a hint of self-pity. Whenever I ask her how things are going, the answer is always the same, 'I can't complain, luvvie. I'm still alive.'

As for *la danse country*, I have to confess that I secretly love the camaraderie that comes from performing the same steps in sync with two dozen other people. There is no rivalry, no bitchiness, no competitiveness. I've warmed to no-nonsense Di with her Brummie accent; Anita who still owns a designer handbag, wears a Cartier watch and like me, is bewildered to find herself line dancing; and Caroline, who loves horses and has enviably slim thighs and a gentle, Sloaney manner. Our paths would probably never have crossed in the UK but here in France, we are a significant part of each other's lives, even if it is just for a couple of hours each week.

One morning it is so hot in the ballroom that we dance outside in the car park instead. I wonder what the villagers make of it, seeing their local bar taken over by a bunch of Brits in cowboy boots. They probably view us in the same way that they did the German occupation. But it's not just the dancing that propels me to get out of bed and drive 20 kilometres on a Wednesday morning. I really look forward to the chat, sitting in the shade of the linden trees in a sweet bubble of lime blossom – just like my favourite Jo Malone bath oil but better – and Barbara's arabica bean coffee during the break. We discuss our respective renovation projects, Ryanair – the latest outrage is the airline's practice of weighing bags at the gate to catch out anyone who has gone over their luggage allowance by indulging in a bit of shopping in the departure lounge – and, more importantly, who's bagged the best cowboy boots on eBay that week.

It is thanks to Ryanair's infamous approach to customer service that I miss the Brettes line dancing festival (for yes, I was persuaded to sign up for it in the end). Returning to France after a work trip to the UK in August, I arrived at Shabsted (Stansted airport) to find chaos and a lot of angry, stressed people, who'd been queuing for hours to drop their bags. It transpired that Ryanair had instituted a new collective bag-drop system and closed down virtually all its check-ins – as you do on one of the busiest travel days of the year.

As a result, I feel quite left out the following Wednesday, when nearly everyone shows up to the dance session wearing matching scarlet cowboy hats, studded belts, feathers and fringed leather tassels clipped to their hats or belts. But I have succumbed to cowboy boots. While in London I splashed out on a pair by Frye, an American brand with pukka credentials, since it once supplied the American cavalry and was favoured by Wild West pioneers. I tell myself even the fashion world would approve of the understated chocolate brown boots in 'distressed' leather. The only problem is that the leather is so stiff – it gets better with age apparently – that it takes me an extra twenty minutes to get ready for line dancing class, lying on my back and performing some complicated maneouvres – pulling, pushing, twisting and wriggling – to get the boots on. But it's better than dancing in flip-flops, which has become almost impossible as the moves get faster and jumpier each week.

Inside the bar, the coffee machine lies dormant again as Barbara has run out of coffee beans, but over an orange juice in the break I chat to Sarah who, like me, is featherless and hatless, having also missed the Brettes festival.

'How's Biff?' I ask.

'Very naughty,' she says. 'Yesterday, he managed to escape and he didn't come back for three hours. We've no idea where he went but he took himself for a very long walk.'

'Really?' I say, trying not to smile as I wonder if, just possibly, he was trying to make his way to Villiers to see me.

'Yes, Steve's really fed up with it. He's done his best to reinforce the gate but Biff keeps figuring out how to open it. We're thinking we might have to get an electric fence to keep him in.'

This removes the smile from my face. 'An electric fence?' I repeat, feeling like I've just received an electric shock myself.

'Yes,' says Sarah. 'It's the only way to keep him in. He's a little devil.'

I later discover that electric fences deliver only the mildest of shocks and are not as cruel as they sound, but I have a horrible vision of Biff with his paws stuck in the fence, his shaggy black hair electrified and standing on end. I can't bear it.

'How's Jon?' asks Sarah.

'Still in the UK. Back on Friday morning.'

'Where does he stay in the UK?'

'In a B & B near Oxford, close to the company he works for. Or that's what he says. I'm beginning to wonder if he might be seeing Jennie again,' I say. My 'boyfriend' has been gone for most of the summer, and Oxford just happens to be where his ex-girlfriend Jennie lives. Past experience should have taught me to make him take a lie-detector test by now – or at least be a little more suspicious – but I still can't help giving people the benefit of the doubt.

'OK, EVERYONE, LISTEN UP,' shouts Jocelyn. 'I've got an announcement to make.'

'Buffalo Bill's arrived,' Barbara mutters behind the bar. (It's clear she still can't get her head around *la danse country*.)

Jocelyn tells us that she has arranged for us to do a line dancing 'demo' at an agricultural fair in Clussay, the last weekend in August. Along with some state-of-the art tractors and combine harvesters, we will be the star attraction.

Anyone who is interested – wild horses wouldn't stop most of those present from taking part – must put their name down on a list, before the end of today's session. 'We also need a name for our group,' says Jocelyn. 'Any suggestions gratefully received. And we've only got a couple of weeks, so we might need to get in some extra practice sessions. Oh and one more thing. For those who don't already know, Jill and I are hosting a quiz night here on Friday. Barbara is making chilli con carne. It's seven euros for the meal and one euro for the quiz. It should be a good night, so it would be very nice if you could all support it.'

This is obviously another kind-hearted initiative by Jocelyn and Jill to drum up custom for Barbara. Since they are a hugely popular couple – they seem to travel always with a little entourage of friends and neighbours – there is bound to be a big turn-out on Friday. And so, before the end of the session, I've signed up both Jon and me for the quiz night, along with Delphine, who never misses an opportunity to socialise with expat Brits. I draw the line at the demo however, as it is *not* the sort of thing a former fashion editor does in public. God knows, there might even be pictures taken.

'What are you doing this evening?' asks Sarah, as we head out towards the car park in the ferocious heat. 'Do you want to come over for supper and a walk with Biff?'

'Ah, I'd love to,' I say. 'But I'm already going out.' Normally, I'd leap at the chance to see *le petit* Biff, but I'm committed to going to dinner chez Annabel and Charles this evening. Annabel pinned me down a week or so ago, while I was having a coffee with Delphine and Mathilde in the Liberty Bookshop, inviting me in a way that brooked no argument.

Apparently, she and Charles have also bludgeoned their neighbour Andy Lawton into coming, which I have to admit, makes the invitation more alluring. (Strictly speaking I am 'taken' but it would be nice to acquire another friend who is not drawing the state pension, and, as one of my friends in London would say, 'There's no harm in looking'.) I drive home, my mind flip-flopping between the possibilities of tonight's dinner party and a terrible mental image of an electrified little Biff.

Chapter 7

Mugged

AS ALWAYS, I enjoy the early evening drive out to dinner. Speeding through the countryside on a sunlit evening, with the windows down and music playing loudly, is one of my favourite things about living in France. It is just so liberating, so exhilarating, to see the sweeping patchwork of yellow, green and red-brown fields stretching to the flawless blue horizon on either side of the narrow, curving road. Apart from a solitary farmer tilling the field in his tractor, there isn't a soul around for miles.

On the passenger seat next to me are two baguettes (which Annabel asked me to get from the bakery) and a really nice bottle of champagne, sent to me by a handbag designer as a thank you for an article I recently wrote. My first thought was to drink it with Jon when he gets back, but that would be a waste of vintage Krug as he doesn't much like champagne. So, I decide to bring it to Annabel's on the spur of the moment, as it will get the evening off to a better start than Chateau Lidl.

It will be interesting to meet Annabel's other friends. I'm particularly looking forward to meeting Andy Lawton in a normal situation – in other words, while sitting at a table rather than lying in a heap on the floor. When I arrive, Charles, dapper in beige trousers and a pink shirt, comes out to open the gates and greets me warmly. The dogs fortunately, are nowhere to be seen, although I can hear Button yodelling somewhere in the distance. Charles ushers me into the kitchen where Annabel, in ankle-length green chiffon and gold gladiator sandals, is making a salad dressing. Her blonde hair has been pulled back into a rigorous chignon, secured with a jade beaded clip.

'Hello Corinne, how lovely to see you. Did you bring the baguettes? Oh is that for me? How marvellous!' Her eyes light up and before I can reply, she grabs the bottle of Krug out of my hands and stows it away in a kitchen cupboard. 'Better hide it before any of the other guests see it,' she says with a conspiratorial wink. I'm appalled as I've actually bought it for us to drink. 'Actually Annabel, wouldn't it be better to put it in the fridge to chill?' I say, hoping she will get the hint. 'It's not quite cold enough to drink yet.' But she chooses not to hear, and carries on beating the salad dressing, causing her brandy-coloured cleavage to crease up and her bracelets to jangle. 'Now what can Charles get you to drink? Red, white or rosé?'

I honestly feel like I've been mugged, as I think of the very expensive Krug, that I will probably now never get to taste, languishing in Annabel's cupboard. Instead of an ice-cold glass of pale gold, premium bubbles, I accept a lukewarm glass of Lidl rosé and follow Annabel and Charles out to the terrace overlooking the pool, where the other guests are already seated at a long table. It is beautifully laid, with a beige tablecloth and crisp white linen and little glass jars along the centre of the table, each containing the head of a single white rose. White fairy lights have been strung around the cherry and apple trees in the garden and hurricane lamps have been placed around the swimming pool, which is bathed in pink light from carefully placed spotlights. It looks beautiful, reflecting Annabel's talents as an interior designer. It is however, a mystery why she and Charles have landed in the Poitou-Charentes rather than St Tropez. Even though Annabel appears to be quite a successful interior designer, money, I figure, probably has a lot to do with it. Their elegant house and pool would cost at least ten times as much on the Côte d'Azur.

Annabel introduces me to the other guests. They include Travis, 'part-time resident and terribly successful TV producer', and 'Monsieur Lawton, our brave new neighbour, whom I think you may already have met'. To my very great surprise, Annabel introduces me to the assembled group as, 'Corinne, an award-winning investigative journalist'.

Andy Lawton stands up to shake my hand and says, 'Hi, how's it going?' in his laid-back way. His gold-blonde hair seems to have got lighter, his face and arms reddened slightly by the sun. When he smiles, the crinkles round his eyes look more pronounced, the result, no doubt, of being perched on a roof under the Poitevin sun for several hours a day.

Travis, who looks like a highly-groomed version of the Ross character in *Friends*, also seems very friendly. Dressed in a pair of up-to-the-minute dove-grey cotton trousers and a crisp white shirt with the sleeves rolled up, everything about him looks freshly-pressed and laundered. It's obvious that he is not yet a full-time resident in rural France as he is still maintaining London standards of dress.

'What kind of things do you investigate?' he asks, pushing his Dolce & Gabbana sunglasses back on his head.

'Er... At the moment, vibrating mascaras,' I reply.

'That sounds interesting,' says Travis, with a glint in his eye.

'I'm actually a fashion and beauty journalist,' I say.

'So sorry, of course you are,' says Annabel. 'I'm mixing you up with another friend of ours who recently won an award for a piece on the Tamil Tigers.'

'I'd rather read about the vibrating mascaras,' says Travis.

Annabel does not find the comment amusing. 'And this is Moira and Geoffrey, who are currently staying in our gîte,' she continues, unsmilingly.

Moira is a nervous-looking woman – who can blame her, sharing outside space with two mad dogs for a week – in a droopy sundress with circles of sweat under the arms; while Gordon, her husband, has a moustache and a stern demeanour. Neither of them seem happy to be here, but I guess they couldn't avoid it if they are living in Annabel's backyard for a week. Charles indicates for me to take the seat opposite Andy and to the left of him, at the head of the table.

'You've recovered from your recent experience then?' says Andy, alluding to the assault by Button. 'Good to see you've got no bruises.'

'None that are visible,' I say, archly. 'How's the barn conversion going?'

'Yeah, it's going,' he says. 'I've just finished the roof and I might even have a kitchen soon. I've got some mates from the army coming out to help me the week after next,' says Andy.

'Really?' says Travis, his eyes lighting up across the table, suddenly looking very interested (he's not the only one). 'Do you think they might be able to help me shift some oak beams in my place?'

'Yeah, I don't see why not,' says Andy.

Over the first course (half an avocado and a prawn each, beautifully presented on black plates scattered with flakes of red chilli), I chat to Travis, who works for a well-known news channel in the UK. He tells me that he bought his house with an ex-boyfriend five years ago, and tries to visit at least once a month for a long weekend, as his job in London is very stressful. Mostly, he comes out to supervise artisans (as French tradesmen are poetically called) to do the various works. He's had quite a few disasters with tradesmen, it seems, and for this reason alone, I spot a kindred spirit.

I'd like to ask Travis more about his job in London and I'd like to talk to Andy about what it was like serving in Afghanistan but this proves impossible, as the conversation is entirely dominated by Annabel. It soon becomes apparent that we are all there to pay court, and to respond appropriately, to her long monologues. She mostly tells stories of neighbours here in France, borrowing things and returning them broken or not at all; of people with 'other sides' to them; and acquaintances who are always abusing her unfailingly generous nature. Her life in France seems to have consisted of a parade of people who have been outrageously rude, badly behaved, mean or duplicitous in some way.

The monologues very quickly become exhausting to listen to, not least because they are littered with some of my least favourite words in the English language: ghastly, classy (a word, in my view, only ever to be used ironically), dishy, golly, terrifically and, at one point – while describing an interior design scheme – wacky. Whenever she describes an acquaintance for the first time, it is always in a binary way: either '*jarst* delightful' or '*jarst* awful' or – if she's had a real clash with them – '*abs-yo-lootly* vile'.

It rapidly becomes clear that there is no possibility of an actual conversation, or any opportunity for others to speak. Instead, we mutely sip our wine, as her sonorous voice cuts through the warm night air, relaying the story of 'a rather dishy' friend of theirs who has just married someone he met on the Internet. 'She really is *soo-per*, a terribly classy lady,' she says, showing us a picture of an attractive woman in her late thirties. 'We simply couldn't find fault with her, *at all*.' She says this as if she had made it her mission to find one, examining every pore and personality trait of this poor woman as if she were used goods, ordered on eBay.

Charles, to his credit, says nothing. He sits with a patient, good-natured smile on his face. I get the impression that he's sat through Annabel's stories many times before. The main course is served: beef tomatoes stuffed with sausage meat and herbs. There is also a side dish of rice salad. We each help ourselves as the chic black platters are passed around. As we tuck in to our tomatoes – only Gordon, I notice, has dared to take two – Annabel switches the conversation to her gîte and the guests who have stayed there. They all seem to have been odd or flawed in some way, or to have had unreasonable expectations of the accommodation. One of the stories concerns a couple who withheld payment until the final day and I wonder if this is a coded message to Gordon and Moira, who exchange an uncomfortable look across the table. Annabel triumphantly relates how the rent-dodgers tried to sneak out at dawn on the final day, but alerted by the barking of the dogs, she managed to rush out semi-naked and thwart their getaway.

I glance around the table and notice that Andy looks unimpressed, while Moira and Gordon look like they'd rather be on holiday in Helmand province than here. The rest of us are looking at the four tomatoes that remain tantalisingly on the plate but Annabel doesn't offer them around and no one dares help themselves. Travis appears to be plucking up courage but just as he leans towards the plate, Annabel, seemingly oblivious, whisks it away.

'Now, who would like another glass of rosé?' she says, standing up.

'Actually Annabel, I was wondering if the champagne I brought might be chilled by now?' I ask, knowing full well that it's not even in the fridge. 'If not, I'm sure you could just shove it in an ice bucket for a few minutes and that will do the trick.'

'Champagne? Fantastic! Bring it on,' says Travis, sitting up and looking noticeably cheered.

'Oh yes, of course,' says Annabel, with a pinched expression. As she goes back through the patio doors, jewellery jangling, I congratulate myself on forcing her to serve the Krug. But I have underestimated the woman. When she reappears, it is with a bottle of champagne by an unknown brand. I look more closely and see that it is actually a Crémant de Bourgogne, a sparkling wine from Burgundy, made using a similar method as champagne. I have nothing against Crémant de Bourgogne – it is usually good quality and, at around €7 a bottle, excellent value – but it is not quite the same as vintage Krug.

'This one is ice-cold,' she says, unpopping the cork, her walnut cleavage crinkling like the skin on cold custard with the effort. 'Might as well serve this now and we can have yours later with pudding.'

My victory becomes a dispiriting defeat. I'm driving and I'm going to have to squander my last allowable unit on a glass of pretend champagne.

It's not just my spirits that have been sapped. Travis is now looking borderline suicidal and poor old Andy Lawton looks like he has no idea what he is doing here (I suspect it might be the lure of a hot meal, as he doesn't yet have cooking facilities); while Moira and Gordon look utterly miserable. It's a pity, because the setting – a lilac-scented terrace overlooking a pink-lit swimming pool, on a seductively warm summer evening – couldn't be more convivial.

Charles tries to launch a breakaway conversation. 'So what exactly did you do in Afghanistan?' he asks Andy, and I for one, await the answer with interest.

'Ammunition disposal,' he says.

'You mean bomb disposal?' says Charles.

'Yes, but not only. I dealt with all kind of ammunitions: bullets, missiles, as well as enemy explosives,' says Andy, who seems to be downplaying his role.

'Are you trained as a fighting soldier?' asks Travis, looking impressed. (He's not the only one.)

'Yes,' he replies.

'Why did you leave?' asks Travis.

'I took early retirement. With a shoulder injury.'

Andy seems reluctant to talk about his army career, and Charles picks up on this and changes the subject. 'You know, you two should get to know each other better,' he says, nodding at Andy and me. This would probably be a good point to mention the fact that I have a boyfriend, but I don't. (I justify this on the basis that Jon is starting to feel more like a pen pal – albeit an electronic one.)

'Karen could help you out with translation from time to time,' Charles continues. 'And she plays tennis. [I've absolutely no idea why he thinks this.] The two of you could get together on the courts in St Hilaire.'

'Oh, Charles, do stop boring everyone with your silly ideas,' says Annabel. 'Just because you play tennis, doesn't mean that everyone else is interested.'

'Actually, I am,' says Andy, while the rest of us collectively squirm at the verbal rap on the knuckles Annabel has just given her husband. 'Good idea, Charles. I didn't realise that there were tennis courts in St Hilaire.'

'The only problem is that I play tennis *comme une vache espagnole*,' I joke. 'Like a Spanish cow' is the humorous response when someone asks if you speak French, but in this context, it doesn't quite work. Everyone just looks at me blankly.

The sky is a captivating violet-blue, but it is still as warm as a hammam outside. Annabel jangles back indoors and returns – oh joy – with a lavish looking chocolate gateau. I sense the mood around the table pick up but then fall again as Annabel proceeds to serve each of us a doll-sized slice of what she declares to be 'Black Forest gateau revisited'.

'Wow, this is wonderful,' I say, tasting the luxurious combination of chocolate, cherries and cream, liberally laced with kirsch. Annabel flashes me a regal smile and says nothing, while Moira, I notice, flushes pink.

'Oh, I'm so glad,' she says, suddenly plucking up the courage to speak. 'I was delighted to make a pudding when Annabel asked, but it was quite a struggle to find the right kind of cream out here.'

There is a momentary silence around the table as we all digest the fact that Annabel was about to take the credit for someone else's dessert. Rumbled, our hostess eyes Moira as if she would like to push the remaining cake into her face and says, 'Oh yes, I was about to say, that it is Moira that we should thank for this wonderfully decadent treat.'

There is a flurry of approving comments from around the table and Andy Lawton asks if he might have another slice, causing Moira to turn pink again with pleasure.

'To Moira, the queen of puddings,' says Annabel, with more than a hint of sarcasm, as she raises her glass to signal the end of this particular conversation. She then embarks on a story about a gîte guest who accidentally left the iron gates open, allowing Button to escape. '"YOU. STUPID. FUCKING. MAN." I yelled at him,' she recalls. There is dead silence as we all digest this surprising little anecdote. It sounds doubly shocking delivered in Annabel's ridiculously posh accent. She goes on to explain that, spurred on by her anger, the poor guest sprinted across several kilometres of fields before finally managing to catch Button.

I scan the table for other peoples' reactions. The smile has disappeared from Moira's face. She is probably making a mental note always to close the gates for the duration of their stay.

'Good lord,' says Gordon. Andy Lawton shifts uncomfortably in his seat, while Travis is drumming his fingers nervously on the table. There is another awkward silence, filled only by the sound of crickets and a fly buzzing around the remaining Black Forest gateau.

'Better put this back in the fridge,' says Annabel. 'We don't want the flies to get it.' She asks if anyone would like coffee – the Krug never did appear – and Andy looks at his watch and announces that he had better be going. This, despite the fact that he lives less than 50 metres from here and it's barely 10.30 p.m. 'It's been a long day and I'm ready to hit the sack,' he says.

'Yeah, me too,' says Travis, faking a yawn. 'I've got a builder coming early tomorrow morning.'

I start to panic at the idea of being left behind, wondering what excuse I can come up with to join this early exodus. Clearly, no one wants the responsibility of being the last through the infamous gates. Fortunately, inspiration strikes. 'I'd better be off too, as I promised to walk Biff, a friend's dog, early tomorrow morning,' I lie.

'Oh that reminds me, Corinne, I'd like to ask you a little favour before you go,' says Annabel. 'Charles and I have to go back to London for a few days next week and wondered if you might be able to pop in and walk Jenson and Button again?' She makes it sound as easy as popping into water some plants. Across the table, Andy Lawton's eyes widen in disbelief and he looks like he is awaiting my response with interest.

'I'm so sorry Annabel, but I think I might have to go back to the UK myself next week,' I lie.

'Well, if you hear-yah of anyone who might be able to look after Jenson and Button, do let us know,' says Annabel. 'We're happy to pay up to fifteen euros a day for a suitable person.'

There is a strange snort on the other side of the table. I think it might be Andy.

'I'll bear it in mind,' I say, wondering what she means by 'suitable'. Presumably someone who puts a very low value on their personal safety. Travis and Andy are already standing up to leave and I quickly join them. After saying our goodbyes we leave Annabel and her remaining guests sitting by the pool, while Charles goes to check on the dogs, who are locked in the study. As we pass back through the house, I briefly contemplate running into the kitchen and grabbing back my bottle of champagne, but Annabel has probably locked it in the safe by now. I bet Moira won't be seeing her Black Forest gateau again either.

It's a relief to exit on the other side of the house, to breathe in the warm scent of a summer evening and to be free of Annabel and her uncomfortable memoirs. Above us, the sky is stitched with glittering stars – a summer night to savour. But suddenly, I hear an ominous panting, a snort and the unmistakable sound of pounding paws approaching fast from behind. 'Jesus Christ,' shouts Travis, who was just about to open the gate, but instead bears the full brunt of the 60 kilogram force as Button charges straight into his neatly pressed trousers. *'GET DOWN!'* Andy runs over and pulls Button away from Travis, just as Charles comes running out of the house, in hot pursuit.

'So sorry, old chap. He charged out before I could stop him.'

At the back of the house, there is suddenly a volcanic eruption by the pool. *'I TOLD YOU NOT TO LET THE FUCKING DOGS OUT!'*

'Oh great,' says Travis, surveying the dirty paw marks on his trousers with an exasperated sigh. I'm so glad that we're leaving. Safely on the other side of the gate, once Charles has disappeared indoors with Button, the three of us stop to draw breath in the darkness. It's a bonding moment. Andy Lawton says: 'If she had spoken to me the way she spoke to that gîte guest I would have told her what to do with her bloody dogs.'

'Hmm,' says Travis, brushing the dog hairs off his trousers. He curls his lip in disapproval. 'And I think I'd like to hear the other side of some of those stories.'

'How long have you known Annabel?' I ask Travis.

'Oh, I don't really know them very well at all,' he replies. 'I met them last winter when Annabel knocked on my door to say that they had run out of wood and could she possibly borrow some.'

'Did you ever get it back?' asks Andy.

'Now you mention it,' says Travis. 'I don't think I did.'

The three of us agree to meet up soon, either for a drink or a game of tennis – Travis is also keen to play – and we wish each other a warm goodnight. Tonight's experience has definitely broken the ice. And as I drive home, windows wound down in the warm evening air, I feel cheered by the thought that, when Andy Lawton told Annabel that he was 'unavailable for the forseeable future', it probably had nothing to do with me.

Chapter 8

Quizzed

THE PORTUGUESE HOUSE has been unusually quiet since the beginning of August. It feels strange being able to come and go without an audience. My French neighbour Monsieur Moreau, a retired *sapeur-pompier*, or fireman, is monitoring the situation closely. Normally a very happy chap – he and his wife are always smiling and wave energetically when they see me – he seems more bothered by the noise than me, even though I am at the epicentre of it and he lives on a different street. He informs me that the builders have gone back to Portugal for the month and that, 'many, many' people have complained, forcing the mayor to issue a written warning. Our Portuguese neighbours, Monsieur Moreau concludes, might be a little quieter when they return. That, I think to myself, is about as likely as Bordeaux running out of wine.

Another Portuguese man also seems to be causing problems in the village. On Thursday lunchtime, I am walking down rue St Benoit when I see René Matout, the baker, coming out of the side entrance of the bakery, carrying a Swiss-cheese plant. I wave cheerily, not thinking anything of it, but René fails to acknowledge me. I look more closely and see pain furrowed into his face: he looks utterly bereft, his normally tanned skin as pale as his bakers' whites. It takes a further second or two to work out why: his tanned, muscular hunk of a Portuguese boyfriend is loading clothes and various other personal possessions into the back of an estate car and is in the process of moving out of the flat that they share above the bakery. René is standing on the steps at the side of the kitchen, watching his lover leave. Oh dear! This might explain why the bakery keeps closing unexpectedly.

Meanwhile, Jon calls to confirm that he will definitely be returning on Friday morning. He asks if I will pick up him up at Limoges airport. It is a good hour and a half drive away, but the flight to Limoges, he explains, was considerably cheaper than Poitiers.

'No problem,' I say. 'Oh, and I've booked us in for the quiz night at L'Auberge de Claviers on Friday evening.'

'Isn't that where you do your line dancing?' he asks, suspiciously.

'Yes, but don't worry, there won't be any. Sarah and Steve are coming. And Delphine, my mayor friend.'

'OK,' he says. 'That sounds good.'

On Friday morning, I arrive at Limoges airport just before 9.00 a.m, an hour early, to pick Jon up, and sit in the cafe with an espresso, waiting with a little flip of excitement for him to arrive. (Although I generally run late for most things in life, I can always be relied upon to pick friends and relatives up from airports on time.)

I start to worry that Jon has missed the flight, however, when everyone else pours through the arrival gates and after nearly half an hour there is still no sign of him. I call his mobile but it clicks straight into answering service. Finally, when the airport has emptied and I'm the only person left waiting at the little cafe, he saunters through the arrivals gate, dressed in jeans and a dark polo shirt with a jumper tied around his waist.

'Hello minx,' he says, kissing me.

'I was starting to worry that you weren't on the flight.'

'My bag didn't come off until the very end.'

'But everyone came through ages ago.'

'I know. My bag was last. And I had to make a quick phone call,' he says, a little defensively.

'To who?'

'Oh, just another company that's offered me some work. Where is the car parked?'

I walk with him to the car, talking about Barbara and the bar in Claviers, about my adventures with Jenson and Button – which makes him laugh – and how I've been 'borrowing' Biff.

'If I were Sarah I'd be worried,' he says, with a chuckle. 'And how are the Portuguese neighbours?'

'They're away at the moment, thank God.' I leave him the keys so that he can put his bags in the boot, while I go and pay for the car park ticket.

'So did you have a good time in the UK?' I ask, as we drive away from the airport.

'I was working.'

'Not all the time, surely?'

'Pretty much.'

'Did you see Jennie?'

'No.'

'So how long before you have to go back again?'

'Not sure yet.'

Maybe it's the August heat, the fact that I'm hungry or that I had to get up early, but I feel vaguely irritated as we drive home. And not just because Jon is so cagey about the details of his trip to the UK. I was looking forward to meeting him at the airport, and I haven't seen him for nearly two months, but it feels disappointing and I can't quite pinpoint why. I drive him back to his house, where, annoyingly, Jean-Jacques, his local butcher is waiting.

'Are you expecting him?' I ask, as we pull up beside a barn dressed in a purple apron of wisteria.

'Yes, he mentioned he'd drop by this morning. He knows someone who can sell me some sheep.'

'Well, in that case, I won't stay,' I say, annoyed that I'm playing second fiddle to some sheep. 'I have to get home and finish off a feature that's due in this afternoon.'

'All right,' he says, making no attempt to stop me. 'I'll pick you up around seven shall I?'

Delphine arrives at 6.30 p.m. – all red lipstick, dark hair and ruffled gypsy dress. I make us both a *diabolo fraise* (Perrier with a dash of strawberry syrup) and we sit in the courtyard chatting. She tells me that she had another meeting with her divorce lawyer in Poitiers today and that the papers will soon be signed. Divorce seems to agree with her, although I think to some extent she is putting a brave face on the fact that she and her husband are splitting up after twenty years of marriage and two grown-up children.

'So you must be very happy that Jon is back?' she says.

'Well, it's weird. He tells me how much he loves me but his actions and behaviour don't quite live up to his words.'

'How do you mean?'

'Well, this morning, after I'd picked him up from the airport, I was thinking that we'd go out to lunch, that he'd want to spend some time with me after being away for so long...'

'Yes, that's normal,' says Delphine.

'But actually he'd arranged a meeting with his butcher.'

'Oh la la!' says Delphine, shaking her hand limply in front of her chest in the funny gesture that she does to suggest something or someone is not quite right. 'That is not so smashing. Men can be very strange.'

'Yes, I was expecting a passionate reunion. And the whole thing just seemed so… lukewarm.'

'Well, it will be interesting to meet him,' she says.

The doorbell rings and Jon's arrival cuts the conversation short. I introduce him to Delphine and we drive to Claviers talking about the exotic sheep that he is planning to buy. He even has some pictures of them on his phone. (They're cola-coloured and have disturbing-looking horns.) Delphine, who is from a family of farmers dating back generations – her brother Gilles still farms the land – is very knowledgeable on all matters to do with livestock and agriculture and Jon, I can tell, is enjoying talking to her.

'I know a lot about sheep especially,' she says, 'because when I was a little girl, about ten years old, I used to guard them for many hours at a time. My father had a flock of sheep and if we moved them to a field to graze, I would be sent to watch them with a big stick.' It conjures up a lovely image of my raven-haired, lipstick-loving friend, as a latter-day Bo-Peep, sitting in a field in the Poitou with her flock. I can't imagine many ten-year-olds I know (admittedly not many) sheep-sitting for an afternoon – or at least not with good grace.

It's an excellent turnout at L'Auberge de Claviers. Sitting outside in the flattering light of early evening are fellow Brits who have come to this watering hole from miles around for tonight's quiz. They are dressed in the classic expat *à la campagne* look – cropped trousers and short sleeves being the preferred uniform of both sexes during the summer months. Many people – the men particularly – nod hello to Delphine and seem delighted to see her. A committed Anglophile, she has no fear of events where expats congregate in large numbers and seems to know more of the people gathered here than I do. But I wonder aloud what the ageing French population of Claviers thinks about the village bar being taken over in this way? 'I am sure they are not getting on their high horses [sic] about it,' says Delphine, diplomatically. 'They are probably very happy that it is open at all. Before this lady took it over, it was closed and boarded up for a very long time.'

I spot Sarah and Steve, who are standing in the throng by the bar. To be honest, in rural France three or four people might be considered 'a throng', but tonight there are at least twelve people waiting, which could be described as a mass gathering. On the other side of the bar, Barbara is pulling pints in her white chef's jacket. She looks more terrified than ever, all big panicked eyes and pink face, as she struggles to cope. Despite her panicked expression, she moves at a sedate pace, with no sense of urgency as people wait patiently, and full of good humour, to be served. I'm surprised that Barbara is not in the kitchen stirring the chilli con carne. I really hope that she has figured out how to use the gas rings.

'If I'd known it was going to take that long to get served, I'd have brought a camping chair and a good book,' says Steve, when we've finally got our drinks and are sitting at a table outside.

Jon laughs. 'I wonder why she hasn't got anyone helping her.'

'It is probably because of the social charges,' says Delphine.

Ah yes, the dreaded 'social charges'. I remember Dylan and Lola in the Liberty Bookshop telling me about this crippling tariff that all entrepeneurs and business people must pay, before they've earned a single euro. Not only do they have to pay these charges for themselves, but whatever they pay their employees, they must pay again to the state. It's a powerful deterrent for anyone wishing to start their own business.

'It's a lot for her to be doing on her own,' says Sarah. 'Serving behind the bar and cooking a meal for thirty people.'

'But I'm sure she knows what she's doing,' I say. 'She certainly looks the part in her white chef's jacket.'

'Well, I could wear a Formula One suit,' says Jon, with a squeeze of my knee. 'But it doesn't make me Jenson Button.'

'Please,' I say, wincing at the memory of Annabel's dogs. 'Don't mention those words.'

'Sorry minx,' he laughs. 'I forgot.'

'ALL RIGHT, EVERYONE. WE'RE READY TO START,' yells Jocelyn.

We file through into the ballroom and take a table furthest away from the swing doors that lead to the kitchen. If there's a disaster going on in there, I don't want to see it. Jocelyn comes around to take the €1 quiz fee from each of us and to ask for our team name. A brief argument ensues between Jon and Steve as to whether we should call ourselves 'The Simple Minds' or 'Snow Chance'. Delphine finds 'Snow Chance' amusing, so we go for that.

I look around and see many familiar faces from line dancing, this time with husbands in tow. There are about nine tables in total, ranging from two lovely silver-haired couples who've chosen to call themselves the 'No-Hopers' to a table of five, very combative looking types, who've called themselves, for reasons known only to them, the 'Wise Bats'. Sarah tells me that two of them are accountants and one is a former tax inspector. 'They look like they memorise Trivial Pursuit cards in bed at night,' says Steve.

Joceyln and Jill have set themselves up at a little table in the centre of the room. 'I'll be asking the questions and Jill will be scoring,' Jocelyn announces. 'Who with?' someone quips, to which Jocelyn immediately fires back 'Not you!'

'OK, the first round is general knowledge,' she shouts, in total command of the room. 'Question number one: phonophobia is the fear of what? And I'll give you a clue. It's not something that I suffer from.'

'Fear of your own voice,' whispers Sarah. 'Or fear of sounds in general.'

'Question number two,' yells Jocelyn. 'What is the world's third highest peak?'

'I know this,' whispers Jon, immediately writing down the word 'Kanchenjunga'.

'How do you know that?' I ask, impressed.

'I used to go climbing, remember?' he replies with a wink. 'I know about mountains.'

'Oh yes,' I say, remembering that his love of the outdoors was one of the things that first attracted me to him. I guess it's true that opposites attract as I'd rather spend a weekend locked in a lift with Michael O'Leary than go rock climbing.

'Question number three: loriners take care of what animal?'

Jon, who loves animals, smiles and writes down 'horses'. Steve nods. The Wise Bats, I notice, also seem sure of the answer and are confidently passing around a bag of nuts.

'Where did they get those from?' asks Steve. 'Barbara didn't have any when I asked earlier.'

'They must have brought them with them,' says Sarah. 'Look, they've got olives too.'

'Blimey,' says Jon. 'And pork scratchings. I might join their team next time.'

At the end of the first round – which includes an obscure football question that Jon also answers correctly – we're in second place, behind the Wise Bats, who got all ten answers right. It's a promising start. But the questions are more difficult than I imagined. And by the end of the second round (film and television) we are at the bottom of the table, second only to the No-Hopers. The Wise Bats are the highest scorers, closely followed by Gin'll Fix It (five members of the Civray Singles Club).

'I bet they memorise Trivial Pursuit cards in bed at night too,' says Jon, nodding towards the table of three women and two men, all in their fifties and sixties.

'They look like they're having a good time, though,' says Sarah, nodding to the three empty bottles of wine on their table.

Dinner is served and Jocelyn and Jill switch from quizmaster to waitress mode, delivering the food from the kitchen. Barbara's chilli, served with a piece of garlic bread wrapped in foil, is very good but there isn't very much of it – her portion control is as rigorous as Annabel's – and she hasn't made enough garlic bread to go around. But no one complains. After all, this is the first quiz night, so there are bound to be some glitches. Then it's the final two rounds before the Wise Bats are pronounced the winners, with Gin'll Fix It the runners-up. Jill divides up the €34 prize fund between the top three. We manage seventh place, which might not sound too bad, but there were only eight teams.

The evening is deemed a success, mostly down to the wit and charm of our quizmasters. Afterwards, Jocelyn comes over to our table to look for volunteers to do the next quiz in a fortnight's time. She looks directly at me as she asks. I hesitate. The only lists I've ever compiled are 'best-dressed lists' and 'this season's top ten must-haves'. Plus I've got important deadlines looming – namely an article on 'the new nude'. This is not as exciting as it sounds as 'the new nude' is actually the colour beige. I am trying to put a positive spin on the fact that it's back in fashion, when in reality, it drains the wearer's complexion, making them look like they've contracted the Norovirus. But I do want to help Barbara out. And anyway, part of the idea of moving to France was to slow down and get involved. I'm just about to say that we'll do it, but Jon has already accepted.

'And don't forget,' says Jocelyn, as we leave. 'We're doing an extra session of line dancing on Thursday morning to practise for the show.'

I wince that she has mentioned this in public. 'Um… but I'm not doing the show,' I say.

'Oh come on,' says Jocelyn. 'It's obvious that you want to.'

'Please tell me,' says Jon, as we drive home to Villiers, 'that you're not going to be doing this line dancing thing in public.'

'Absolutely not,' I say. 'There is no way that I am going to be dancing on a stage in front of farmers at the agricultural fair in Clussay.'

'Are you sure?' says Delphine, smiling in the back of the car.

'Yes. Totally sure,' I say.

We drop Delphine in front of the *mairie* in Villiers where she has parked her car, and I think how great it is not to be returning home alone. Life is definitely easier as half of a couple – and not just because Jon knows about mountains, horses and football.

'That was fun, minx,' he says, as we walk down rue St Benoit. 'And when we do the quiz it will be even better.'

The following morning we cycle to a *vide-grenier* in the nearby village of Brion. I'm not plannning to buy anything –

there is no space left in my little house – but the car boot sale, in an old farming community, turns out to offer unexpectedly rich pickings. Leaving our bikes against the wall of the church, we join the French locals browsing in the sunshine and realise almost immediately that one of us will have to cycle back to fetch the car and more cash.

As *vide-greniers* go this is the real deal. Most of the vendors are French and, by the looks of it, they really have been emptying out their grandmother's attic, rather than just gathering up old toys, clothes and other junk. All the clichés of French country style are here: the mismatched crockery, copper saucepans, old earthenware pots, willow baskets and crystal decanters – and at bargain basement prices. Jon has soon bought a set of copper saucepans, a bread basket and some large serving dishes for his B & B. He also puts a deposit down on a huge black cauldron, which the vendor tells us was originally used for cooking pig feed.

'What on earth are you going to do with that?' I ask.

'I'm going to turn it into a fire pit in the garden,' he replies.

'A fire pit?'

'To sit around in the evening. You put wood in it, like a woodburner and you can also barbecue food over it.'

I spot an old Louis Philippe-style mirror and almost fall over when told the asking price: €15. Admittedly, the glass is mottled – actually a good thing as it proves that it is old – and the intricate brown moulding is chipped in several places exposing the white plaster underneath, but the going rate for such mirrors, as I know from having looked at lots of them, is €80–100. The vendor, a pretty twentysomething, appears to be enjoying a day out with her mother and grandmother, who both look very jolly, chatting and drinking coffee.

'It's very cheap,' I say.

'It's a little damaged,' she replies with a shrug and a smile.

A coat of chalky white or grey paint will easily hide the damage to the frame and I like the idea that all three generations of women present may have checked their reflections in this mirror over the years. I hand over the €15 before the vendor changes her mind. As Jon picks it up, she warns him to hold it from the bottom in case the glass falls out, as it's not secure in the frame.

'That's easily fixed,' says Jon, as we walk away. 'But I don't believe you,' he laughs. 'You're supposed to haggle about the price, not tell the vendor that it's too cheap.'

'It was only fifteen euros. What's the point?' I say.

A refreshment tent consisting of a makeshift bar and long trestle tables has been set up in the corner of the square. Jon suggests that I wait there with the mirror and other booty, while he cycles back to Villiers.

'I'll come with you. We can leave the stuff with the girl who sold me the mirror. I'm sure she won't mind.'

'It's really hot. There's no point in us both going,' he persists. 'We can put your bike in the back of the car.'

It's a long wait – nearly two hours. I amuse myself by playing my favourite game, 'Spot *l'anglais*', although in fact, there aren't many of them. As lunchtime approaches, the crowd starts to thin and just when I'm starting to go mad with boredom and wondering where on earth Jon is, I see a familiar face. It's Andy Lawton looking at an old wooden sack trolley on a stand opposite. He's wearing khaki shorts and surfer sandals and has a rucksack over one shoulder. He appears to be on his own, which suggests he has not yet been snapped up – a fact that pleases me greatly, although I know it shouldn't. But then I notice that no, he isn't on his own. He has a male friend with him. The friend has a shaved head and is lean, tanned and super-fit looking. Possibly a friend from the forces, I think to myself, who's come out to visit.

I'm following their progress around the fair with interest when Jon reappears.

'Sorry minx. I had to stop for diesel,' he says.

'But you've been gone ages. I thought you'd only be an hour.'

'Yeah, well I had to take a work phone call.'

'On a Sunday?'

'It was important.'

'Are you sure you didn't sneak off to visit someone else?' I say, only half joking.

'*Oh please*,' he says – a response which strikes me as ambiguous.

The cauldron won't fit in the car, so Jon makes arrangements to collect it later in the week with his four-wheel drive, or 'the tank' as he calls it. When I get home, I take a closer look at the mirror and discover that it is just the backing paper that is loose on the back. Underneath, the glass is firmly held in place by wooden baguettes, and ready to hang. Jon offers to do it. Holding it up against the wall in the guest room, I decide it doesn't even need a coat of paint. It's perfectly imperfect and if anything, the damage adds to its charm. Amazing, I think to myself, what you can discover at a car boot sale.

In the week ahead I see a lot of Jon – if I'm honest maybe too much, given that I have several work deadlines looming. In the evening he comes over for a walk or a bike ride and afterwards I make dinner. Often he drops by in the daytime too. Although he lives 10 kilometres away, most mornings he finds a reason to come to Villiers – to visit the bank, buy plants and look at livestock if its a *foire* day or to meet Mathilde in the Liberty Bookshop for his twice-weekly French lesson. Afterwards, he invariably pops round 'just to say hi', and although he is supposed to be installing guest bathrooms in his B & B, he never seems in a hurry to leave.

My work–life balance, already a little off kilter, becomes even more unbalanced. As a freelance fashion and beauty writer, I should, in theory, be spending seven hours a day at my desk; but the reality is that in France, in the summer, there are days when all I manage to do is check my emails. If Delphine or Mathilde call to say that they are in the Liberty Bookshop, for example, I need little persuasion to join them, and it's amazing how an entire morning can then just disappear. Ditto if I go into Poitiers to visit Zara or look around the shops; or if I drive 25 kilometres to Civray for the weekly yoga class at La Grande Galerie, a cultural space with a busy little cafe attached. In addition, there are line dancing classes to attend, plants in the courtyard to keep alive, friends to visit and a little dog in Romagne to walk.

But when a deadline looms, I work day and evening until it's done. This infuriates Jon. 'You need to organise your time better' is the terse response when I phone one afternoon to say that I won't be able to go for a drink at the bar in St Secondin that evening as planned. I decide to ignore this comment and the lecture that he gives me about my time-management. After all, I *am* glad to have him back.

On Thursday morning, against my better instincts, I return to L'Auberge de Claviers for the demo practice session – for the exercise, obviously. I've lost several kilos since taking up line dancing and I'm not the only one. All the regulars look slimmer and fitter, while Jocelyn has undergone a dramatic transformation. She has dropped several dress sizes – or rather trouser sizes since I've never actually seen her in a dress – in about six weeks.

The troupe now has a name – the Civray Stetsons, named after the nearby town – and it will soon have matching T-shirts paid for by the Entente Cordiale committee. It's also been decided that it will perform three dances at the agricultural fair: the 'Texas Slide', 'God Blessed Texas' (which includes a raunchy little hip shimmy) and another dance, called, ahem, the 'Boot Scootin' Boogie'. All we have to do is perfect the steps. I say 'we' because at the last moment, I am persuaded to join in order to make up the numbers. Twenty-three people have signed up for the demo but twenty-four are needed to make matching lines, and Jocelyn can be *very* persuasive.

The T-shirts arrive the following Tuesday but excitement soon turns to disbelief as Vivienne distributes them at the end of the class. One of our number, a comfortable size sixteen, turns as pale as a *fromage de chèvre* as she pulls hers out of its plastic wrapping and holds it up against her ample chest. It's not much bigger than an iPod and there is little to no chance of it reaching beyond her armpits. I'm not thrilled about the idea of wearing a white T-shirt with 'The Civray Stetsons' picked out in diamanté across the chest anyway, and even less delighted when I discover that mine (supposedly size 'medium', but actually size 'toddler') barely reaches my navel.

'Jocelyn,' I say. 'We are none of us Britney Spears. And we don't want to frighten the horses at this farm festival.'

'Speak for yourself,' she replies, pulling her own 'large' T-shirt from its bag. 'And anyway, there won't be any horses. Just cows and some llamas. And maybe sheep.'

'*Quand même,*' I say. 'The idea is to attract some French people to take up line dancing. If we appear in these T-shirts, they're likely to run for their barns.'

'Bloody hell,' she says, as she holds up her own T-shirt. 'You're right. The sizing is completely out.'

In the end, a compromise is reached. The larger ladies will be allowed to wear plain white T-shirts or shirts of their own; while the rest of us will have to wear the shrunken diamanté ones but layered over another white T-shirt or vest top for decency's sake. Since the T-shirts are already as tight as elastic bands, that's not going to leave much room to maneouvre. It's a good thing that *la danse country* doesn't involve much movement above the waist.

On Friday afternoon I collect Biff and his overnight bag from Romagne and bring him back to Maison Coquelicot for yet another mini-break. Sarah and Steve readily agreed as he's been up to no good again – escaping, digging up the garden and chewing Steve's highly prized ornamental clogs (I've no idea what they are but apparently they were on display next to the woodburner before Biff tucked into them). It's odd because Biff always behaves impeccably when he is with me. I promise, as always, to deliver him back on Sunday with his paws worn out and hopefully too exhausted for any Houdini-like antics with the (recently reinforced) garden gate.

I've planned a special treat for him. Early on Saturday morning I drive to St Hilaire. Thanks to my adrenaline-charged escapades with Jenson and Button, I know a lovely walk leading to a pond that is deep, very clean, and quite perfect for a little dog to swim in. Obviously, the fact that I might bump into Andy Lawton has no bearing on my decision to walk Biff there. None whatsoever. Still, it's a high risk plan as I might bump into Annabel. And if I do, she might try and foist Jenson and Button on me again. I park my car in a clearing that can't be seen from her house, and follow the narrow track that runs along the side of Andy's barn. I notice as we walk by that his shutters are closed and his car isn't there. He must be away again.

Once we're through the hamlet, I unclip Biff from his lead and he's off like a little black bullet flying between yellow fields. I follow behind, captivated by the tranquil scenery, the clean green scent of a July morning and the gentle warmth of the low-slung sun. It's not yet 8.00 a.m and there is a subtle haze over the fields, throwing everything into soft focus and signalling the heat to come. I feel so lucky to be part of this perfect morning. It's like nature's equivalent of Prozac (or several shots of tequila). With or without a dog, I tell myself, I should set my alarm earlier and do this more often.

Until now, most of my forays into the French countryside have taken place in the evening. When I first arrived, I made it my mission to follow every unexplored farm track to its end, often cycling until the sun slipped out of the sky and darkness fell over the surrounding fields. In this way, I got to know every *petit chemin* and every hidden hamlet within 20 kilometres of Villiers. And even now, my favourite antidote to a day writing about the comeback of the kitten heel or the return of the polka dot is to jump on my bike and cycle for a few hours. But in the early morning light, and with Biff for company, it's like discovering the French countryside anew.

We follow the dusty track up and down, past sun-coloured crops and green fields, towards an old church spire in the far distance. I clip Biff back on his lead as we approach a small farming hamlet, passing several stone cottages with bleached blue-grey shutters and pots of coral-pink geraniums outside. Eventually, we reach a narrow road with a hedgerow and a field of sheep on one side; and, slightly incongruously, a shady green dell and the pond on the other.

I set Biff free and watch as he heads towards it. He looks uncertain for a moment and then slides into the deep, clean pond with a little splash. *'Allez, Biff!'* I shout, as his big paws propel him through the dark water, his head bobbing up and down on the surface. He looks a little panicked when he discovers how deep the water is but then gains in confidence as he swims to the other side, and I can't stop myself clapping and shouting encouragement. 'Well done, Biff,' I yell, grateful for the fact that deep in the French countryside, no one can see or hear me. '*C'est très bien.*' He scrambles out of the water on the other side, as black and shiny as a baby seal, looking as pleased with himself as I am proud. Returning to the hamlet, there is no sign of Andy Lawton and thankfully, no encounter with Annabel. I drive home singing along to Lily Allen, a damp dog tucked under the seat in the back of the car.

Back in Villiers I stop at the *boulangerie* to buy some cakes – Jon is coming over for lunch along with some other friends – and am delighted to see that René Matout himself is serving. He hasn't been the same since his boyfriend left. Several times recently I have seen him on rue St Benoit, sitting on the side steps to the bakery, anxiously drawing on a cigarette and staring into the middle distance. And it must be said that the once well-stocked cake cabinet is looking very lacklustre these days. In place of the vibrant patchwork of colour and texture, there is now a sparse selection of eclairs and fruit tarts. Where, I wonder are the Mont Blancs – those firm and tantalising mounds of puréed chestnut and whipped cream on a meringue base – or his rose-almond *bûche*? There is no sign of his famous *religieuse ananas* – two pastry puffs in a frilled skirt of yellow custard, topped by a jaunty slice of pineapple – or his sumptuous *tarte citron meringuée*. René's choux buns have lost their bounce, along with the baker himself.

'*Ça va, René?*'

'*Pas vraiment,*' he replies, his voice cracking with emotion.

I pull a sympathetic face, not sure what to say. It can't be easy being a single gay man in a small French village, where other gay men are a rarity. The rumour in the village is that Miguel, his ex-boyfriend, who is a window dresser by profession, has gone to live in Paris because there wasn't any work for him in the countryside. I remember once complimenting René on his wonderful Valentine's Day windows and he looked so proud as he told me that his boyfriend had done them.

'You look very tired,' I say. 'Maybe you need a rest.'

'I can't sleep at the moment,' he says, looking as if he might burst into tears.

I pull another sympathetic face.

'Things are... very difficult,' he says.

'I'm sorry,' I say and ask for two baguettes. 'But I'm sure it will get easier soon.'

This time he looks like he really will cry and I'm really grateful when a little old lady in a floral pinny with a pull-along trolley comes into the shop behind me. I pick up my baguettes and leave, wishing that there was a way, not just for René but for the sake of the village, that Miguel might be persuaded to come back.

A week before the agricultural fair, or the *Comice Agricole* to give it its French name, disaster strikes. Vivienne, a petite Scottish lady, who is the new and very dynamic social secretary of the Entente Cordiale and one of our star dancers, hobbles into the bar in Claviers for the Wednesday morning practice session with her foot in plaster. 'This is just a ploy to get out of wearing your child-size T-shirt isn't it?' I joke, as everyone gathers around.

'What happened?' asks Barbara, eyes as wide as soup plates, behind the bar.

'I was knocked over by a very big dog,' says Vivienne. The story, as she begins to tell it, sounds very familiar. Vivienne was seconded into looking after two dogs, whose owners had been let down at the last minute by another dogsitter. 'One of the dogs, a sort of black pit bull-like thing, came running towards me and hit me full force on the knees,' says Vivienne, still looking haunted by the memory. The other women shake their head and tut in sympathy.

'These dogs,' I say. 'Were they by any chance called Jenson and Button?'

'How on earth did you know that?' says Vivienne.

With or without Vivienne, the show must go on. Those French farmers are counting on us. And by a strange quirk of fate, we recruit a replacement by lunchtime. Her name is Gloria, and she wanders into L'Auberge de Claviers during our break. Jocelyn rushes forward to explain that we are actually practicing for a demo on Saturday, and that while she is welcome to watch, the steps might be too complicated for her.

'Oh, I have done a little bit of line dancing before,' says Gloria, with what turns out to be considerable understatement. 'Perhaps I can just watch and join in if I know the steps.' Jocelyn agrees but looks sceptical. 'How did you get to know about us anyway?' she asks.

'Oh, I walked by the bar a few times and heard the music,' Gloria explains. 'I've only just moved here.'

Gloria has shoulder-length, white-blonde hair and a gap-toothed smile. She is in her late fifties but seems much younger, thanks to a mischievous smile and a naughty laugh. Drawing up a bar stool, she explains that her husband recently died. (Another one, I think to myself. What is it about all these husbands dying like wasps that have flown into a honey pot on arrival in France?) But rather than go back to the UK, where she has children and grandchildren, she has decided to stay on in France alone. At the end of half an hour's chat, we all feel like we've known her forever, though Jill, I note, seems more than a little dismissive of her new neighbour.

Undeterred, the newcomer follows us back into the ballroom for the second half of the session. 'This one is called "Boot Scootin' Boogie",' explains Jocelyn, looking at Gloria. 'You might want to sit it out, as the steps are a little complicated.'

'That's OK, I know it,' says Gloria.

Jocelyn puts the music on, still looking sceptical. But within a few minutes, she is staring at Gloria, open-mouthed, as indeed we all are. This white-haired grandmother, dressed in loose-cut trousers and a baggy white shirt, is utterly mesmerising to watch. The way that she moves her hips is almost indecent; while your eyes cannot help but be drawn to her sassy little wiggle.

It defies all the laws of line dancing – which, unlike most forms of dancing, suppresses individuality in favour of group conformity. Yet, somehow Gloria manages both. She conforms, in that she knows the steps perfectly, but she performs them with an extra dose of charisma or *je ne sais quoi*. And unlike the rest of us, who are grimly focused on the steps, Gloria's shoulders are back, her head held high. She seems to be enjoying herself enormously and above all, goddamnit, she looks sexy.

'That wasn't bad,' Jocelyn tells her when the dance is finished.

It turns out that Gloria also knows the other dances we are doing. Jocelyn, I can tell, is impressed; Jill, less so.

'OK, are you free on Saturday afternoon?' Jocelyn asks, at the end of the session.

'I think so,' says Gloria.

'Great,' says Jocelyn. And so, just like that, Gloria Roper, a gap-toothed, recently-bereaved grandmother from Plymouth, with a saucy grin and a sassy little wiggle, becomes the Civray Stetsons' newest recruit.

By the final Friday practice session, thanks to Jocelyn's ruthless coaching – 'Karen, yer ruining it by doing an extra step,' she yells at me at one point – we're as ready as we're ever going to be. Even Barbara abandons her post behind the bar to come and watch the final run-through in the ballroom, although she puts a bit of a dampener on things when she declares, with typical Yorkshire bluntness, that we all look 'a bit bluddy glum'.

Jocelyn reminds us that the uniform is jeans, white T-shirts, and brown cowboy boots, and tells us to meet at the Entente Cordiale stand at tomorrow's fair at around 1.30 p.m. 'Oh and don't forget, everyone. Karen's doing the quiz here tonight. But don't let that put you off. At least the food should be good.'

Compiling the quiz is harder work than I imagined. I manage to put together a section on English literature and, fortunately, Jon does the rest. On Friday afternoon he arrives at my house with his laptop and more questions than *University Challenge*. His *pièce de résistance* is a section on the Poitou-Charentes. Unfortunately, I can't answer any of them. 'These are a little difficult,' I say. He flashes me The Look, which means that things could get tricky if I argue with him.

'They're staying,' he says, firmly.

'Well maybe we could just swap a few of the questions for something simpler?' I suggest.

'If you mess with any of my questions I won't do the quiz with you,' he says. I think he's joking but I'm not sure.

Getting ready to go to Claviers that evening, I feel quite nervous. The only public speaking I've ever done was at a shopping event in a fashion boutique in Manchester, organised by the magazine I was working for at the time. Only one person showed up, an old lady in a knitted hat who, thinking that no one was looking, swept all the sandwiches from the buffet into her plastic carrier bag, before attempting to shoplift a sequined skirt. Meanwhile, I wandered around with a microphone talking about the season's key trends, for the benefit of some bored-looking shop assistants. At least there should be a better turnout this evening. Barbara's fish pie – 'no wun does a fish pie like my fish pie,' she boasted earlier – is going to be the star attraction. As for the quiz, Jocelyn and Jill are going to be a hard act to follow. No pressure or anything but I'm well aware that if the quiz doesn't go down well, people might not come back.

Jon and I have agreed that I will ask the questions and he will do the scoring.

'Do you need a calculator?' I ask, as we are getting ready to leave.

'No,' he says, flashing me The Look. 'I don't need a calculator to work out some quiz scores.'

'Up to you,' I say. 'But remember, everyone takes this very seriously. No room for any errors. Get it wrong and we'll be in trouble.'

News of the previous quiz night must have spread, because when we arrive at the L'Auberge de Claviers, there are twice as many people as last time. Sarah and Steve are sitting outside in the sunshine and there are lots of members of the line dancing group there with their husbands. I see Jocelyn and Jill standing at the bar with a big group of friends, including our new recruit Gloria, who is looking quite minxy in dark indigo jeans with rhinestones on the pockets and lizard cowboy boots the colour of Dijon mustard. Despite only having met them that morning, she appears to be laughing and joking with Jill and Jocelyn as if they were old friends.

I also spot Annabel and Charles drawing up in the car park, which is surprising as I wouldn't have thought that an expat quiz night would be their thing.

Barbara, meanwhile, appears to have gone to ground and, worryingly, there is no one serving behind the bar. Jocelyn, whose reservoir of goodwill towards Barbara appears to be running dry, shakes her head in disbelief. 'Where the bloody hell is she?' she says, taking charge of the situation as usual. 'Honestly, she's expecting this bar to run itself.'

We find Barbara in the spotless stainless-steel kitchen, staring belligerently at the oven. 'There's a problem with us fish pie,' she says. 'Bluddy oven wun't heat up. It's bin in there for 'ours and it's still stone cold.'

Jocelyn and I both immediately glance at the electrical socket but this time, the appliance appears to be plugged in. We open the oven door and it's true that it is emitting very little heat. If Basil Fawlty had a bar in France, I think to myself, this would be it.

'I don't know what to say,' says Jocelyn, after playing around with the temperature dial for a few minutes.

'Why don't I get Jon to come and have a look,' I say. 'He's good at stuff like that.'

'Barbara, you need to do something about the bar,' says Jocelyn. 'You can't leave it unattended like that. Do you want me do it?'

'If you want,' says Barbara, who is not big on gratitude.

'Oh dear,' says Jocelyn, shaking her head as we go back into the bar. 'Still,' she says with a wink, 'I've always fancied being put in charge of a bar.'

As Jon goes into the kitchen to try and help with the oven, and Jocelyn takes over behind the bar to a round of applause, I join Steve and Sarah and ask about my little friend Biff.

Unfortunately, it sounds like he's been naughty again, escaping and taking Milou with him. Worse, last night he apparently cocked his leg against the fireplace, while looking Steve directly in the eye, in an overt gesture of disobediance. It sounds to me as if Biff is trying to make himself as disagreeable as possible, perhaps in the hope that Sarah and Steve might give him to me.

'I'm not sure what's going on,' says Sarah. 'He's really acting up at the moment. But if you want him this weekend, I could drop him off tomorrow morning, as we're going into Poitiers for the day.'

'Oh, yes please. I'm doing the line dancing demo at Clussay tomorrow afternoon but I'll bring him with me.'

'Not you too?' says Steve, with a look of disbelief. 'Good God, it seems like this line dancing thing is turning into a cult.' He looks at Sarah, who dropped out of the class a few weeks ago when the steps started getting too complicated. 'Thank goodness you got out in time darling,' he says.

A little beige van draws up in the car park and Delphine, Mathilde and Sebastian roll out. Mathilde, her dark hair in a chignon, looks very elegant, wearing a little cotton dress in the exact shade of 'new nude' that I have been writing about. On her, the colour actually works, enhancing her brown skin rather than making her look anaemic. Her partner Sebastian is an artist. Tall, charismatic and with long grey hair in a loose ponytail, nine out of ten people would guess that by looking at him. I invited my French friends along as I thought it might be fun for them to experience an English pub quiz and some hearty Yorkshire cooking. Now, as they come over to join us, I'm wondering if I've made a terrible mistake, not least because I have really 'bigged up' Barbara's fish pie, making a big deal of the fact that she is a Yorkshire woman and this is her signature dish.

'I really cannot wait for this fish pie,' says Mathilde, after I've introduced everyone. 'I imagine it is very filling, so I didn't eat any lunch today.'

'Yes,' says Sebastian, eyes twinkling. 'I am really looking forward to some English cuisine.'

'Me too,' says Delphine. 'It should be very good.'

Aaghagh! I scream silently, hoping that Barbara has managed to get the oven working.

Jon reappears. 'I think the fish pie is going to be a while,' he says.

'Well, I hope it's not going to be too long,' says Steve. 'I'm starving. And I'm not the only one.'

At least Jocelyn has the bar under control. In a checked shirt and jeans, and a face entirely free of make-up, she is not your stereotypical barmaid. Nonetheless, she is proving a hit with the customers, laughing, chatting and poking fun at them. At 8.00 p.m. she claps her hands together and tells everyone to move next door into the ballroom as the quiz is about to start.

My first duty as quizmaster is to go around the various tables, recording team names and taking the quiz fees. The teams include the Wise Bats, who won last time and the Eggheads (Annabel and Charles plus the latest occupants of their gîte). Sarah and Steve have teamed up with my French friends and are once again going by the name of Snow Chance; while the No-Hopers, the two absolutely charming elderly couples, who came last in the previous quiz, are obviously good sports as they have returned for potentially more public humiliation.

'That'll be one euro each then,' I say, when I get to Annabel's table. The gîte couple hand me €2 and then watch as Annabel rummages in her purse. They are not going to help her out. Annabel, like the queen, never seems to carry any cash. She is a type that I've met many times in the fashion world: all fur coat and no funds – or at least none that she is prepared to part with.

'Oh dear,' she says. 'I don't have any change. I might have to wait for Charles to get back from the bar.' I get the impression that she is hoping I will waive her quiz fee or that someone else will pay it.

'I'll come back,' I say.

When I do, Charles is chatting to Delphine and it's still a battle to get money out of Annabel. But I'm determined. Eventually, she hands me a €50 note, which is annoying because I don't have any change, as I'm sure she knows. I take the note anyway, and promise to come back later. I've been told by Jocelyn that we should do two rounds and then stop for dinner. My English literature questions do not go down very well. I notice that there is a lot of head shaking and staring into space. 'Karen, it's supposed to be a pub quiz,' shouts Jocelyn, as rumbustious as ever. 'Not a bloody A-level exam.' She's got a point. Even the Wise Bats only get four of my literature questions right. Fortunately, Jon's general knowledge round is more successful, triggering lively debate, and lots of audible whispers of 'I know that!'

Predictably, at the end of the first two rounds, the Wise Bats are comfortably in the lead and the No-Hopers are in last place. I go into the kitchen hoping to find dinner is ready to be served. But Barbara tells me, unapologetically, that the fish pie is not yet cooked. So I go back and ask another set of questions. Half an hour later, I return to the kitchen hoping to see plates laden with fluffy fish pie, lined up and waiting to be ferried through to the ballroom. But there is no sign of anything emerging from the oven, let alone making it onto a plate. 'It's going to be at least another half an hour,' says Barbara, staring at the oven. 'They'll just have to bluddy well wait.'

Back in the ballroom everyone looks… ravenous. Mathilde, who normally eats at 7.00 p.m. on the dot, is starting to look as pale as her dress. 'Is everything OK?' asks Jon, looking worried.

'No,' I whisper. 'She needs another half-hour. At this rate we're going to run out of questions.'

'Fortunately,' he says. 'I did an extra set.'

'Oh thank goodness. Where are they?'

With a flourish, he hands me another list of questions. 'Oh dear,' I say when I see the subject matter – French cuisine.

'OK folks,' I shout. 'One more round before dinner.' The mood in the room sinks like a soufflé. They were hoping for dinner, not more questions. I look up nervously. The assembled throng looks hungry enough to eat their scoresheets. 'Question number one: name the fruit traditionally used in a *tarte tatin*.'

'Question number two: if you ask for your steak to be cooked *"saignant"* what does that mean?' (The answer, I know, is 'rare' or 'bloody' which is what this situation is likely to become if Barbara doesn't get a shove on.)

I go through the questions at the speed of a combine harvester crawling along a country road in a *convoi exceptionnel*, and include many long pauses.

'Would anyone like me to repeat any of the questions?' I ask hopefully, at the end of the round. Silence. No one does. 'OK, please swap papers with the table next to you,' I say. While everyone is doing this, I hotfoot it back into the kitchen to check on Barbara's progress. I find her casually washing some wine glasses. 'Barbara, we're going to have to get a move on here.'

'There's nowt much I can do if us oven isn't working properly,' she says.

It's all right for Barbara, I think as I go back into the ballroom. She can hide behind the swing doors and doesn't have to deal with a hungry mob. I know it's not my fault, but as quizmaster I feel somehow responsible. 'Excuse me love,' says a woman sitting at a table near the kitchen door. 'Any chance of some bread? My husband suffers from low blood sugar. He needs to eat soon.' I look at the pale-faced chap sitting next to her. He looks like he's losing the will to live. God, this quiz is becoming a medical emergency.

'I'll see what I can do.' I rush back into the kitchen. 'Barbara,' I say. 'People are asking for bread.'

'Bluddy 'ell,' says Barbara. 'They'll be wanting champagne and caviar next. What do they expect for seven euros?' She might just as well have said, 'Let them eat cake.'

'I think we're going to have to serve up soon,' I persist. 'People are starting to get a bit restless.'

'I'm doing us best luvvie. They'll just 'ave to 'old their horses. It's not the bluddy Ritz.'

She's got a point, but so have they. This is a restaurant after all and a basket of bread doesn't seem like that much to ask. I go back into the ballroom and tell the lady with the sugar-starved husband that the food won't be long.

'Please tell me the food is ready,' says Jon, when I return to the quiz table.

I shake my head. 'How many more spare sets of questions have you got? We could still be here for breakfast at this rate.'

Jocelyn gets up from her table and comes over. 'Is everything all right? It's ten o'clock. I don't think we can expect people to wait much longer for their meal.'

'Perhaps you can go and have a word,' I say. 'She doesn't seem to sense the urgency.' I plod on with the answers to the French cuisine questions, torturing the hungry crowd with mentions of coq au vin, rare steaks and and beef *bourguignon*. By the time this round has finished and each table has called out its score, it's nearly 10.30 p.m. The Wise Bats are still in the lead and looking very smug about it, while Annabel's team is in second place.

Back in the kitchen, I am overjoyed to find that there is a big metal catering dish sitting on a stainless-steel worktop.

'Now where's us ladle… ' says Barbara, looking around the kitchen.

'Oh come on, Barbara! Get a move on!' I want to scream.

Instead, I watch as she wanders around looking for a serving spoon. I'm almost tempted to start scooping up the fish pie and dolloping it onto plates with my hands. Eventually, she finds a ladle and starts to dish up the food, all in her own good time, with no concept of the discontent on the other side of the door. I'm surprised to see that she is serving the fish pie into soup bowls rather than normal plates, and that the portions are more like *amuse-bouche* than main course size. Even more worryingly, Barbara's fish pie looks more like fish soup, with bits of hard boiled potato and pink salmon dropped into it.

'Can I help?' I ask, wanting to snatch the ladle from her and serve it more speedily.

'Nooh, I'm all right, pet,' she says.

'Is there another tray in the oven?' I ask, worried that there doesn't look like anywhere near enough food to go round.

'No pet. This is it,' she says.

There are murmurs of discontent on the quiz-room floor as Jon and I deliver the small bowls to the various tables. It's Michelin-sized portions of greasy-spoon food – the worst of both worlds. I walk away quickly before anyone has chance to protest, but I can sense the collective dissatisfaction.

One of the Wise Bats – or the Stupid Prats as Jon has quietly taken to calling them as he adds up the scores – calls me over to complain.

'I can't eat this,' she says. 'The potatoes aren't cooked.'

I can't argue. 'Um, yeah... Sorry about that. I think Barbara had a problem with the oven.'

Annabel is also very unhappy (even though she and Barbara seem to have the same approach to portion control). 'Corinne, what on earth do you call this?' she asks, summoning me over. 'It's not what I'd call fish pie. Or value for money. I'm very loath to pay seven euros for this. Even a ham sandwich would have been better. And have you got the change from my fifty-euro note yet?'

My French friends try to put a positive spin on the tiny portions that I set in front of them.

'At least we will not be gaining any kilos,' says Mathilde, patting her already flat stomach.

'Yes, I am glad that the food is not too 'eavy,' says Delphine.

Unfortunately, there isn't enough food to go around, so Jon and I don't get to taste Barbara's famous fish pie, but as I'm clearing the plates away, several people complain that they are still hungry and ask if there is any possibility of dessert. I go back into the kitchen, confident that, as a Yorkshire woman, Barbara is bound to have a few Bakewell tarts or treacle puddings stashed away in her larder, but she blinks uncomprehendingly when I ask and an outraged expression flashes across her face.

'I'm not bluddy well doing pudding as well for seven euros,' she says.

'Oh no, I know that. People are prepared to pay extra for it. They just want to know what the options are.'

'There aren't any,' she says. 'No one mentioned doing afters as well.'

I desist from pointing out that she *is* running a restaurant and it's not that unreasonable a request as I don't want to add to her stress. Instead, I relay the news back to those who've asked, fully expecting them to start eating their scoresheets sometime soon. I decide to get through the last round as quickly as possible, before it all goes really badly wrong. Halfway through the questions – Jon's round on the Poitou-Charentes – I remember that I must give Annabel her change. As I approach her table, I see that she has got a mobile phone out and is googling the answer to the question 'What is Le Vigeant famous for?' (Car-racing, if you're wondering.) I am shocked – surely no one needs to win a prize of €27 that badly – but say nothing.

Fortunately, when Jon adds up the final scores, Annabel's Eggheads are in third place, despite scoring full marks in the final round. Instead, according to Jon's scoresheet, the No-Hopers have won, with the Wise Bats in second place. 'Are you sure?' I say. 'I don't think that's possible. Here, let me check.'

'No,' he says, pulling the scoresheet away. 'You'll just have to believe me.' He gives me The Look, telling me I mustn't question him further. But I am absolutely sure that the No-Hopers could not possibly have won. They were trailing in seventh place at the end of the previous round. But it falls to me to make the announcement.

'In third place, the Eggheads.' I hand them their prize of €5. Naturally, it is Annabel who takes the money.

'In second place, the Stupid Prats.' There is silence in the room and I glare at Jon, who has written down the results using his unflattering nickname for the team of retired accountants. 'Sorry, I mean the Wise Bats.'

'And the winner is... The No-Hopers.'

There is a murmur of surprise at this news and a delay before the room breaks into a polite ripple of applause. The Wise Bats look stunned – one of them starts making calculations on a piece of paper – while no one looks more surprised at the outcome than the No-Hopers themselves.

'Are you sure, dear?' one of them whispers as I hand them €27 – their share of the prize fund.

'Yes, just take it,' I plead, before anyone else questions the decision.

The evening has not been a huge success. There are vague whispers and disgruntled looks as people file back out through the bar and into the car park. Hardly anyone hangs around. As Jon says, they've gone home to make themselves something more substantial to eat. Several people stop to say that they particularly liked the Poitou-Charentes questions – the section that I was worried would be too difficult. 'Honestly?' says Jon, looking very pleased with himself and flashing me a told-you-so grin. No one congratulates me on my English literature questions; although Mathilde, Sebastian and Delphine thank me politely for a *'super bon'* evening. (Their team, Snow Chance, came a very respectable fourth, helped by the Poitou-Charentes round for which they scored full marks.)

'I'm sorry about the pie and the wait,' I say.

'Oh, it's not your fault,' says Mathilde, shrugging her slim brown shoulders.

'I'm a little embarrassed all the same.'

'It's no big deal,' says Sebastian in French, shaking his head to emphasise the point.

Eventually, it is just Jon and I left. We pull up some bar stools for a nightcap with Barbara. Although many of her customers – most notably Annabel – have gone home this evening muttering about never returning again, I can't help but have sympathy for her. 'It must be stressful doing this on your own,' Jon ventures.

'I'll bluddy kill 'im when I get up there,' she says, referring to her husband and gesticulating skyward. Frankly, whatever you think of her fish soup – sorry, fish *pie* – you've got to admire the woman's spirit.

'I really like her; she's excellent,' says Jon with a chuckle as we head into the car park, the night air still warm and sweet with the smell of the linden trees.

'Though I'm not sure that she can do this on her own for much longer. I'd hazard a guess that at least half of tonight's customers won't be going back.'

As we pull out of the car park, Barbara locks the door behind us and turns the lights off, plunging the little bar into darkness. It must be so lonely dealing with all of that on your own, I think, as I drive home, grateful to have Jon at my side. Barbara is the expat dream gone horribly wrong and you'd have to be very hard-hearted not to have sympathy for her.

Later, Jocelyn tells me that she had a quiet word about the fish pie. 'Barbara, I don't think you can serve that again. People weren't very happy,' she said.

'I know love. The recipe were bloody useless. I won't be using it again,' she replied. Typical Barbara: never to blame. And she's not the only one. When we arrive back in Villiers, I look at the scoresheets and see that Jon has made a mistake, double-counting the No-Hopers' score in the final round. They should, in fact, have come second to last.

'I told you, you should have let me check the scoresheets,' I say.

'What does it matter?' he says, shrugging his shoulders. 'It's only a quiz. And anyway, the No-Hopers deserved to win. Apart from Sarah and Steve's table, they were the only ones not to complain about the fish pie. And better them than the horrible Eggheads. I couldn't bear that Annabel woman. What a snobby cow.'

'But you can't just let a team win because you like them.'

'Can't you just forget it?' says Jon. 'No one cares.'

'No one cares?' I repeat incredulously. 'You saw how annoyed the Wise Bats looked. It could have turned really nasty in there.'

'Well do the quiz on your own next time,' he retorts.

Even when Jon is in the wrong, I've noticed, he behaves like he's in the right. But I change the subject – mentioning there will be llamas at tomorrow's agricultural fair, which I know will interest him – as I don't want an argument. It's too early in the relationship to be bickering like an old married couple.

Chapter 9

Rhinestone Slope

THE FOLLOWING MORNING Sarah and Steve drop Biff off early. He comes running into the house, all big paws and wearing his eager-to-please expression. He sniffs Jon's ankles suspiciously and looks frankly a little miffed to find an interloper in his holiday home, but Jon soon wins him over by throwing a sock around the *petit salon* for him to fetch. After breakfast in the courtyard, we take the bikes out for an hour, Biff running behind us, all bouncing ears and flashing white teeth. Then I get ready in my too-tight T-shirt, cowboy boots and borrowed Stetson and, ignoring a couple of quizzical looks from my French neighbours (the Portuguese are still away) the three of us set off for Clussay. Despite the fact that it's hotter than a pizza oven, Biff climbs into the back of my car without hesitation, assuming his usual position with his head tucked under the driver's seat. It's another of the things that I adore about him – the way he adopts this brace position and stays there until we get to our destination.

'He's heard about your driving then,' says Jon.

'Ha, ha! Very funny,' I reply.

The agricultural fair, or *Comice Agricole* to give it its correct French name, takes place in a large meadow close to Clussay and is in full swing when we arrive shortly after midday. We spot the white marquees from the road and are directed into a car park in a bumpy patch of field. The *Comice* dates back to the nineteenth century, according to Delphine, and was originally designed for farmers to showcase their talents in animal husbandry and cultivation, as well as the latest technology. As Delphine charmingly explained, 'Normally some animals should be there and you can also expect hunting dog demonstrations and some speeches and examples of all the skills that a farmer should have.'

Such events used to be a hot social ticket, she explained, directing me to a famous *Comice* scene in Madame Bovary, where the protagonist enjoys an illicit flirtation as the awards for best manure and merino rams are handed out. In Emma Bovary's day countryfolk dressed up in their best finery to mingle with the bleating lambs, snuffling pigs and bellowing calves, before enjoying a huge communal feast.

It's not quite such a junket or big deal today, although there are lots of rural types milling around, all ruddy complexions, flat-caps and Simon-Cowell-style – i.e. pulled-up-to-the-armpit – jeans. Despite the *parfum* of manure on the warm air – which as a beauty journalist I would describe as a 'lingering, animalistic scent' – there are not many animals on display. Walking around we find a field that has been assigned to a tractor ploughing competition and an area that has been fenced off for a quad car race. In another field, a display of shiny new tractors and terrifyingly large combine harvesters has drawn a small, admiring crowd. Disappointingly, most of the wooden huts and stands dotted around the fair are devoted to agricultural associations and farmers' cooperatives, rather than tantalising displays of local produce. And where are the prize-winning ewes, the 'prancing stallions' and 'the great black muzzled bull' of Madame Bovary?

Despite the lack of livestock, both Jon and Biff seem very happy to be here. (I was worried, when Jon first saw my outfit, that even the llamas might not be enough of a pull.)

'Oh, look,' he says, pointing towards a set of sharp horns in the distance (belonging, it transpires, to an exotic breed of goat). 'The animals are over there.'

We head towards the horns, Biff straining on his lead, nose to the ground, wildly excited by all the interesting new sights, smells and distractions. I notice his nostrils twitching as we pass the food tent, which is diffusing the scent of sizzling meat and barbecue smoke into the air.

We manage to locate the llama pen and Jon immediately goes to the fence and holds his hand out to the llama's nose. The animal fixes him with its big, beautiful eyes and submits to having its neck stroked. The llama breeder is a studious looking man in smart clothes and spectacles, and seems an unlikely candidate for animal husbandry. It turns out that he is British and from the Limousin. Jon chats to him for what seems like ages, asking about their upkeep, diet and breeding habits. Who knew there was so much to ask about llamas? I hang back with Biff in the hot sunshine, drawing some odd stares in my unflattering outfit. Biff sits patiently at my side, quite unembarrassed to to be seen with me. Eventually the llama man mentions that female llamas cost around €2,500 and Jon's interest wanes dramatically.

Pulling Biff's nose out of a (no doubt *delicious*) pile of llama straw, we head towards the Entente Cordiale stand, where I have arranged to meet Delphine, here in a semi-official capacity as mayor of a nearby commune. Dressed in a flouncy turquoise skirt and black cardigan, she is already waiting for us. She is chatting to Vivienne, the Entente's new social secretary who is running the stand today even though her foot is still in plaster.

Despite its stated aim of bringing French and English together via cultural activities, the Entente Cordiale has only persuaded one *Français* to join since its launch four years ago – the mayor of Clussay, for whom it would have been rude not to. *La danse country* is a fairly new addition to its repertoire of activities, and Vivienne, who is also in charge of recruitment, is hoping that today's performance will encourage some real-life French people to sign up. (Though personally, I wonder about the target audience: I can't see many of the farmers here rushing to learn the 'Tush Push' or the 'Electric Slide'.)

We are due to perform at 1.30 p.m., in half an hour's time, and many expats in cowboy hats are already milling about the Entente Cordiale stand, the designated meeting point. It's reassuring to see so many other Brits also looking ridiculous. I watch as Jocelyn and Jill arrive with Gloria, whose cowboy hat is so big that it hides most of her face. Nice one Gloria, I think to myself, wishing that I'd thought of that.

Delphine greets me in a flurry of fragrant kisses, too polite to remark on the fact that I am vacuum-packed into a tiny white T-shirt. 'By the way,' she whispers, as Jon wanders off to chat to a local farmer that he knows, 'your army friend was just 'ere. The one with the blonde hair who was at the night market in Villiers.'

I know immediately who she is referring to.

'You are joking?'

'No, he was 'ere with another friend – a man, also very 'andsome. They just went off to look around. They are both very charming.'

Oh God, oh God, please don't let them come back anytime soon! And even if they do, I can take some comfort in the fact that I'm in the back row.

'There's been a last minute change of plan,' says Jocelyn, coming over and putting her arm around my shoulder. 'You're now at the front.'

Aaghagh! This cannot be happening.

'Why?'

'Because Jill is going home with a headache.'

'But you said I could be at the back,' I protest.

'Well you're in the front now, between me and Gloria, so don't forget to smile,' she says. 'And try not to fall off the stage. It's very small.'

She points to the wooden platform that has been set up in the middle of the field for us to dance on. It is indeed very small. Jon reappears and starts to laugh. 'It's going to be a tight squeeze if you're dancing on that,' he says.

'Exactly,' says Jocelyn. 'So look where you are going.'

'Are you OK?' says Delphine. 'Shall I get you some water? You look a bit stressed.'

Almost an hour after we were due to perform – time spent hanging around the Entente Cordiale stand with Jon and Biff and privately debating whether or not to make a run for it – there is a sudden flurry of activity. Jocelyn tells us to take our positions on the stage as quickly as possible. An old boy with a microphone then appears and we think he is about to introduce us, but instead he gives a long speech about agricultural achievements in the Poitou and is joined by some officials who proceed to hand out prizes. It takes about half an hour. We stand patiently in our lines, shoe-horned together and bearing the full brunt of the Poitevin sun.

It doesn't help that most of us are wearing two layers – in my case, the Entente Cordiale T-shirt over a long white vest. I feel like I've been wrapped up in parcel tape, so tight is the fit. Just as I'm thinking how nice it would be to have a long lie-down on the grass, I hear the chap with the microphone saying, '*Messieurs, mesdames, voici les Civray Stets-urns.*' A small audience has gathered, mostly consisting of embarrassed husbands, looking like they'd rather be drilling through dry stone walls than watching their wives dance in public. I also see Delphine, in her big straw sunhat, flashing me a smile of encouragement. Jon is doing his best to look like he is nothing to do with this spectacle, while Biff, who is about to witness his first ever display of line dancing, is watching with interest.

Poised in our lines, ready to launch into 'God Blessed Texas' – very appropriate for a French farming fair I think to myself wryly – I'm running through the opening steps in my head (step, touch and clap; back, touch and clap… Step, kick, flick, half-turn, step, scoot, scoot, step, kick…) and… nothing happens. The sound system has failed. Vivienne's husband, who has helpfully come along dressed as a cowboy, is fiddling with the amplifiers, while we slowly fry on stage. Appliance failures seem to follow us around. Over on the Entente Cordiale stand, I see Jon grinning, while Biff, black eyes cast downwards, looks embarrassed on my behalf. And standing beside them… is Andy Lawton, with the friend that I saw him with at the *vide-grenier*. Great.

The sound system kicks into life suddenly with a squeal like a pig being slaughtered – it's possible, given the nature of the fair, that somewhere a pig is being slaughtered – and we're off. Half our audience, which wasn't that big to begin with, drifts away after the first few minutes and we only get to perform two out of the three planned dances, as the man with the microphone intervenes to cut short our repertoire and announce that the raffle (first prize: six bags of pig feed) is about to be drawn.

Over on the Entente Cordiale stand, Andy and his friend are laughing with Jon (probably at me). Reluctantly, I go and join them.

'Woah, it's Annie Oakley,' says Andy, as I approach. His friend – who has piercingly blue eyes and very white teeth – laughs, but in a friendly way.

'Careful, she might have a gun.'

'Très drôle,' I say.

'Actually, it wasn't that bad,' says Jon. 'In fact, the woman next to you, the one with the white-blonde hair was really good. [He means Gloria.] She was by far the best dancer.'

'Thanks,' I say.

'So have you been to dinner at Annabel's recently?' asks Andy.

'No. Have you?'

'I think I'd rather eat my own arm than go through that again.' He looks at his friend. 'That's the neighbour I was telling you about,' he explains. 'By the way, this is Karen; Karen, James.' The friend nods and smiles.

'OK, let's go,' says Jon. 'I think Biff could do with some water.'

'Take it easy both of you,' says Andy. 'And nice to meet you, Jon.'

'How do you know him?' asks Jon, as we head back to the car.

'Oh, he helped me when I had a flat tyre once. And he lives near Travis, my gay friend.'

'He seems like a nice bloke,' says Jon.

'What were you talking about?' I ask, trying to sound as casual as possible.

'Nothing much. He just asked me what I was doing there and I said I was waiting for you. He asked if you were my girlfriend; and I told him that yes, you were.'

'What else did he say?

'He said that you looked like a bit of a minx to be honest.'

'He did?'

'No, I'm joking,' he says with a wink.

'Does his friend live out here?'

'I don't know. But why are you so interested?'

'Oh, you know. It's just interesting to know about other expat Brits,' I say.

Surprisingly, there is no rush to the Entente Cordiale stand to sign up after our performance. Afterwards, Vivienne reports that the farmers were far more interested in the pig feed. But we've had our first taste of performing in public. And the Civray Stetsons have no idea of the force that they are about to unleash on the Poitevin countryside.

It's September, and the Portuguese neighbours are back – browner, louder and more cheerful than ever. It's a good thing that they work such long hours – 5.00 a.m. until midnight several times a week – as it's enough to drive me and the French neighbours to pastis. And just when I thought they couldn't get any more annoying, they start to park a big white van with 'Supodal' written on the side in multi-coloured letters in front of my house. Sometimes, if they've finished work early (fortunately, that's never before 7.00 p.m.) they pull up at speed outside my window and often, if I'm eating my dinner or chilling out with a book on the sofa, I'll look up and see at least three men staring at me as if I'm the main attraction in Monkey Valley, a local tourist destination. I can almost hear the tour guide explaining: 'Here we have a very hostile primate. This primate is not to be provoked.'

One morning I walk up to the *boulangerie* to buy a *pain au chocolat*, only to find it closed and a sign saying *'fermeture définitive'* – final closure – on the door. This is terrible news. Although there is another perfectly good bakery in the village, no one makes cakes with such style and verve as René. Visiting his chocolate-coloured shop, with its scent of sugar, vanilla and warm dough, is a social event and his customers, myself included, will miss his little jokes almost as much as his cakes. The day gets worse. Walking back down rue St Benoit, I notice something odd about the rear of my car. Close inspection reveals a large dent in the hatchback door. Something has rammed into it with force, and that something was not a normal car, as the point of impact is quite high. It has also left a white paint-mark. That something, I think to myself, was probably a large white van. Monsieur Moreau appears while I'm examining the damage and shakes his head. 'It's terrible,' he says. 'But look! There is only one thing that could have hit your car like that. A big white van. Just like the big white van that our neighbours drive.' He nods towards the Portuguese house.

'Do you know why the bakery has closed?' I ask, partly to change the subject but also because I'm concerned about René. This former big bear of a man now looks pale and drawn whenever I see him, which is fairly often as he lives above the bakery, at the end of rue St Benoit.

'The bakery has closed down,' says Monseiur Moreau. 'He couldn't afford to pay his bill for flour because his bank would not advance any more money.'

'That's terrible,' I say. So the closure isn't because of his boyfriend leaving – although that can't have helped. 'Poor Réne. What will he do?'

'No one knows,' says Monsieur Moreau with a shrug. 'But listen! You must call the gendarmes about your car. *C'est clair*. A crime has been committed.'

But while I have my suspicions – in fact, I'm ninety-nine per cent certain, as no one else in my road has a white van – I have no proof that my neighbours hit my car. And the damage, though very noticeable, doesn't bother me that much. It's one of many battle scars that my Golf has acquired during the fifteen rollercoaster years that we have been together. I quite like the beaten-up look. (One of my wing mirrors is currently held together by brown tape.) More to the point, past experience has taught me not to bother having dented bodywork fixed or scratches painted over. Better to take a laissez-faire approach as, chances are, the damage will only occur again.

I change my mind that evening when the neighbours play rock music very loudly while barbecuing merguez sausages in the street. The next day, I march up to the shoe shop on the square and ask the owner, a slim blonde woman in tight jeans and hoop earrings, if I can speak to her husband. She nods and goes upstairs to get him. After a few minutes, the boss of Supodal appears – tanned, good-looking and nattily dressed in jeans, black shirt and snakeskin cowboy boots (is he a secret line dancer too, I wonder?).

He introduces himself as Fernando. I figure he knows who I am as he's attended enough barbecues outside my house. *'Vous êtes?'*

'Madame Wheeler. I live next door to 7 rue St Benoit,' I reply in French.

'Ah, *bonjour* Madame Willer,' he says, grinning and holding out his hand.

'My car,' I say. 'Your workers have damaged it with their van and you are responsible.' Having used the damaged car to get his attention, I then launch, in rapid-fire French, into a rant about the noise, the hell they have created on rue St Benoit in the months that they have been living there. Scarcely stopping for breath, I conclude with *'c'est pénible'* (it's painful/distressing), the phrase most often used by my French neighbours to describe the problem on our street. 'And another thing,' I say. 'Sometimes, it sounds like they are fighting and I'm worried that they are going to kill each other.'

His wife is laughing. 'Oh no,' she says affectionately, as if they were her children. 'They are not fighting. It is just how they are.'

'Well, I don't care. I've had enough of it and I want it to stop.'

'Madame Willer,' says Fernando, still smiling. 'I will ask them about your car and I will speak to them about the noise.' His reasonableness knocks the wind out of my sails.

'When?'

'I will go to rue St Benoit myself on Saturday morning, when they will all be there and I will speak to them. At the moment they are working in Niort, so you should be all tranquil for the next few days.'

Late on Saturday morning Fernando rings my doorbell and presents me with a bottle of port. 'It is an apology, Madame Willer, from my workers. I have spoken to them and they will try to make less noise.'

'And what about my car?'

'I have asked them and they say that they did not do it.'

'Well, of course they are going to say that. Let me show you the damage.'

I walk across the street to my car and show him the rear, which looks like it has been hit by a meteorite.

'Truly, Madame Willer, if they were lying I would know. My workers are good, honest people.'

I look over to number seven and see The Lion emerging, a little sleepy-eyed, from his lair. He lights a cigarette and, leaning with his knee against the wall, looks over with his signature scowl. I scowl back – grateful that I've never had Botox, so I can – certain of his guilt.

'Well I'm going to reflect on this,' I say. 'And I might report the matter to the gendarmes.' The truth however, is that I have no intention of going to that kind of trouble. Given the French love of dossiers and paperwork, there would probably be a library's worth of forms to fill in.

After our modest success at the agricultural fair in Clussay, invitations for the Civray Stetsons to perform start to pour in. (Well, OK, one.) An official from a local tourist office saw us dancing there and subsequently asked if we would perform at a night market in the village of Douhe. This time we have a captive audience, as we dance while people are eating their dinner and, unlike at the agricultural fair, where we were competing with large agricultural equipment, they have no choice but to watch us. Strangely, they seem to enjoy it and the following week Vivienne reports a sudden surge in Entente Cordiale membership as *les français* sign up in droves to learn *la danse country*. This breakthrough owes a lot to the fact that Vivienne, a journalist by profession, also managed to capitalise on our recent performances by writing an article for a local French newspaper. She announces a Monday night beginner's class in Douhe, which is where most of the new French recruits live, and asks for volunteers to help. I know I shouldn't – I know I already have far too much line dancing in my life – but this sounds like a good opportunity to mix with some real French people (lately I've been spending a lot of time at expat events), so I offer to help.

The turnout for the first class, which is held in a community hall as big as the Palace of Versailles (sadly that's the only similarity), is astonishing. Over fifty *français* have signed up to learn the art of stomping and posturing like a Texan. I've always thought of the French as loving graceful dances such as the tango, so it's a revelation to find that so many of them can't wait to climb into cowboy boots and indulge in some thigh-slapping.

The other remarkable thing is that the vast majority of them are young – in their twenties and thirties – and dressed in super-tight jeans, slinky tops and high-heeled boots. There are even some teenagers present. Clearly, line dancing in France does not have the same stigma as it does in the UK. Equally unexpected is the fact there are *men* – lots of them, all ages and one of them very attractive (unfortunately he is there with his wife). Unlike the Clussay class, where the average age hovers around sixty and everyone is *anglais*, here it has dropped by at least three decades and is entirely made up of French people. And everyone looks so *eager*, so excited to be here.

Jocelyn – sturdy, reliable, honest and organised – has volunteered to teach the class. Jill, Gloria and I are going to help. Gloria, who seems to have an extensive collection of cowboy boots in many colours and exotic skins, is tonight wearing a pair in pink lizard, and a T-shirt with 'vixen' written across the front. Jocelyn begins by teaching a beginner's dance, the 'Texas Stomp', and invites the three of us to join her at the front to give a little demo. The entire hall cheers and claps when we've finished and, for a second, I have an inkling of what it would be like to be a member of Girls Aloud.

The class is a joy to teach. Most people – particularly the dozen or so women in tight jeans and full *maquillage* at the front – learn very quickly. But I love the two small ladies in their seventies, who hop around hopelessly in the middle.

'*Encore! Encore!*' everyone demands when we reach the end of the 'Texas Stomp'. So we do it again. And again. And again. And each time the dance comes to an end, they cheer and clap as if Johnny Hallyday himself were in the room. Their enthusiasm knows no bounds and the atmosphere in the room – who would have thought it of a line dancing class? – is electric. And everyone appears entranced by the no-nonsense *Anglaise* in a checked shirt and jeans at the front of the class, teaching them to dance.

'Eh man-tenant, "Achy-Breaky Heart",' she says, speaking very slowly and looking at a sheet of paper that contains the steps in French, downloaded from the Internet. She indicates for me and her two other lieutenants to join her in a demonstration at the front. I groan inwardly. The song, a country-and-western classic, once reached number two on an American list of 'Most Awesomely Bad Songs Ever', and even the most fanatical line dancers in our Wednesday group sit this one out. So it's a shock to discover that here, in this draughty community hall in rural France, it it goes down like chilled rosé at a summer barbecue. *They love it!* As we come to the end of the demo, I fear that mass hysteria is going to break out. This dance is more challenging to teach, as some of the steps such as 'hitch' (a sort of small knee-lift) and 'scuff' (scuffing your foot on the floor) don't translate into French.

At the end of the evening, Jocelyn is surrounded by excited people wanting to thank her or clarify some of the steps. No one seems in a hurry to go home. Instead, several people are laying out paper plates, cake and bottles of cider on a trestle table. Jill and I join them. 'Well, I think that was a success,' says Jill. 'Jocelyn's been panicking like mad all week. Gloria and I were her guinea pigs.'

'Really?'

'Yeah, we've been dancing in the garden every night, so that Jocelyn could practice ordering people about in French,' says Jill, raising her gentle brown eyes skywards. I picture the three of them lined up by the rhododendron bushes in their Stetsons – Jill, tall and slender; Jocelyn short and sturdily-built; and Gloria small but curvy – and am forced to suppress a smile. I look over at Jocelyn, who is demonstrating a cross-step known as a 'jazzbox' to a small group of French women and couldn't look any happier.

Driving home under a new moon, I wonder if I am sliding down a slippery rhinestone slope. I didn't even know what line dancing was before I moved to France. Now here I am helping to teach it to fifty enthusiastic French people. I try to keep my new Monday night activity secret, but later that evening, in a phone call to Jon, who is back in the UK *again*, I let it slip. 'Oh my God,' he says. 'Line dancing is funny enough, but French people doing it… Wow, that's even funnier!'

But what I love about the Monday night class is how friendly it is. Everyone kisses everyone – and when there are fifty people in the room, that takes a long time. I am touched that, when I return the following Monday, people are practically queuing to kiss me, including Coralie, the elfin-faced young hairdresser, Sandrine the spiky-haired *fonctionnaire*, and Ralph the local councillor with dark curly hair. Never have I felt so popular, not even at school when I managed to find the answer book to the maths course we were doing. Jocelyn, Gloria and Jill, who always arrive together in a Renault van, run a similar gauntlet of kisses.

At the end of the class, as we are once again enjoying cider and cake, Gloria, who is wearing baby-blue cowboy boots this evening and a matching fringed belt, declares that she has never felt so fully integrated. She makes herself sound like a kitchen appliance, but I know what she means. Forget boules, birdwatching and conversation groups: line dancing is by far the fastest way to befriend the locals in the French countryside. Overnight, it feels like I have been accepted into some huge French family, albeit it one that only ever dresses in denim and cowboy boots and shouts 'Yee-hah!' a lot.

The Douhe class assumes even more importance in late September with the news that the informal Wednesday morning sessions are under threat. L'Auberge de Claviers, it is rumoured, will soon be closing down, as the bar is not making any money. Stories abound. One couple, for example, booked Barbara's famous fish pie (presumably not the liquid one) in advance. When they arrived, she greeted them in overalls rather than her white chef's jacket and with a paintbrush in her hand rather than a vegetable knife. 'I'm just in t'middle of painting us back room,' she declared. The hungry couple then had to wait nearly two hours while she made the pie from scratch. Such stories travel fast on the expat bush wire. And so people stop booking in for dinner and it becomes a downward spiral. It's a similar situation with the quiz nights, which are limping on, but are not the success that they could have been.

The Lion has bought himself a car. Previously, I have only ever seen him at the wheel of the big white or a red Supodal van, with his colleagues packed in tightly on the front seat beside him. But on Saturday afternoon, he draws up in a little white

Renault Clio, which he parks behind my tatty Golf on rue St Benoit. Drawn to my bedroom window by the sound of U2's 'Beautiful Day' playing on his car stereo, the sight almost makes me smile. The car is as un-macho as its driver is macho. The Lion looks way too big and powerful for the two-seater vehicle and the fact that he is driving such a girly runaround only serves to emphasise his almost caricature-like masculinity. He climbs out of it looking very pleased with himself, and turns round to give it an affectionate backward glance as he heads towards his house. It's all right for him, I think, with his perfectly unscathed Clio. I wonder how he'd feel if someone left a depression the size of the Devil's Punch Bowl in the back of his car.

The following morning, I'm walking Biff around the square, having manipulated my way to yet another overnight pass for him, when I notice that the bakery – which last time I looked had closed down for good – has reopened. Hurrah! René Matout himself is behind the counter, looking tired and drawn.

'I'm so glad that you are again open,' I say. 'It would be very sad for the village if you were to close.'

If I'm not mistaken, René looks like he is about to cry. His voice cracking with emotion, he explains that he has managed to negotiate with the bank to extend his loan but there is no guarantee that he will be able to keep the bakery open. This once happy, smiling man looks really miserable. Even his *pains au chocolat*, which used to be flaky, buttery perfection, now look flat and dense. I buy one anyway and head back down rue St Benoit, Biff prancing along at my ankles (he loves these little shopping expeditions).

The sky is a bath-crystal blue but there is a definite autumn nip in the air. In front of my house, I see The Lion tending to his Clio, even though it is already spotless. He is polishing it with a cloth, the sleeves of his orange-and-white T-shirt rolled up to expose his magnificent forearms, which look really brown as they move gently over the gleaming white bodywork. Shame, I think, that he and his crew do not show such respect for other people's cars.

He looks up as we approach and bids me the usual, gruff '*Bonjour*'. I ignore him as usual. Biff, however, stands stock-still as if he has seen something menacing. And then he starts barking at The Lion, as if he too has identified him as 'The Enemy'. He pulls sharply on his lead, causing me to lose my grip, and before I know it he is standing at The Lion's ankles, growling. It's a ridiculous sight: a small black terrier trying to threaten a powerfully built man. The Lion stops working on the passenger door for a moment and looks down at Biff, as if he can't quite believe the dog's audacity. He doesn't smile or pat him, as most people would; he merely looks him in the eyes for a second and carries on working, ignoring the feisty little animal growling at his feet.

'He's not vicious,' I say in French, and immediately realise what a laughable statement this is. It's not as if The Lion looks worried.

'Really?' he says, with more than a hint of irony. '*Très bien.*'

I'm not sure what to do, as I don't particularly want to start groping around The Lion's legs, trying to catch Biff by his lead.

'Biff, stop that, *now*!' I shout in French, from the opposite pavement. 'Come here!'

Naturally, he doesn't respond. After I've been shouting 'Biff, come here. NOW!' for a few minutes without any success, the neighbour stops polishing, casually picks up his lead and gives it to me.

'*Merci,*' I say, avoiding any eye contact, as I really dislike this man. '*Merci beaucoup.*'

'It's nothing,' he says, in a voice so deep that it sounds like a growl.

I try to march purposefully back into the house, dragging Biff behind me.

'Good boy, for growling at him,' I say, once we're inside. 'That nasty man and his friends damaged my car.'

After breakfast, I call Jon to find out when he might be returning to France. As often happens, his phone clicks straight to the answering service. What could he possibly be doing on a Sunday morning, I wonder, to prevent him answering his phone? I am beginning to think that he might be having an affair. To even contemplate the possibility is something of a first, as being suspicious does not come naturally to me. It ought to, as I've got form when it comes to cheating boyfriends. I've managed to attract two of them into my life so far. Naturally, I'm keen to avoid a third. Jon is spending more time in the UK than he is in France and, although he is there on the pretext of work, he could very easily be leading a double life. Is he, I wonder, seeing Jennie, his ex-girlfriend, again, or even someone new? And how, short of hiring a private detective, can I possibly find out? Maybe, I think, I will confront him when he comes back, whenever that might be. Only one thing is certain: if Jon keeps spending this much time in the UK, the springs of Evian will have run dry by the time he opens his B & B.

In fact, I speak to my new friend Travis more often than I speak to Jon. Since exchanging numbers at Annabel's dinner party, we have been in constant touch by phone, even though he is based in London. Travis dreams of moving to France full-time, but that would mean giving up his very well-paid TV producer job. Even though this job funds a house in London and a *maison sécondaire* in France, Travis hates it – and not just the 4.00 a.m. starts and having to be in bed by 8.00 p.m.

on weekday nights. His colleagues, who include an uppity newsreader called Kelly Drubber, sound like a terrifying bunch. But I love hearing the tales of his back-stabbing co-workers and the underlings with their over-developed sense of entitlement. It reminds me of my days as fashion and beauty director on the glossy magazine and makes me really glad that several years, hundreds of miles and the English Channel lie between me and that job now. Travis, meanwhile, loves hearing the details of my daily life in France, no matter how mundane. 'You're so lucky! I'm so jealous,' is his constant refrain, even when the most exciting thing I've done that day is stack the woodpile, visit the tip or pull weeds out of the flowerbed.

As lunchtime approaches, the usual crowd starts to congregate next door, but as promised by their boss, the noise levels are significantly lower than usual. There is laughter but no loud music. I run their gauntlet mid afternoon as I take Biff out for a short walk, noticing that Fernando, the boss, is there with his wife – unusual, as these gatherings are nearly always male, with wives and girlfriends left at home. The Lion, as usual, is in charge of the barbecue.

'*Bonjour Madame Willer,*' says Fernando. '*Ça va?*'

I smile weakly and keep walking. 'Madame Willer,' he says, when we return a short while later. 'My workers and I would like to invite you to join us for a coffee.'

'*Merci, mais c'est pas possible,*' I reply, thinking I'd rather eat veal's head (a rural French delicacy currently undergoing a revival) than sit down with The Enemy for a coffee. Biff, however, has other ideas. As I turn to close the front door, he slips past my feet and bolts for the house next door. Drawn, no doubt, by the smell of barbecued food, he heads straight into their kitchen, his tail wagging hopefully. No barking at The Enemy this time. With food in the offing, he seems to have swapped sides. I stand on the enemy border (the doorstep), watching as he sniffs around their immaculate white-tiled floor, shouting 'Biff. Come here. *NOW*!'

'He's funny!' one of them says in French. Another makes a clucking noise and holds out a small piece of ham for him. And as I am clocking their very neat and clean kitchen – not at all what I expected of a house occupied by three single men – Biff does something appalling. He rolls over with his paws in the air, while one of them tickles his belly – the canine version of waving the white flag of surrender. I stand on the doorstep watching, my cheeks an hibiscus pink as my dog flirts shamelessly with The Enemy. Obviously, I can't go marching into their kitchen. And obviously, given that there is food in there, Biff is not going to come out. Everyone is laughing, apart from me. Finally, after what seems like an age, Fernando scoops him up and places him in my arms. '*Voilà, Madame Willer. Votre chien,*' he says. 'I think he likes our company.'

The Lion, who is leaning against the kitchen sink with a beer in his hand, says nothing. But, as always, he watches everything with those devil-black eyes.

Later that afternoon, I'm packing Biff's overnight bag, ready to drive him home – it's getting harder and harder to give him back – when I hear a loud bang. It's the harsh, unmistakable noise of metal impacting on metal. What the hell are my neighbours up to now, I wonder? I rush to the window in time to see a white van making a speedy exodus from rue St Benoit. Monsieur Moreau's old Renault, meanwhile, has been visibly damaged. I recognise the van immediately. But it is not the clean, shiny white Supodal van driven by my neighbours. Or even their big red van. It is a dirty, shabby looking vehicle belonging to a man who owns a hunting shop in Clussay, and who is known to love Ricard as much as he loves rifles. Oh dear, I think to myself, as The Lion and his friends, appear at their door to see what the noise is. Maybe, just maybe, I owe The Enemy an apology. But obviously, that's out of the question.

Chapter 10

9.23 p.m.

IN EARLY OCTOBER, Jon returns. It's nice to have him back. Together we go for long bike rides in the weak autumn sunshine, following the remote farm tracks of the flat Poitevin landscape. The vivid blue, yellow and green of summer has faded now to dull earth tones, though occasionally the autumn landscape is lit up by a burst of coppery light or a benign blue sky. If I've managed to get custody of Biff for the weekend, we walk for hours between churned fields, straggly hedgerows and occasional pockets of forest, where unknown animals – rabbits, deer or possibly wild boar – rustle in the thickets. One of my favourite walks is around a reservoir, near a little hamlet called Bastard (really!). In the Poitevin countryside, it is possible to walk for miles without seeing a soul, the only sound the soft thud of acorns falling to the ground or the sudden pop of gunshot on the distant horizon (the hunting season is back in full swing). Returning from a walk in the late afternoon, we close the shutters, light the woodburner and open a bottle of wine. And more often than not, I will cook dinner.

Usually, I go to a great deal of trouble (and everything is organic) but he is never very appreciative, which is irritating. One evening, after I've made a really delicious lamb stew followed by a Delia Smith chocolate soufflé, I find myself angling for compliments but 'very nice' is the best I can extract. 'You know, maybe it's your turn to cook dinner for me?' I venture.

As to whether or not Jon might once again be seeing Jennie on his many trips back to the UK, I bide my time on that one, hoping for some sort of clue or sign. One Saturday afternoon, about a week or so after his return, he phones to say that he's on his way over and has something important to tell me. Oh, dear. I brace myself for the worst. I still haven't fully recovered from 'Pastagate' a few evenings ago, when I arrived at his house expecting a romantic, candle-lit dinner, only to be served packet tortellini that was nearly a month out of date. I noticed this by chance, while checking the list of ingredients (the packaging said *tortellini viande* but worryingly did not specify what kind of meat.)

'Everyone knows that use-by dates are just a guide,' he said, looking really annoyed and implying that I was being unreasonable for not wanting to eat potentially poisonous pasta. But I wasn't prepared to take the risk. I think he felt bad about it because the following day he showed up with not one but two Terry's Chocolate Oranges.

Now, I know that out-of-date pasta is hardly a reason for splitting up with someone. But in my mind, food and love are very closely linked – I go to a huge effort to prepare meals for friends and people that I care about – and it seemed like a message of sorts. No doubt, he is thinking the same thing; and the message for him is that I am too difficult.

I imagine that Jon will look very stern as he tells me it's over, citing the 'Pastagate' incident as the reason. Or maybe he has decided to go back to Jennie, or met someone else on his frequent trips to the UK? But when he arrives, he looks surprisingly cheerful for a man about to deliver bad news. 'So what is it that you wanted to talk to me about?' I say, after some small talk about the L'Auberge de Clavier, which looks like it will be closing down before the end of the month.

'Ah yes,' he says. 'The thing is, I've been doing a lot of thinking lately.'

'You have?' I brace myself, noting that his expression has suddenly become very serious.

'Yes.'

'And?'

'I've realised how much I love you. When I was in the UK I couldn't wait to get back to you.'

'Really?' I say, waiting for the 'but', as in 'but you are too high-maintenance/difficult/obsessed with organic food'.

'The thing is, I'd really like you to marry me.'

'Really?' I say, a little stunned. This is not at all what I was expecting. 'You mean you're not having an affair?'

He looks at me astounded. 'Having an affair? What on earth makes you think that?'

'All those visits back to the UK. I thought you were secretly seeing Jennie again.'

'I go back to the UK for work. And why would I ask you to marry me if I wanted to get back with Jennie?'

'Er... yes, I guess that's true.'

He starts to laugh. 'You are so blonde sometimes. But that's what I love about you.' He looks me directly in the eye. 'Mrs Wakeman has a nice ring to it, don't you think?'

'Um...' I say, while thinking that Miss Wheeler, or even Madame Willer, has a nicer ring.

This is not the first time he has proposed to me. He did that when we initially got together, in the first few days of the year. Jokingly, we decided that our wedding would be in a flower-filled meadow, barefoot, with simple food (*steak frites*) and lashings of pink champagne. But it feels like a huge amount of time has passed since then – in reality, only ten months – and now, I am not sure that I want to be married to anyone. Having made it to nearly forty without officially aligning my future with someone else's, I'm just not that into the idea any more. Lately, I've seen so many people struggling to tunnel their way out of the institution amid such acrimony, that marriage has lost a great deal of its allure for me. (For some reason, a very high proportion of couples seem to split up soon after moving to France.)

'Say something,' says Jon.

'Aaghagh...' I reply.

'Is that a yes, or a no?'

'I'm not sure. Can I think about it?' I ask.

'Well, don't think for too long,' he replies, looking offended.

Later that afternoon, he leaves to go to Castorama, the DIY store in Poitiers, to buy some bathroom tiles. I follow him out into rue St Benoit to say goodbye. There is a wonderful aroma of cooking wafting out of the house next door and I see that The Lion is taking advantage of the unseasonal October sunshine to barbecue lunch for himself and the rest of his pack. (It must be a Portuguese thing but they never seem to eat lunch earlier than 3.00 p.m.). I notice that he and Jon exchange glares. Then Jon puts his arms around me and kisses me goodbye, as if sending a pointed message to The Lion.

'I'll call you this evening,' he says before jumping into his sports car, revving the engine dramatically and roaring away. As I go back into the house I can't help but notice the expert way that The Lion delicately flips the fillets of fish with his big hands. I also notice that he looks like he is in a bad mood and he doesn't bother with the usual *'Bonjour'*.

I go inside and think about this unexpected development. I like Jon enormously but I can't imagine myself married to, or living with him. I'm actually very grateful for the fact we've got separate houses and both have somewhere to storm off to. Storming off, in the short time we've been together, has become quite a regular occurrence, often over very minor things. Recently, for example, he went into a major strop because I arrived at his house half an hour late – not great timekeeping, I agree, but we were only going for a walk.

Still, I've chosen to focus on the fact that Jon is kind and good and well liked and, because of his gamekeeping background, knows lots about country stuff. (I like the fact that he knows the names of all the wild flowers and plants on our frequent forays into the countryside.) And so I decide to ignore my niggling doubts for a while longer and together we attend the final quiz night at the bar in Claviers. It is Barbara's swansong before returning to Yorkshire. She goes out in style with a delicious paella, followed by lemon meringue pie, proving that she is, in fact, an excellent cook after all. 'If only she had done food like that all along, and tried to smile at the customers from time to time, she wouldn't be in this pickle now,' I hear Annabel say, while standing by the bar.

Give the woman a break! I want to shout. If Barbara had done food like that all along, for just €7, she would have been bankrupt by now.

Everyone from the Wednesday line dancing session is there to see Barbara off. Although she hasn't yet sold her house or the bar, the removal van is coming to ferry her stuff back to Yorkshire tomorrow, and Jocelyn, Jill and Gloria have volunteered to come back in the morning to help her pack up her last remaining possessions. L'Auberge de Clavier will then be boarded up indefinitely as there have been no other takers so far. It's a great shame as I'll miss Barbara and we won't be able to continue our Wednesday sessions there; and so far, Jocelyn has had no luck finding an alternative venue. Although there are many *salles des fêtes* in the area with suitable dance floors, hiring a village hall for a group activity is a complicated affair. You must be an association (which the informal Wednesday class isn't) and have public liability insurance, and no doubt many other *dossiers*, for it to be allowed. And so a good thing comes to an end. Fortunately, there are still the classes in Douhe to look forward to.

As Barbara closes the door behind us for the last time, I'm tempted to give her a big hug but, stoic and unsentimental until the end, she is just not the type. Many people, on finding themselves unexpectedly widowed and stuck in a small village in a foreign country with only a cat and a grumbling clientele for company, would have crumbled. But Barbara, made from sterner stuff, didn't. Less than a year after moving to France, her dream is over. But I will never forget the Yorkshire woman whose French adventure coincided with mine for such a short but enjoyable period of time. 'I'll miss Barbara and her funny Yorkshire ways,' says Jon as we pull out of the dark car park.

'Me too,' I say.

A week or so later, I am due to go on a day trip to Paris for a lipstick launch. Jon offers to give me a lift to and from the station. 'Are you sure?' I say, delighted by the offer, as if there's one thing that I really hate – and I've done it many times – it's arriving back at Poitiers station alone. 'It would mean leaving here early, about eight. And I won't be back till about nine in the evening.'

'No problem,' he says. 'I've got to go into Poitiers anyway to buy some tile grout.'

The evening before, Jon comes for dinner and stays the night. The following morning he nips out to the bakery to buy *pains au chocolat* to eat en route – unfortunately René has forgotten to put the chocolate in the middle – and we set out in the darkness for the 25 kilometre journey to the station. As we drive along, he squeezes my knee and gives me one of his cheeky winks. 'Everything OK, minx?'

'Yes, I'm just so happy that you're going to meet me later. I've done this journey alone so many times, driving home to an empty house. It's just lovely to know that you'll be waiting for me at the station this evening.'

'No problem,' he says. 'Just give me a call when you're on the train and let me know what time you'll be arriving.'

'Oh, I can tell you that now,' I say, rummaging in my bag to find the ticket. 'My TGV gets in at exactly nine twenty-three. Maybe I could buy you dinner afterwards as a thank you?'

'OK,' he says. 'Just let me know when you're on the train.'

'Well, it's a non-changeable ticket,' I say. 'So I'll definitely be on that train and it gets in at nine twenty-three. TGVs are nearly always on time.'

Jon pulls up in front of Poitiers station. I kiss him goodbye and jump out into the cold, harsh light of an October morning. 'Look forward to seeing you later,' I say. 'Don't forget: nine twenty-three.'

'OK. See you later.'

I buy *une petite noisette*, an espresso with a splash of milk, at the Paul patisserie on the station concourse and join the people shivering on the platform for the Paris train. As I stamp my high heels to keep warm, I think how nice it is to be travelling light in every sense. It might be cold but it gives me a warm feeling to know that someone loves me enough to meet me at the station tonight. Arriving in Paris an hour and a half later, even the dismal grey bunker that is Montparnasse station cannot drag down my mood. Instead, I breeze through and into a waiting car and cross Paris – passing the Seine and the beautiful glass pyramid in the grounds of the Louvre – all the while thinking of Jon and the fact I have someone who cares about me back in the French countryside.

I arrive at the chic Avenue Montaigne headquarters of the beauty brand that is holding today's launch. A dozen or so immaculately groomed British journalists are already waiting, having come straight from the Eurostar. Whenever I come up to Paris for these launches, I always feel like the country bumpkin in comparison – an imposter among this hyper-groomed clique, with hair that looks like it's been ironed and skin so radiant that you almost need to shield your eyes from the glare. I still have my John Frieda highlights (more or less a beauty editor prerequisite) but I'm not carrying a handbag or wearing an outfit that has recently starred in a major advertising campaign. This morning it was even a struggle to brush my hair as Biff hid my hairbrush on a recent visit and so I had to use his metal grooming brush – that I recently bought for his overnight stays – instead.

We file into the glossy white meeting room, where a giant pair of glistening red lips has been projected on a flat-screen TV on one of the walls, and where a rather rigorous looking Frenchwoman in a white lab coat and high heels, is already waiting. We take out our notebooks and get down to the serious business of super-hydrating lipstick.

Now you might think that there is a limit to how much you can say about a lipstick, but you'd be wrong. I know, from having attended previous lipstick launches – and on one occasion, a lipstick symposium – that (unfortunately) some people can talk for hours on the subject. And so it proves today. The R & D woman, Madeleine Gambetta, leads us through a highly scientific presentation complete with charts, figures, statistics and diagrams about the latest nanotechnology that will allow tiny spheres of moisture to be delivered deep into the dermis of the lips. At least I think that's what it all boils down to.

Often in these presentations I look at my fellow journalists, whose beautiful faces are a study in inscrutable blankness, and wonder what is going on in their minds. Are they really thinking nano-spheres of 'sophisticated silicons' and 'new-generation polymers' or are they mentally compiling Sainsbury's shopping lists, wondering how they can jump the waiting list for the new 'must-have' bag, or figuring out how to slap down an overly ambitious assistant or scheming colleague. As for me, my mind bobs back and forth between 'glide-on' formulations and where to go for dinner with Jon this evening.

'And now,' Madeleine Gambetta is saying, 'I will hand you over to Ludovic Fillon who will explain to you the philosophy behind the new packaging, which he has designed.' The room collectively sits up as Monsieur Fillon – attractive in a clean-cut, chiselled kind of way – takes the stand. There is a flurry of earnest note-taking as a big, black tube is projected onto the wall behind him.

The packaging for the new super-hydrating lipstick is matte, black and ribbed, with a rubberised finish, but Monsieur

Fillon waxes lyrical for nearly forty-five minutes about the tactile appeal, the contrast between the dark outer casing and the bullet of colour within, between masculine (presumably, the phallic tube) and feminine (the colour), and the satisfying click of closure. With the exception of Larissa, the PR, who is sucking on her pen with a faraway expression on her face, the gathering continues to make copious notes. The great irony is that when a write-up of the lipstick appears in newspapers and magazines it will be a small picture with a two line caption, half of which is the price and stockist enquiry number. No matter. When Ludovic has finished he is bombarded with questions about the stylish phallus... sorry, tube.

Next up is Rodrigo Ferrari, 'the renowned make-up artist', who has recently been signed as the brand's artistic director. Wearing tight leather trousers, a billowing black shirt and pixie boots, Rodrigo talks us through the colour palette and tips on how to achieve superlatively glazed lips. Unfortunately, by the time he has finished it is eyes that are glazing over rather than lips, as it's almost impossible to understand his thick Italian accent. My mind has already drifted away from the glossy white room at this point to a dimly lit restaurant in the Poitou, where I will be enjoying a bottle of wine and a rare steak with Jon later.

And so the day continues. There is lunch in a super-posh restaurant and then a dreaded 'lab visit' – something that all beauty journalists hate, but all big beauty companies believe to be fascinating and insist on foisting on them. Later, as a cab whisks me back over the Seine towards Montparnasse, I think how much friendlier Paris seems when you have a significant other in your life. Many times I've visited this beautiful city and been struck by a strange melancholy. It's as if all the beauty and romance – encapsulated so brilliantly by the famous

Robert Doisneau photograph of two people kissing – acts as a cruel reminder of your loveless state. Romance is the whole point of Paris and if you don't have someone to walk hand-in-hand along the Seine, snog under bridges or sit in candle-lit restaurants with, the city can seem like an exclusive club, to which you are not welcome. It gives me a warm glow to think that this no longer applies to me.

The warm glow lasts for the whole journey home: in the mob of people standing before the departure board at Montparnasse, waiting for the platform number to be announced; boarding the train through the usual fug of cigarette smoke, as the nicotine-addicted grab a last hit before the train departs; and battling my way to my seat. Once there, I phone Jon to let him know that I'm on the train. He doesn't answer on either his landline or his mobile, so I leave a message reminding him that the train gets in at 9.23 p.m. As the TGV powers south, I settle back and fall asleep. When I wake up we are just ten minutes away from Poitiers. Fellow passengers are calling their loved ones. As the air rings with 'À tout à l'heure' or 'À bientôt chéri', I think of calling Jon again. But he will almost certainly have left home by now, and I don't want to bother him on his mobile while he's driving.

The TGV screeches to a halt and I descend, through a little clique of smokers seizing the opportunity for another quick cigarette, onto the cold platform, eager for a glimpse of Jon. As usual the platform is a melee and a cacophony of unwelcome sounds: slamming doors, screeching whistles and borderline hysterical train announcements (endlessly and urgently repeated just to add to the stress levels). Then, another screech of a whistle, more slamming of doors and the TGV pulls out of the station with a painful scream. Any minute now, I think, I'll see Jon's smiling face, coming towards me in the crowd.

But I don't. Nor is he waiting on the station concourse. I go outside, expecting to see him running across the station forecourt or his car drawing up outside, but, again, no sign of him. I join the forlorn little crowd of people whose lifts are also late, waiting outside the station, stamping their feet to stay warm or grabbing another sneaky cigarette. I stamp my feet too as I wait with them. The warm aura that has been following me around all day has disappeared. Instead, it feels as if someone has thrown a bucket of icy water over me.

Gradually, the other people slip away until I am the only one waiting outside the station. I look at my watch: its 9.40 p.m. If Jon doesn't get here soon, it will be too late for dinner, even at the *routier*, the trucker's cafe that we normally go to. I am cold and hungry. But most of all, I am horribly disappointed. Being met at the station might not seem like a big deal to many people, but for me, it was very symbolic. I feel hugely let down that he couldn't make the effort to be here on time, especially since it is such early days in our relationship. And in my view, a man who has just proposed might reasonably be expected to haul his ass to the station on time, as promised. And then a horrible thought occurs to me: what if he has had an accident en route? Panicking I phone his mobile but it clicks to answer machine immediately. And then because I can't think of what else to do, I phone his landline, even though I know he won't be there. Except he is.

'Jon?' I say, shocked.

'Hello minx. Where are you?'

'I'm at Poitiers station,' I say, almost too upset to speak. 'I thought you were going to pick me up.'

'OK, I'm leaving right now.'

Leaving right now? I can't believe he is still at home.

'But what happened? You were supposed to be here at nine twenty-three.'

'Well, I was expecting you to call from the train, remember?'

'Did you not get my messages? I called from Paris to say I was on the train. I told you over and over that my train got in at nine twenty-three. And I really can't believe that you are not here.'

'I'm sorry. I was round at my neighbour's, so no I didn't get your messages but don't worry, I'm leaving right now. I'll be there in forty minutes.'

'You know what? Don't bother. I'll take a taxi instead. I can't believe you've let me down like this.' By now, disappointment has turned to anger. I am furious that he has left me hanging around in a cold railway station.

'Look there's a cafe in the station, isn't there? Just go and get a coffee and chill out and I'll be there to pick you up in no time at all.' *Chill out?* How dare he? I'm already so cold that my hands could chill a bottle of wine. Again, I am speechless with disappointment and anger. He lives 40 kilometres from the station, most of that on narrow country roads, and he hasn't even left home yet. The cafe that he is talking about is a charmless place, frequented only by people in transit and it closes at 10 p.m. This is worse, so much worse, than arriving here alone. If I'd relied on myself as I've always done, at least I'd be travelling without expectation, and more importantly, with my car waiting in the multi-storey car park adjacent to the station. And I'd be halfway home to Villiers by now.

I haven't felt this angry since my fashion editor days, when I was sent to Miami for a week, accompanied by a very strange female photographer. After lunch, on the final day of the trip – with four magazine covers still to shoot before catching the flight back to London – she disappeared. As I sat in the location van in the middle of Miami with the rest of the crew, watching the light fade and black clouds gather, my feelings of anger were matched only by feelings of impotency. When she finally returned, I asked where she'd been. 'I went to buy organic muffins for the flight home,' she replied. 'Here's the receipt. You can pay me back later.' Then, as now, there were no words that could have adequately expressed my feelings.

'Minx, are you still there? I'm on my way now, as soon as I've found the car keys. I might have to stop for diesel but it shouldn't take long.'

'You know what? Really don't bother. By the time you get here, I'll be gone.'

I'm so angry with Jon that even if I did wait another three quarters of an hour for him to pick me up, it would be a miserable ride home. I hang up and wonder what to do. I could call Delphine or Mathilde, both of whom can be relied upon completely and would come willingly. But it's nearly 10 p.m. and most of my French friends go to bed early. And I really hate to inconvenience anyone. A taxi from here to Villiers will cost about €80 but I'll just have to bite the bullet and pay it. I look over at the taxi rank and of course, there isn't a single bloody taxi there. And it's started to rain.

I pick up my little carrier bag, laden with super-hydrating lipsticks and stiff glossy press releases, and head over to the rank, forming a queue of one. I stand in the rain for fifteen minutes – which in my current state of mind seems like forever – before a taxi arrives. I climb in gratefully, and as we drive in the rainy darkness back to Villiers, silent tears roll down my cheeks. The worst thing is that Jon knew how much this meant to me. But it teaches me a lesson – namely, that there is a lot to be said for relying on myself. On any other evening I would have jumped in my car and, assuming that I hadn't left the lights on, rendering the battery flat – unfortunately, this has happened on several occasions – I would have been home by now. Better to travel alone and without expectation, I think to myself, than to travel with high hopes and have them spectacularly smashed. But it is not just hopes that have been dashed this evening. The relationship has too. Jon wasn't waiting for me as he promised and no amount of declarations of love – or Terry's Chocolate Oranges – are going to make up for that.

I've been home half an hour, and am rifling through my empty cupboards for something to eat, when the doorbell rings. I'm too upset to speak to Jon, but he is persistent so I eventually open the door.

'What do you want?'

'Minx, I'm so sorry. I didn't realise what time it was.'

'I've got nothing further to say to you right now.'

'Please. I love you so much,' he pleads.

'Then you should have picked me up like you promised.'

I close the door on his useless declarations of love. I am still boiling with rage and I'm not sure where Jon and I go from here.

There is one person, however, who always seems to be waiting for me: The Lion. On weekends, whenever I leave the house, it feels like he is always there, on his doorstep, lying in wait for me with those penetrating black eyes. If he's not drawing up next to my window in his van, or polishing his car opposite my house, he is standing on his doorstep, watching, it seems, my every movement with his gimlet eyes, as a lion might watch a gazelle, before moving in for the kill. But The Lion doesn't scare me. Or Biff. In fact, my little furry friend seems magnetically drawn to the den next door.

One Saturday afternoon, Biff bolts out the front door while I'm pulling on my riding boots and when I come out of the house there is no sign of him anywhere. I run down the hill towards the river in a blind panic shouting his name. But he's not there. I run back up the hill to see if he has gone in the opposite direction, towards the square, and find The Lion and his housemates, standing in the doorway, watching me. 'Have you seen my dog?' I shout. 'The little black dog.'

'*Il est là*,' one of them says, pointing to their kitchen. I rush up to the door and sure enough, Biff is in there having a casual sniff around. I almost cry with relief to see him in there. I also notice that the table in the spotless kitchen is laid for three, with a big bowl of a quite delicious-looking salad in the middle. For three single men it is all suspiciously clean and tidy.

The (young) Nicholas Cage lookalike, whose name I have worked out to be Piedro, goes into the kitchen and brings Biff – who comes reluctantly, dragging his big paws along their white-tiled floor – out by his lead. As he hands it to me, he says something in Portuguese and the other two laugh loudly. The joke, I'm sure, is at my expense. But I don't care. I'm just relieved to have Biff back, not least because I promised Sarah I'd return him by 7.00 p.m. this evening. As I'm dragging Biff back indoors, Jon's car draws up outside.

Under the scrutiny of The Lion, he walks towards me, looking sheepish.

'Can we talk?' he asks.

'There's nothing to say,' I reply.

'Look, I've been an idiot,' he says. 'The reason I didn't get to the station on time was that I was on the phone to Jennie.'

'What?'

'Look, can I come in?'

'No. I'm sorry, there's no point'

'Well, the thing is, Jennie and I promised to remain friends…'

'That's not a problem,' I say, 'because it's over.'

'Please. I don't want to have this conversation on the doorstep.'

'There's nothing more to say. Sorry.'

I go inside my house and slam the door. The Lion and his pack are watching with interest, but I really don't give a damn.

Inside the house, the phone is ringing. It's Travis to tell me that he's just booked a flight to France for Halloween. Thank God. The cavalry is arriving. It's the first time he's been out since Annabel's dinner party, but we have become good friends just by speaking on the phone two or three times a week. The news of his imminent arrival cheers me up hugely.

'Excellent!' I say. 'Shall I book you in for the Halloween party in Douhe?'

'Hmm,' says Travis. 'Didn't you say that there was going to be line dancing there?'

'Just a very little bit,' I say.

Travis groans.

'Listen,' I say. 'While you're out here, we should have that game of tennis with Andy Lawton. My French friend Mathilde plays very well, so we could try and do doubles.'

'OK,' says Travis. 'I'll speak to Andy and try and arrange it. I was planning to call round anyway to see when his army mates are coming out.'

Things can only get better, I think, as I hang up the phone.

I have been a little economical with the truth, however, as far as the Halloween party is concerned. In fact, the Civray Stetsons – whose ranks have been massively boosted by the Douhe contingent – are set to perform half a dozen dances. Progress has been very rapid at the Monday night class, moving quickly from slow beginner shuffles to more dynamic, fast-moving numbers. The demand among the French for learning new dances is voracious and poor old Jocelyn is struggling to keep up. So too are the less coordinated members of the group, many of whom have stopped coming as the routines have become more complicated. It's a shame, as it was the fact that the class encompassed all age groups that made it so much fun.

Three of the front-rowers – Coralie, Sandrine and Hélène – are particularly enthusiastic. The dance that they really want to learn, having seen us perform it at the night market in Douhe, is 'Copperhead Road'. It's actually more of an Irish jig than a line dance and involves jumping and hopping to a song about a Vietnam war veteran who turns to heroin smuggling (obviously no one realises this) by Steve Earle. The front row girls pick it up immediately and are so ecstatic, it's as if they've been given the formula for eternal youth rather than a few dance steps. We perform 'Copperhead Road' – which speeds up halfway through – five times in succession, on the insistence of Coralie and the clique in the front row. I fear for the few elderly folk who have yet to be scared away from the class.

But in the weeks that follow 'Traingate', practising for the Halloween party provides a welcome diversion from the latest failure in my love life; as does a work trip to London in the final week of October. Before I leave, Jon shows up at my house unannounced at least half a dozen times to ask for forgiveness. He also phones and emails constantly. But in my mind, it is over. As far as men are concerned, it is, unfortunately, back to the drawing board, but when the next one comes along, they're going to have to make a far bigger effort to win my heart than the occasional box of Ferrero Rocher. And I'll probably make them fill in time sheets too, for the hours that they are out of my sight.

Chapter 11

Bewitched

IF YOU HAD told me two years ago that I would be donning a pair of cowboy boots and dancing to Shania Twain in front of a crowd of people in a *salle des fêtes* in rural France on Halloween, I would have replied that there was more chance of me marrying Nicolas Sarkozy. But on the appointed evening, I stash my Stetson and diamanté T-shirt in a bag like a guilty secret, and set out in driving wind and rain to pick up Travis in St Hilaire, which is just a few kilometres away from Romagne, the village where the party is being held. Looking very metropolitan in designer jeans, and a dark fitted shirt, he invites me in for a glass of Halloween champagne, which he serves in fluorescent orange champagne flutes that have been chilling in the freezer, giving them an opaque frost.

It's this kind of attention to detail that makes Travis so endearing. Yet on first impressions, there is nothing camp about his demeanour. He might chill his champagne flutes and ensure that his clothes are always wrinkle-free, but I've also seen him chopping firewood and digging ditches in his garden and he can actually look quite blokeish – an impression reinforced by his lean physique and hair that is ever so slighty greying at the temples. 'You won't catch me dying my hair like an old queen,' he once told me. (He does however, have a rather less blokeish habit of pursing his lips and narrowing his eyes to convey disapproval.)

We drink the champagne in front of the log burner in his terracotta-tiled sitting room. 'God,' he says. 'I can't tell you how happy I am to be here for a week. My job is really doing my head in.' He fills me in on the latest Machiavellian developments in his office and, in particular, the saga of Kelly Drubber, the newsreader who keeps changing the script at the last minute, often with disastrous consequences. 'Unfortunately, she's shagging my boss,' he says. 'So no surprises as to whose side he is going to take.'

'Such is office life,' I say, with a sigh. Sometimes I do miss the cut and thrust of having a job in the metropolis, but then I speak to Travis and remember all the reasons I quit mine. 'There are many Kelly Drubbers in the world,' I say.

'I know, but I hate it. If it wasn't so well paid, I'd chuck it in tomorrow and come and live out here but I'm just not brave enough.'

En route to Romagne, a village that has been almost completely colonised by Brits, he asks me about tonight's party.

'There might be a little *danse country*, but not a great deal,' I say, deliberately avoiding the words 'line' and 'dancing' since they distress Travis so much. 'Then a buffet dinner and a disco.'

'Line dancing and Halloween: a natural combination,' he notes wryly. 'One is about the dead, the other, the almost-dead.'

'*Travis!* That's such a horrible thing to say. Why do you hate line dancing so much?'

'Because the sort of people who do it wear unbranded jeans and shapeless jumpers,' he replies. 'It offends all my aesthetic sensibilities.'

'Not here in France,' I say. 'And just for the record, my jeans are by Seven For All Mankind and I don't wear shapeless jumpers.' *Au contraire*, I think, picturing the tight-fitting diamanté T-shirt hidden in my bag. But I decide not to mention that just yet, as I think it might be too much for Travis, who is, also, it must be said, a bit of a looks fascist. (He has a magnet on his fridge saying 'no fat chicks'.)

At the community hall, we pay our €12 entrance fee and walk into the huge hall, which is one of the most upmarket *salle des fêtes* in the area, with a beautiful, polished wooden floor and a stage. A huge effort has gone into decorating it with giant cobwebs suspended from the ceiling and carved-out pumpkins with tea-lights in them, dotted around the room. I had no idea, until I moved here, that Halloween was such a big deal in rural France. Earlier today for example, all the shopkeepers in Villiers had organised a 'trick or treat' event for the children in the village, putting bowls of sweets and other treats on their counters. Even René Matout managed to get it together to put out some pumpkins and hang a few black bats and cobwebs in his window, despite his depressed state.

I spot the Civray Stetsons, sitting together at two long trestle tables – approximately thirty women and one guy, Colin, a British carpenter, who recently joined. (Yes, it sounds odd, but he seems quite happy with the arrangement.)

'Why are all those people waving at you?' asks Travis.

'That's my line dancing group.'

'Really?' he says, surprised. 'Some of them are quite good-looking. And they don't all have grey hair.'

'I told you. It's different in France. And anyway, grey hair is very fashionable right now. As seen at the recent catwalk shows.'

We go over and I embark on a marathon round of kissing. Each person that arrives must greet and kiss the other thirty members of the troupe before they sit down. It does wonders for your ego. I missed the last practice session as I was in London, so I'm greeted like a long-lost relative. Travis is also given a warm reception, especially as, apart from Colin, he is the only man among us. We sit down next to Coralie and her twentysomething friends, who look like members of a girl band this evening in tight jeans with heavily kohled eyes and glitter sprinkled in their hair. They've even managed to find cowboy boots with high heels.

On the next table, I see Jocelyn, Jill and Gloria. Ever since Gloria walked into the saloon in Claviers that day, and wowed everyone with her dancing, the three of them have become inseparable. Recently, I even spotted them shopping together in Intermarché. It must be nice, I think, for Gloria, a recently bereaved widow, to have Jocelyn and Jill living a few doors away in the same hamlet.

'*Ka-renne, ça va?*' I look up and see a glamorous witch, whose ruby-red lips, raven hair and jolly smile I would recognise anywhere. She is wearing a black cloak over her voluptuous figure, high heels and a tall pointy hat.

'Delphine! You look amazing.'

'*Merci*. Are you doing *la danse country*? I am very much looking forward to seeing this.'

'Whose table are you on?' I ask.

'Oh, I'm over there, with the mayor of Romagne and some of his councillors. But I will come and find you later.'

'Who was *that*?' asks Travis.

'Oh, that's my friend Delphine. She's the mayor of a nearby commune.'

'She looks *fabulous*,' says Travis. 'You must introduce me later. Oh God, look who's over there.' I look over and see Annabel, who is not specifically dressed as a witch but looks like one, thanks to her scrawny frame and sour expression. 'I really hope she doesn't see us,' says Travis. 'I'm just not in the mood for her tedious stories.'

'Karen, where's your T-shirt?' yells Jocelyn across the table.

'Don't worry, I've got it with me,' I say.

'Well, you better put it on. We're about to dance.'

I go to the bathroom and swap my civilian black top for the regulation T-shirt. I really, really hope that no one takes any pictures.

'DON'T. SAY. ANYTHING,' I warn Travis, as I return to an almost empty table.

'Nice!' he says, with an ironic smile. 'You'd better hurry up. They're all on the stage.'

I join my fellow conscripts just as the master of ceremonies is announcing, '*Mesdames, mesdemoiselles, messieurs, voici les Civray Stets-urns!*'

I try to inveigle my way to the back but someone pushes me forward, so that I'm next to Coralie in the front row. She is tall, skinny and looks like a model, so is absolutely the worst person to be next to. At least I know the steps so well that I could do them in my sleep. What could possibly go wrong?

As the opening bars of the first dance become audible, I look over to see who is responsible for the sound system – which is impressively free of feedback and unexpected crackles – and standing next to the DJ, beer in hand, is... Andy Lawton. Again. I'm starting to think that he is following the Civray Stetsons around. Strangely, he looks as though he is enjoying himself. While Travis, sitting alone at a long empty table, is wearing a moody 'What the fuck am I doing here?' expression, Andy looks quite happy and is even tapping his foot in time to the music – 'Addicted to Love' by Robert Palmer.

It doesn't take long for things to go wrong – the second dance, in fact. I'm waiting to launch into the opening steps of 'Party for Two' by Shania Twain, when I realise that I don't recognise the music. At first, I think the DJ has made a mistake and chosen the wrong track, but everyone else has already started dancing. '*Ce n'est pas* "Party for Two",' I hiss at Coralie.

'It's a new dance,' she mouths back, in between several kick-ball turns and a grapevine. And then, stating the obvious: 'We have changed the schedule.' I stand stock-still while everyone else does a half-turn to face a different direction. Across the room I see Travis smirking. Andy Lawton is also looking amused. Shame-faced, I do the only thing possible in the circumstances, which is to clamber down from the stage and make my way back to the table.

Travis is doubled up laughing. 'You didn't tell me this was a comedy act too,' he howls.

'Very funny.'

'What happened? Was it stage fright? Did you forget the steps?' He clutches his sides, laughing so hard he looks like he's in pain.

'It's a completely different dance to what I was expecting,' I say. 'They substituted it at the final practice session while I was in London. And no one thought to tell me.'

'Oh dear God,' says Travis, wiping mock tears from his eyes. 'Your face! That was priceless. I haven't laughed so much in ages.'

I sit out the remaining dances, too embarrassed to draw attention to myself by getting back on the stage. Anyway, who knows what other last minute substitutions they have made? 'I'm ever so sorry, Karen,' says Jocelyn, once the performance has ended. 'I completely forgot to tell you we'd changed one of the dances. It all happened very quickly – nothing to do with me. Gloria taught it to the class at the last practice session and they all wanted to do it tonight.'

'Don't worry.' I say. 'It's not the first time I've looked like a total banana. And it won't be the last.'

'You know Andy Lawton is here?' says Travis, after we've collected our first course (pâté) from the buffet. 'I bumped into him at the bar earlier. I said we'd go and talk to him later.'

'Yes, I saw him. He was standing next to the DJ.'

'I mentioned about that game of tennis but he said he's very busy at the moment. He's got a friend coming out from the UK next week.'

'*Tant pis!*' I say, disappointed that we won't be playing mixed doubles anytime soon.

'He seems like a nice guy though,' says Travis. 'We should get to know him better.'

'Is he here on his own?' I ask.

'No,' says Travis. I think he knows the DJ, plus he had another friend with him. A guy with close-cropped hair, very fit looking.'

'Oh,' I say, thinking that it sounds like James, the friend that he was with at the *vide-grenier* and the *Comice*.

'It's a shame they're both straight. You should go over and talk to them.'

'Travis, I've just made a complete prat of myself.'

'Honestly, you need to be bit more forward,' says Travis. 'Neither of them look like they've got girlfriends. I'd get in there if I were you.'

I point to my outfit. '*En plus*, as you might have realised, this is not my best look.'

'OK, you're right. Maybe another time.'

The main course is served – a cassoulet, followed by lemon tart, cheese and coffee. Even Travis, who is a bit of a food snob, is forced to admit that for a community hall meal, it's very good. Jocelyn then takes the microphone and invites the audience to line up on the dance floor to learn *la danse country*. A surprising number of people do. As Jocelyn talks them through the steps of the 'Texas Stomp', first in French, then in English, I look around the room. Lined up on the dance floor are people of all ages, from adorable *enfants* and teenagers to silver-haired septuagenarians. I think to myself how refreshingly non-ageist the social life in rural France is. But it's a bizarre mix: the Civray Stetsons dressed as cowgirls (and a cowboy), mingling with witches, ghouls, wizards and characters from 'Areee Pott-air' (as J. K. Rowling's work is known in France). It's particularly surreal to see Delphine gamely trying to perform the 'Texas Stomp' in stilettos and pointy hat.

'God,' says Travis. 'I can't believe how popular this dancing thing has become. It's like some weird cult.'

'Come on,' I say, trying to pull him up from the table. 'Just give it a go.'

'No chance. *No way*. I absolutely do not do line dancing,' he says.

'Oh, you're such a spoilsport,' I say, before going to the bar to get some water. I leave him with Coralie and the other French line dancers desperately trying to sign him up for the Monday night classes.

While waiting at the bar to be served, I hear a familar, super-posh voice. It is Annabel, who is standing near the bar with

Charles. It looks like she has cornered Andy Lawton, who is waiting with his friend James to get served. Dressed in jeans and grey V-neck sweater rather than the shorts and vest top that he was wearing at the *Comice* and the *vide-grenier*, James still looks fit enough to run up Mont Blanc and back without pausing for breath.

'This line dancing is all very well,' Annabel is saying, 'but must we be subjected to it everywhere? I'm getting rather tired of it. Oh hello, Corinne, how are you?'

'Great, thanks,' I say, disappointed that she has spotted me. Andy and James both smile and nod hello and Charles greets me with a warm, 'How delightful to see you.'

'We were just talking about the line dancing phenomenon that seems to be sweeping through the French countryside,' says Annabel. 'But I gather you are one of the… er, participants.'

'Um… sort of. Or I would have been, if someone hadn't changed one of the dances at the last moment.'

'Yes, I did wonder what happened,' she replies.

Charles gives a hearty laugh and puts his arm around my shoulders. 'You handled it very well, considering,' he says. 'And I do like that T-shirt.'

'Well, I really enjoyed tonight's performance,' says Andy. 'Everyone looked like they were having a good time. I'm all for it.'

Surprisingly, he seems like he's being sincere and is not just saying this to wind Annabel up. For a second, it occurs to me that maybe, just maybe, we could recruit Andy to our troupe. I'm sure that Colin would appreciate the company. Unfortunately, it's not possible to ask him as, no doubt desperate to escape from Annabel, he excuses himself, saying that has just spotted someone he urgently needs to talk to. While Charles is distracted by another *Anglais*, I grab my water and also run, before Annabel invites me to dinner or asks me to look after Jenson and Button again.

When I return to the table, Travis is no longer there. My first thought is that he has bolted, but he wouldn't get very far, as he's relying on me for a lift home. I scan the room, thinking that he has probably gone off to talk to someone, but no. To my very great surprise, Travis is on the dance floor performing a strange little jig with Coralie, to 'Man! I Feel Like a Woman!' by Shania Twain. Coralie has obviously taught him some of the steps. I allow myself an ironic smile. Travis, of all people, doing *la danse country*.

Unfortunately, neither of us gets the chance to talk to Andy again, as he always seems to be surrounded by people. Then the disco starts up and I spend the rest of the night dancing, as does Travis, who seems to have acquired an entourage in the form of all the front-rowers from my line dancing group. Hips like syrup, he makes quite an impact on the dance floor, especially when 'Night Fever' is played and he does a mean impersonation of John Travolta. He doesn't even flinch when the DJ plays 'Rasputin' by Boney M – a song played at every *bal populaire* in the French countryside that I have ever been to. Later, I spot Jocelyn, Jill and Gloria doing the steps of the 'Texas Stomp' to Phil Collins 'You Can't Hurry Love', another rural fave.

As we leave, Coralie and her friends bombard Travis with kisses – he's obviously made quite an impression on them – and remind him that the next class is on Monday evening at 8.30 p.m., should he change his mind and want to come along.

'Well,' I say as we drive through the curving back roads to St Hilaire, 'I never expected to see you dancing to Shania Twain.'

'I only did it under duress. Your friend Coralie made me do it.'

'But you looked suspiciously like you were enjoying it.'

'OK, I admit it,' says Travis, grudgingly. 'I've had more fun this evening than I could ever have imagined.'

I drop him off and drive home alone. So, no progress on the Andy Lawton front – he's like a carrot that keeps being dangled in front of my nose and then pulled away – but it's been a fun evening and I always feel buoyed by having spent time in Travis's company.

Monday is my least favourite day in rural France, as everything is closed. It's as if the 'pause' button has been pressed on normal life. You can't even go out for a coffee, as the Liberty Bookshop, the Café du Commerce and the little bar on the corner are all closed. So to say I don't like Mondays is a bit of an understatement. Sometimes I drive 26 kilometres to La Grande Galerie in Civray, an art gallery with a little tea shop attached and the only place I've found that makes cappuccinos made with real milk as opposed to the horrible long-life stuff. There are nearly always people around, especially in the summer when people sit outside and chat in the courtyard, which is reassuring, because if you visited Villiers on a Monday, and weren't familiar with life in rural France, you might well think that all human life had been wiped out by some freak virus or flu strain.

My other ploy for beating the Monday blues is to drive to Romagne, 20 kilometres away, to see the great love of my life. When my car draws up in front of the farmhouse, he invariably comes pelting down the garden path to the little wooden gate designed to keep him in, and tries to hurl himself over it, such is his joy at seeing me. The sight of his animated black eyes and big gorilla paws on top of the gate always sends my seratonin levels soaring. Milou, his 'sister', also comes running out to greet me, but Biff is never very happy if she gets too close, nudging her out of the way.

Usually, I take Biff out on his own as Sarah reckons that Biff is a bad influence on Milou, and if you let them off their leads together, they tend to 'pack up' and run away. Much as I like Milou, I prefer it when it's just Biff and me, rambling through the countryside together.

And on those walks, I notice the evenings, and then the afternoons, grow shorter; while the fields near my village, once a vivid yellow or lush green, revert to a dormant expanse of red-brown earth. The willow baskets outside L'Épicerie, meanwhile, now contain parsnips, sweet potatoes and beetroots rather than the glossy tomatoes, bell peppers and paintbox colours of summer. In the mornings there is a cold nip in the air and the plastic tables outside the Café du Commerce have been taken indoors until the spring. And it is the smell of woodsmoke or rain on concrete that pervades rather than the subtle drift of wisteria and lilac from a nearby garden.

The greyest days sap the energy and it's hard to feel enthused about anything.

One Monday afternoon in late November, after one such low-energy day, I phone Sarah and Steve on the spur of the moment and ask if I can come over to walk Biff. Sarah readily agrees but tells me to hurry as it is already getting dark. The sky is a menacing dappled grey when I arrive, so Steve gives me instructions for a short circular walk, lasting about half an hour, which should get me back before it is dark. The walk should take me along a path by a damp green field, past an ostrich farm and a family of donkeys, and bring me back to their farmhouse. Only it doesn't and after over an hour and a half of walking, I'm lost in a forest with the light fading fast. I have no idea where I am. Somewhere in the forest to the left of me, a man is chopping up tree trunks with a chainsaw. I'm certainly not going to stop and ask him for directions.

So we plough on along the muddy track, in the grey half-light, me trying not to fall over in the deep tractor furrows, Biff blissfully unaware that we might be spending the night outdoors as he trots along ahead of me. It reminds me of the Sunday when, armed with a copy of *Time Out Guide to Country Walks* and no compass, I over-confidently led a group of London friends on a fifteen-mile foray into the Sussex countryside. We took a wrong turn at an oak tree and it all went wrong from there. It culminated in a scene reminiscent of the horror film *The Blair Witch Project* when at nightfall we found ourselves lost in a scary forest miles from the train station. 'Did you not think to bring a proper map or a compass?' one of my friends asked. Then, as now, the answer is 'No'. (Stupidly, I haven't brought my mobile phone with me either.) Instead, I do what I always do when lost, which is keep going in one direction in the hope that a signpost or landmark will appear.

The problem is that when darkness falls in rural France, it is like someone has dropped a black velvet throw over the surrounding countryside: you can't see your hand in front of you. But suddenly, that's the least of our problems. As if out of nowhere, a grey, liver-spotted beast charges towards us, teeth bared. I'm glad at first that he decides to chase Biff and not me, as Biff can run faster. But as the *chasse* dog closes in and Biff lets out an anguished yelp, I am forced to intervene to save him, hurling myself towards them and yelling at the big grey bully to go away. Fortunately, it does. Although I do have experience in the dog department – after all, I survived Jenson and Button – I'm not normally this brave when faced with a snarling hound. But I would have wrestled that beast to the ground with my bare hands if necessary, in order to save little Biff.

A few minutes later, just as I'm seriously contemplating a night huddled under a tree with Biff, and wishing I'd watched more Ray Mears (the survival expert) on TV, we emerge from the woods by a pig farm. And in the distance, several fields away, I can see a village. After attempting an ankle-twisting walk over a brittle, ploughed field – a major breach of countryside etiquette – I return to the road and eventually find a small wooden sign. The village in the distance – hallelujah – is Romagne, where Biff lives.

It's dark when we finally make it back to the farmhouse. 'What happened?' asks Sarah, looking really anxious, as she opens the door. 'Steve was about to go out in his car to look for you.'

'I don't think that would have done much good as we were lost in a forest,' I say. 'I took a wrong turning somewhere. And I had to throw myself between Biff and a really vicious hunt dog. It was quite a walk.'

This very same dog, it transpires, recently gave Sarah a very nasty bite, necessitating several hospital visits. But Biff seems unbothered by his brush with death. While I take a seat by the roaring log burner, he stretches out on top of the sofa, eyes fixed on the range cooker, where Steve, tall and with a slight stoop, is cooking his special 'dog stew' (not made *from* dogs, I hasten to add, but *for* them). I love the fact that Sarah and Steve make their dogs a hot meal every night. Biff's really landed on his feet here.

They invite me to stay and eat with them, which I do, feeling a little envious of their cosy set-up and the fact that they get to curl up on the sofa with Biff at night. Sarah and Steve came to France five years ago with different partners and split with them shortly after arrival – sadly, an all-too-common story, I've noticed – before meeting each other when Steve, a carpenter, came to make kitchen cabinets for Sarah's farmhouse. He never left (although he has several houses of his own that he is renovating). They've since become one of the most popular couples in the Poitou-Charentes and are booked up several weeks in advance (unheard of in the French countryside, where most of us are free at a moment's notice) with everything from 'Sixties nights' (as in the decade, not the age group) and charity events to dinner parties and string quartet soirées. I honestly don't know where Sarah finds the time. (She also does volunteer work for a charity that helps lonely, depressed or clueless expats). And on the rare evenings when they're not out, they usually have a gang of friends gathered for three genial courses in their cosy terracotta-coloured kitchen. Sarah is an excellent cook (tonight: butternut squash soup, roast lamb with two kinds of veg and lemon meringue pie for dessert) and Steve really knows his wine.

After a really enjoyable evening – much of it spent talking about Biff – I drag myself reluctantly away from their roaring woodburner. I kiss my beloved goodbye and set off home in the darkness, wishing that he was tucked under the seat behind me.

It's getting more and more difficult to give Biff back. On Friday afternoon I collect him for an overnight stay. After a long walk, I close the shutters, light the fire and make him half a beefburger, peas, carrots and basmati rice for dinner. Then he drags a cushion under my desk – you have to admire his chutzpah – where he lies, his wet nose nudging my ankles, while I finish a feature on the shaggy (fake fur) coat. (Travis suggests that I call it 'Anyone for a Shag?' when we chat on the phone later.)

I work most of Saturday too, again with Biff curled up at my feet, and reward him for his good behaviour with a windswept, two-hour walk in the rain. I then leave him lying in front of the log burner to dry his shaggy coat – yes, he's wearing winter's must-have – while I get ready to go out. (I've promised Sarah that I'll drop him back early evening, en route to dinner at Travis's house.)

He sighs ostentatiously when I come downstairs in sprigged green chiffon and a mist of Chanel Cristalle, rather than my usual muddy riding boots and outdoor gear, for it's obvious that we are not going for a walk. Instead, I bundle him and his beanbag into the car and drive him back to Romagne.

Sarah invites me into the kitchen and offers me a glass of wine but, as much as I love talking to Sarah – like Biff, she has a very mischievous sense of humour – I'm late for Travis's dinner party. I thank them for letting me have Biff and then try to sneak out of the house when he isn't looking. But suddenly, he bolts through the narrow gap in the door and up the garden path ahead of me. Smooth as a Guérlain lipstick, he jumps up onto two legs and deftly opens the gate with his paws, then steps back so that he can walk through it. 'He's going with you!' cries Steve, aghast. And then, as we watch open-mouthed, he runs through the gate and sits by my car door, waiting to climb in. I laugh and feel secretly thrilled, but also embarrassed. Sarah and Steve love Biff as much as I do, and this must feel like a big betrayal. But as I drive away from my beloved, I feel sad as I think of the beseeching look on his face as I opened the car door. How I wish I could have taken him with me.

The fact is: life is just not the same without Biff. The car feels empty without him curled up behind the driver's seat and there is something missing on the beaten-up leather sofa in the evening without his big black paws stretched out beside me. I think of him a billion times a day – which, if I'm being truthful, is way more than I ever thought of Jon. Delphine, who has seen the two of us together many times, usually in the Liberty Bookshop, says it is obvious that I have fallen completely

194

in love with him. And he with me. Oh dear! He is, after all, someone else's dog.

Travis's dinner party is great fun. Despite being a part-time resident in France, he has managed to assemble a really interesting group of friends, all of them under forty. They include a DJ who lives locally, a television set designer who commutes back to London once a week while his wife and young son live in St Hilaire, and Tina, a highly groomed expat with her own catering business, who has just split up with her husband (another!). The evening culminates in Travis cranking up the music and everyone dancing until 2.00 a.m on the terracotta-tiled floor of his sitting room. The great thing about living in a remote rural location, he points out, is you can make as much noise as you like and no one complains.

Driving back from Travis's house that evening, it suddenly hits me: rather than hankering after someone else's dog, what I need is a Biff of my own. Despite the lateness of the hour, when I get home, I surf the net for schnauzer breeders, since Steve is convinced that Biff is part schnauzer. But I quickly realise that they cost almost as much as a Birkin bag and therefore wildly beyond my budget. And then, lying in bed that night, I have a better idea: why not get a rescue dog?

The following morning I contact Phoenix, the dog rescue in Bergerac, from whence Biff came. It's a small operation, run by a husband and wife team, but all the dogs that pass through there – I know several living locally – seem to have lovely temperaments. I register on their website first and then call and explain what I'm looking for – basically Biff mark two.

'Ah yes, we remember Biff,' says Sheelagh, the co-proprietor. 'But it will be difficult to find another small black terrier like him. He was a one off.'

'Could you at least try?' I plead.

I hear nothing for two weeks and then, suddenly, Sheelagh emails to say that she and her husband have found me no less than three Biff lookalikes, all of them in the SPA (the French equivalent of the RSPCA) in Bergerac. She emails me pictures of three dear little black dogs. One of them, Wilf, does indeed bear a close resemblance to Biff – not least in terms of his black button eyes and slightly haughty demeanour. I phone Sheelagh immediately and arrange to drive to Bergerac to see him at the first possible opportunity. Wilf, I think, might just be The One.

Chapter 12

Tongue and Cheeks
(And Ears Too)

ON MONDAY MORNING, the day before I'm supposed to go to Bergerac to meet Wilf, Sarah calls to ask a question that doesn't need to be asked. Her tone is very serious, and she cuts straight to the chase.

'Look,' she says. 'Steve and I have given this a great deal of thought over the past couple of weeks.' She pauses. 'Would you like Biff?'

'What? Forever?' I ask, taken aback. I want to be sure, before I get my hopes up, that she doesn't just mean for the day or the weekend.

'Yes, forever,' she says. 'He would be your dog.'

'Well, I think you know the answer to that,' I say, wishing she was in the same room so that I could hug her. '*OF COURSE* I would like Biff.'

'The thing is,' she says, 'we love him hugely, but that Saturday night when he ran up the path after you and sat by your car, he was giving us a message. He was telling us that he wanted to live with you.'

'Oh,' I say, feeling bad for Sarah and Steve. It can't be great knowing that your dog has tried to elope with someone else.

'Ungrateful little bugger,' jokes Sarah. 'But seriously, I wouldn't part with him or give him to anyone else but it's been obvious for quite some time that you adore him and he adores you.'

'It's true. I do absolutely adore him,' I say, feeling the usual surge of boundless, unstoppable, unlimited love at just the thought of that little black animal.

'There's just one condition,' says Sarah.

'What's that?' I say, ready to agree to anything if it means I can have Biff.

'That we will always have contact with him. We're both really fond of the little fella and we'd want to still be able to see him. If you need to go back to the UK on one of your work trips, the deal is that we would look after him.'

'Of course,' I say, thinking to myself, could this be any better? Not only have I landed the dog of my dreams but Sarah is willing to take care of him when I go away.

'And if, at any moment, you change your mind and decide you don't want him after all, you give him straight back to us,' says Sarah. 'I don't want him being passed from pillar to post.'

'Oh my God, of course,' I say. 'But I can absolutely guarantee that I won't change my mind.'

'It's just that if you're not sure or have any doubts...'

'I don't think I've ever been more sure about anything in my life.'

'Good,' says Sarah. 'I think it's fairer on Milou too. Biff always needs to be the centre of attention and it's been like that ever since we got him. When she had an eye infection I couldn't even put drops in her eyes without Biff rushing over and pushing her out of the way and batting his eyelids as if to say "me, me, me".' I laugh as it's so easy to picture Biff doing this.

'To be honest, Biff and Milou together were a bit of a handful,' continues Sarah, as if justifying her decision. 'When we only had Milou, she was a really good dog. But then Biff came along and he's been a bad influence on her. They pack up together when we go for walks and disappear off into the woods, sometimes for hours. Biff needs to be with one person who will give him non-stop love and attention.'

'Oh I will, I will,' I say, picturing his eager little face and shiny nose and the two of us curled up on the sofa together, night after night.

'Watching you and Biff together reminds me of how I used to be with Charlie,' says Sarah, referring to her now deceased cocker spaniel. 'He was the love of my life and he went everywhere with me, even when I was giving lectures at college. I think Biff needs that kind of relationship too. I can't give him all the fussing and attention that he wants because I've got Milou and Steve.'

'Well, don't worry, Biff will be the most important thing in my life,' I say, aware that this sounds a little tragic. Not that I want to subject Sarah to emotional blackmail or anything…

A couple of days later, I set out, armed with a bag of beauty products, to collect my prize. Sarah and I have arranged to meet outside the vet's in Douhe, where Biff is booked in for his worming treatment. (I don't like the sound of that but it turns out that it just involves a tablet.) Sarah will also bring along his pet passport and the necessary documents to transfer ownership to me. I feel a strange combination of guilt – it feels like I'm stealing someone's husband or child – and euphoria. The thing I have wanted, dreamed about for months is about to be mine. Our bond is about to be made official. I've never quite managed to sign up for the 'for richer, for poorer, in sickness or health… till death do us part' deal with a man, but I can, with all my heart, promise exactly that to this little dog. I love him now at his most youthful and handsome and energetic, but I will love him even more when he is old and grey and no longer able to chase rabbits or do bunny-hops. I will cherish and adore him even if he eats my favourite cherry-red shoes. I'll walk him in fair weather and foul, in sunshine and rain. And in return, I hope that he will love and obey me. (I'm pretty sure of the love; it's the obeying that might take a bit of work.) But one thing is certain: it's the biggest emotional commitment I've ever made.

Sarah and Biff are waiting outside the vet's when I arrive. He gives several barks of excitement and strains at the leash when he sees me, jumping up and trying to lick me. Sarah is laughing. I scan her face for any signs of doubt. I'm anxious that, until the documents are stamped and signed, she might change her mind, leaving me jilted on the vet's doorstep. 'Are you sure about this?' I say, bending down to stroke the top of his head and pull his ears from side to side. 'It feels like I'm stealing your child.'

'I've given it a lot of thought and I've made up my mind,' she says. 'It's for the best. He's a spirited little chap and he needs the kind of walks and attention that I know you'll give him.'

The spirited little chap in question sniffs the air in distaste as we enter the clinic and refuses to go any further, digging in with his large paws. The vet, a tall, serious-looking man, indicates for us to go through to the treatment room.

'Come on Biffy,' says Sarah, dragging him along behind us. When he won't budge, she picks him up like a baby, his head bobbing over her shoulder and carries him into the leek-coloured room before putting him gently down on the examination bench.

The vet's manner is entirely perfunctory as he examines Biff, administers the worming pill and looks up his medical records. How can he be so immune to Biff's charms, I ask myself? Sarah tells him that she is transferring ownership to me and the vet gives me the relevant form to change his registration details and apply for a new identity card. I notice from Biff's current *carte d'identification* that he was once known as 'Tiny Tim', and that his 'racial type' is given as *'croisé cocker'* or cocker spaniel cross.

'He's definitely more of a Biff than a Tiny Tim,' I say.

'I know,' says Sarah, 'an awful name. It makes him sound like a victim. It didn't suit him at all, even when the poor little soul first came from the rescue and was missing great patches of hair. That's why we changed it.'

She hands me the passport and registration documents. 'There you go,' she says, with a gentle smile. 'He's yours now. I know that he'll have a wonderful life with you.' I want to hug her. She has just given me something life-changing. We find a cafe that is open – we are the only customers – and order *deux crèmes*, or white coffees. Sarah also requests a bowl of water for Biff, who lies patiently under the table, unaware that his life is about to change too.

Sarah runs through a list of instructions for his care and upkeep. I must give him half a tinned sardine once or twice a week in order to keep his bones strong and his coat glossy; and, from time to time, ground linseeds for the same reason. I'm to apply a tick and flea treatment called 'Frontline' to the back of his neck once a month, give him a worming tablet every three months, and check for tick bites (yeuch – they sound disgusting) during the summer months. And I mustn't forget to take him to the vet's on the appointed date for his rabies booster jab – if I'm even a day late the whole treatment has to start again. Biff looks up at both of us with a beatific expression on his face. He loves it when people are talking about him, even when it's in relation to worms and rabies.

'Oh and there's just one other thing... the Phoenix Rescue. They're very strict about what happens to their dogs once they've been rehomed and they might be a little upset if they think I've just given Biff away. I'll phone them this evening and explain the circumstances.'

'Well, actually,' I say, feeling sheepish, 'they already know. I had to phone and say that I wouldn't be taking Wilf, the Biff lookalike that they found for me. They couldn't have been nicer. Sheelagh said it sounded like I'd got the dog that I really wanted and she was happy for me.'

I feel a little pang of guilt when I think of Wilf, who has missed out on a new home with me by a whisker. For a second, I did think of taking him too, but then I figured that Biff might not like it. The bond between us is so strong that he might not appreciate a third party coming along and parking his paws on the sofa too.

'Well, I'll phone anyway,' says Sarah. 'It's important that they know I wasn't looking to rehome Biff and that I wouldn't have given him away to anyone but you.'

'I think they know that,' I say. 'I told them I practically stole your dog and it's not like you just gave him away on a whim.'

Sarah looks thoughtful, as if she is having some regrets. I start to feel guilty again. 'Oh, I've just remembered. I've got something for you in the car,' I say.

As I get up to leave, Biff immediately sits bolt upright like a little soldier, his beady black eyes following me and on full alert. And he starts to cry – a plaintive, panicked wail. The sound of his distress follows me to the door.

'It's OK, Biffy,' I hear Sarah trying to soothe him. 'She won't be long. She's coming back.' It must be hard for Sarah to witness this second act of betrayal. As if Biff hadn't stated his preferences strongly enough when he ran down the garden path and tried to get into my car the other night, now he is really slamming home the point. But I am ashamed to say, I can't help feeling secretly pleased by the overt display of his feelings for me.

Well,' says Sarah, when I return from the car clutching a bag of beauty products, including a La Prairie anti-ageing serum (not that she needs it), a Chanel bath oil and some Christian Dior make-up, 'I think that was the proof that I'm doing the right thing.' Biff's wailing, it seems, has validated her decision.

'These are for you. It seems like a good exchange for Biff,' I joke. Only later does it occur to me that this was possibly a crass thing to do, to try and pay off someone for their dog with some blusher and an oscillating mascara.

But Sarah is far too nice, too much of a class act to make me feel bad about taking Biff, or to let me know how sad she is to see him go. She did, after all, nurse him back to health, when he came to her skinny and missing great tufts of hair. Sarah has shown me his 'baby' pictures, which are heartbreaking. With bald patches above his eyebrows, he was far from the handsome chap that he is now. Yet his proud expression suggests that he knew he was destined for better things.

'So shall we get his stuff out of the car?' she says. As we leave the cafe, she hands me Biff's lead. It's going to take a while to get used to the fact that he is my dog now. She gets his beanbag – the one printed with bones and 'woofs' – out of the boot, along with some pulverized-looking toys and his little green Barbour jacket.

'That belonged to Charlie,' says Sarah. 'But it's Biff's now.' She bends down to ruffle his shaggy coat and kiss him goodbye, and he licks her face in return. 'I'll miss you, you little rascal,' she says to him. And then to me: 'I know that you'll love him and really look after him and that he'll have a wonderful life with you.' And I'm going to have a wonderful life with him, I think as I give her a quick hug – I'm worried that I will start to get emotional – and thank her profusely again. She pats his head one more time and then he and I walk back down the high street to my car. He jumps inside happily, assuming his usual position in the footwell behind the driver's seat. And so I drive home through the damp winter countryside with my precious prize in the back. Two weeks before Christmas, Sarah and Steve have given me the best present I could ever have imagined. I cannot believe that Biff is finally mine.

The week before Christmas, I drive to Puysoleil to meet Delphine for lunch at Le Café de la Paix. I've heard a lot about this little rural restaurant mainly because Didier, the owner, is quite a colourful local character. He's also a very good chef according to Delphine, so I'm looking forward to a delicious lunch as I drive along the narrow, curvy road to her village, in the drab winter light. The countryside is sapped of all colour now – churned red-brown earth stretching to the horizon and a milky, moonstone sky. But in my heart, it feels like summer, knowing that Biff is curled up under my seat in the back of the car. It's only a week since he officially became mine, but I am already so attached to him, our personalities already so strongly merged, that I honestly don't know how I would live without him. At first I was worried that he might miss his other family, Sarah and Steve and Milou, and find it hard not having a huge garden and open countryside on his doorstep. But in fact, he has adapted easily to village life and seems very happy in his new home.

We've slotted perfectly into each other's lives. In the mornings, I get up, throw on my clothes and walk or run him around the local lake. In the late afternoon, I take him out for a second long walk, along tracks with deep puddles and muddy furrows that seem to suck boots and paws down into the earth. If he's really muddy when we get back, I give him a warm shower – he walks into the cubicle willingly – and then dry him with heated towels. In the mornings, I place a fleece blanket on top of the antique radiator in the sitting room, so that he can stretch out on that and dry his fur while watching the comings and goings of the neighbours. If it's really cold, I pull the leather sofa in front of the woodburner so he can dry his shaggy hair in front of it. Then, in the evenings, watched by adoring eyes, I cook us both dinner. It's my favourite moment of the day.

I feel such a glut of love for Biff that I surprise myself. When he wags his tail, climbs up on the sofa and wedges his long body next to mine, or steals one of my shoes and runs down the stairs with it in the hope that I'll give chase, I just feel great waves of joy and happiness. Similarly, watching him run at full pelt across a ploughed field gives me more pleasure than any handbag or pair of designer shoes ever did. I even love his little habit of hiding my clothes and shoes. Recently, I was wondering where all my black socks had gone and then I found them in a little pile tucked behind my desk, but he looked so pleased with his stash that it was a struggle to reclaim them.

As a child, with a hard core Enid Blyton habit, I longed for my toys to come alive at night as they did in the various 'nurseries' and 'playrooms' of the well brought-up little children in her tales. It feels as if I finally got my wish. Biff is like an adorable teddy bear, with a beating heart, a bobbed tail and paws that smell like biscuits. The fact that I am capable of feeling such a surfeit of love for another living creature also makes me love myself more. A dog, I discover, is not just good for your calf muscles – mine have never looked skinnier – but your self-esteem. I want to broadcast to the world the fact that I am utterly besotted with Biff, bouncing up and down like a love-struck Tom Cruise on Oprah Winfrey's sofa. I really am that embarrassing.

Biff, however, always looks proud to be seen with me – even when I make him sit through a *danse country* session in Douhe. I clip his lead to a table at the back of the room and apart from a few barks to remind everyone he is there, he is always perfectly behaved. Among my English friends I am often referred to as 'Biff's mummy' – I try not to think about what that makes me – while in my village Biff is greeted with enthusiasm everywhere, from the newsagent to the local restaurant. My French friends even sign off their texts with *'bisous à toi et Biff'* – 'kisses to you and Biff'! It's as if through owning Biff I have become more connected to everyone around me.

When we arrive in Puysoleil, I park in front of the ancient church, opposite the *mairie* – a charming, old stone building, just one storey high, with distressed-looking pale blue shutters and the word *'Mairie'* painted in faded red paint and an old-fashioned typeface above the entrance. In the summer, scarlet roses climb up the stone walls and the blue hydrangea bushes outside burst into life with huge pompom-like flowers. It's as far removed from a drab municipal building as it's possible to be.

The interior is equally charming, consisting of just one room, with ancient flagstone floors and an old fireplace, bearing a mandatory picture of the *président*. But Delphine has really made this domain her own. Alongside Sarkozy's mugshot on the mantelpiece, is the *tricolore* hat, topped with a swirl of red, white and blue netting, that Delphine's milliner in Niort made her to celebrate becoming mayor. The overall effect is cheerful and upbeat – an effect reinforced by the lemon-yellow paint used on the door, window frames and skirting boards. This being France, it's not a lairy yellow but a low-key, subtle shade that, like the various blues used for shutters here, would be impossible to replicate in Homebase.

I first came here for Delphine's inauguration back in May. When the formalities were over and the previous incumbent had handed over the mayoral sash, Delphine and her fellow councillors – and yours truly, the interloper at the back of the room – celebrated with Vouvray, a sparkling white wine, and lemon drizzle cake, which, ever the Anglophile, Delphine had ordered from the Liberty Bookshop. Later, she posed for pictures in front of the lemon fireplace wearing her red, white and blue mayoral sash and spectacular tricolour hat.

'*Coucou!*' I shout.

'*Eh, bonjour Ka-renne. Ça va?*' says Delphine. '*Et bonjour le petit Biff.*' She's sitting at an old chestnut desk with her secretary Agnes. Biff strains on his lead when he sees Delphine. He adores her. In fact, it's become a little joke that he sees in her a kindred spirit, because she too, has long, curly, dark hair. 'I won't be long,' she says. 'We are just going through the post.'

Delphine makes running a small commune look effortless but I know that she is at her desk at 7.30 a.m. most mornings, before heading off to do her job as a supply teacher in various schools and colleges within a 30 kilometre radius. From her lemon-painted, rose-covered power base, she keeps Puysoleil functioning smoothly, marrying the inhabitants, presiding over their funerals, apportioning the annual budget (next year the roof of the small school needs to be repaired) and sorting out their disputes. One villager has recently installed a window that overlooks someone else's courtyard, without permission; another is upset about his neighbour's overhanging laurel bushes; while a local farmer has ploughed a public footpath (not for the first time: he threatened the previous mayor with his gun). All of these problems Delphine sorts out with common sense and good humour, a disarming smile and a large dose of feminine charm, as well as a registered letter.

But her role as mayor goes further than minor disputes about boundaries, illegal ploughing and barking dogs. Perhaps because of her warm, worldly personality, she is also called upon to play the role of confidant, providing pastoral care for her 'flock'. People come to her with problems of the heart – the alcoholic husband, the cheating wife, and worse. Delphine, more often than not, offers a discreet, sympathetic ear and practical advice.

Often, she adopts a multi-faceted approach to solving problems. When the single mother who lives opposite the *salle des fêtes* started to complain about the noise, Delphine took all the usual official steps: she looked into soundproofing, brought forward the official hour of closure for parties and events, and even consulted the lawyer in Poitiers, charged with helping all the mayors in the region, for advice. But her *pièce de résistance* – according to a former Puysoleil resident who now lives in my village – was to appoint the best-looking gendarme for miles around with the task of 'updating' Madame Arnault, the unhappy villager. Later, so the Puysoleil gossip goes, the gendarme reported back to the *mairie*, that 'Madame Arnault had a very big smile on her face when I left. Don't worry *Madame le Maire*, I don't think you will have any more complaints from her.' And to date Delphine hasn't, although when I asked her if the story about the handsome gendarme was true, she flashed me a big smile and replied 'no comment'.

Her commune, of just 300 people, is in many ways typical of many rural villages in France. If you blinked you would miss Puysoleil as you drove by – this small and sleepy village that seems to consist in its entirety of a *mairie*, an old church, a couple of ivy-covered houses and Le Café de la Paix. But there is more to it than meets the eye. Puysoleil boasts no less than three big *châteaux* – all tucked away in thick countryside on the outskirts of the village – and an equally hidden railway station, from where you can travel directly to Poitiers and Angoulême. This 'secret village', as I like to think of it, is home to several grand and aristocratic families and several Parisian bigwigs, including a hotshot lawyer, who returns to his wife in Puysoleil at weekends; and a high-ranking female *'fonctionnaire'*, or official, in Sarkozy's government, who spends her weekends here.

I glance around the little room. Even the festive tinsel – a vivacious mix of purple, red and green – draped around the mantelpiece seems to reflect Delphine's personality.

'Do you like our tinsels?' she asks. 'We did the decorations last night. We have been making some new ones – those fake parcel things.'

'I saw them as I arrived.'

'Oh yes. We have 'ung them everywhere… lamp posts, the church door, the nets of the tennis court – anywhere they can be tied to.'

The mayor of a small commune, it seems, is very hands-on. 'We 'ad two big rugby players who live nearby come to help,' says Delphine. 'It was very funny. With their big paws they were doing all the dainty things like tying ribbons.' She paints a wonderful picture of everyone gathered around the large wooden table, singing old French songs as they wrapped and tied and glued. Then later they stopped for cider and home-made walnut cake. Even good works are fun in Puysoleil, it seems.

She tells me that later today, she will return to the *mairie* to prepare the Christmas 'packets' – I think she means 'packages' – for the elderly. Everyone in her commune who is over sixty-five will this year receive a half-bottle of champagne and a box of chocolate truffles – last year it was a really good bottle of vintage Bordeaux and a slab of foie gras – hand delivered by Delphine and some of the children from the commune. This evening, some local firemen have volunteered to come to the *mairie* and help wrap the presents and write Christmas cards for the elderly. I'm almost tempted to volunteer myself. And when I'm sixty-five, I definitely want to live in Delphine's village.

'Didier is in a very good mood today,' says Delphine, pulling her signature red Guerlain lipstick from her large red patent-leather handbag. 'I went in early for my coffee this morning and he was drinking brandy with the hunters.'

'There was a hunt today?'

'Oh yes, all these old boys, they meet very early in Didier's cafe, looking very macho in their hunting clothes, before they go off to shoot deer.' She rolls her eyes. 'They are like little boys with their guns and their army outfits.'

We cross the road to Le Café de la Paix, a well-maintained building – owned by the commune and leased to the proprietor – with a smooth, sand-coloured facade and a French flag fluttering outside. Inside, I'm expecting your usual, sparsely decorated French country bar with a tiled floor and functional tables. But it's immediately apparent that this cafe has character. The bar to our right is very small – there is standing room only

– with old flagstone floors. There is an enormous pair of deer antlers on one wall; a stuffed stoat, or something similar, in a glass case on another. All evidence points to the fact that this is a hunting hotspot. And just in case you haven't picked up on the vibe, there is a little crowd of oldish men standing at the bar in hunting vests, military-style trousers and caps.

But it's the cosy, pink-lit dining room to our left that really catches my eye. There are wall lights with red, fringed lampshades and tables laid with pink tablecloths and red napkins. The small, intimate room is home to a bohemian array of bric-a-brac, including another set of stag horns, a collection of antique crystal decanters on a sideboard, and an old wooden easel displaying an oil painting of a naked (and very voluptuous) woman. A string of red fairy lights has been wound around the rails of the old wooden staircase – I get the impression that they are a permanent fixture and not just for the festive season – while brightly coloured Christmas baubles dangle from the light fittings and ceiling. It's all effortlessly quirky and inviting. Fashionable restaurateurs in London would pay a small fortune for an interior designer to create a decor as chic as this. But Le Café de la Paix is totally uncontrived.

Didier doesn't disappoint either. His face breaks into a big smile when he sees Delphine. 'Ah, Madame le Maire,' he says, coming out from behind the bar to greet us. Wearing jeans and a white chef's jacket over a smart, striped shirt and a bulging tie, he is roughly the same height as the big turquoise beads dangling in Delphine's cleavage. His face is very pink – the colour of a kir – and his hair is dyed an unconvincing yellow-blonde and teased into a bouffant. He reminds me of an ageing *Petit Prince*, but more worldly looking than the disarming hero of Antoine Saint-Exupéry's French fairy tale.

Delphine, who loyally starts most days with an early morning coffee here, has painted an evocative picture of Didier's customers. There are no tourists wielding maps or Michelin guides to be found here. Instead, the clientele is overwhelmingly male, local and French. A handful of the 'old boys', as Delphine affectionately calls them, remain for most of the day, complaining that their wives have left them or that they are not getting any sex. This is an authentic local cafe and restaurant, run by a genuine French person – a rarity in my region where most of the *auberges* are now run by Brits, offering burgers and chips and quiz nights with no prior culinary experience. It feels like a privilege to have been brought here by the local mayor for lunch.

Didier takes us through to the small dining room and asks if we would like an aperitif. Following Delphine's lead, I say yes. Hell, it's almost Christmas and that feature on the death of the alligator handbag can wait. But, as I've already been warned, Didier does not produce a wine list or ask us what we'd like. There are no menus at Le Café des Bons Amis. Instead, we are to have whatever Didier has prepared. He disappears and returns with a bottle of red Pineau, the famous sweet brandy of the Poitou-Charente, and two glasses which he fills, almost to the brim, with garnet-coloured liquid, which he declares to be *'de très bonne qualité'*. I'm actually not a fan of Pineau, as it's too sweet for my tastes but I don't say anything as I don't want to appear impolite. *'Mon Dieu,'* says Delphine. 'The old divil is trying to get us drunk.'

The starter arrives. It's a slab of chicken liver pâté, the size of a block of butter, served with a basket of thickly-cut bread. 'It's enormous,' I say, hoping that I'll be able to eat it as I don't want to offend Didier.

'The trick is to eat very slowly,' says Delphine, who is not your usual carbohydrate-fearing or calorie-counting Frenchwoman. Instead, she loves earthly pleasures such as food and drink, which is part of the reason why we get on so well.

'So are you missing Jon?' she asks.

'Well, I think the plan is that we will remain friends,' I say. 'Though in practice, that's a little difficult at the moment. He's phoned and emailed asking to see me but I think it's too soon.'

'Yes, I agree,' says Delphine.

'And the truth is that we weren't right for each other.'

'Relationships are like boats,' says Delphine, whose insights and knowledge of human nature are nearly always spot on. 'They always seem better viewed from afar, than when you are actually in them.'

I laugh at the truth of this. For although it was nice having someone to do things with, Jon would often turn up out of the blue, usually just as I was making dinner, and hang around expecting to be entertained. Then he would get stroppy if I had to work or didn't give him my undivided attention. And having once spent a week in the cramped confines of a wooden sailing boat in Turkey with twelve other people and a coffin-sized bathroom, I know exactly what she means about boats.

Didier returns to clear our plates. He looks very pleased when we say how good it was, and tells us that he made it himself. 'Let's hope the main course is something light,' I say, as he disappears into the kitchen. It's actually very liberating to be free of the tyranny of menus and choices. And I quite like the element of surprise – of not knowing what we are going to be eating. As long as the main course doesn't feature brussel sprouts or *andouillette* I'm confident I'll be able to eat it, as I like to think of myself as an unfussy eater. Like many an *Anglaise*, I can make a decent display of enjoying such French delicacies as escargots. In fact, fried with garlic and parsley, or served in a flaky pastry, they're quite delicious – like mushrooms, only chewier. Frogs' legs and pigs' trotters don't appeal (all bones and gristle surely?) but I could, if required, eat them to be polite. The gastronomic line that I cannot cross, like many Brits, is *andouillette,* made from chitterlings (the small intestines of a pig). I have tried it but the smell was so pungently evocative of the material it's made from that I almost gagged. Nothing could be worse than that.

'He is looking very pleased with himself today,' says Delphine, nodding in Didier's direction. 'The rumour in the village is that the *fonctionnaire* from Paris is pregnant with his child.'

'Really?' I say, astonished.

'I know,' says Delphine, as if reading my thoughts. 'He is only in his fifties but he has had a lot of problems with alcohol and his heart. And this woman, she is forty-six. And married to a very influential man in Paris. She comes here at weekends.'

'*Mon Dieu,*' I say, marvelling, not for the first time, at the stuff that goes on behind closed shutters in small French villages.

As we are waiting for our main course, two of the other three tables fill up with the hunters from the bar. Delphine tells me that they will be having exactly the same as us – whatever that might be. Didier appears from the kitchen and places the dish of the day in front of us – a big steaming silver plate of what looks like Irish stew. Only it's not.

'*Tête de veau,*' declares Didier, triumphantly. '*Bon appétit.*'

'What?' I ask, thinking I've misheard.

'*Mon Dieu,*' says Delphine. On the table in front of us, if I've understood correctly, is a French speciality and something that

I can confidently say I have never, ever seen on a British menu: calf's head.

Although I've heard that the dish is undergoing a resurgence in the Poitevin countryside, this is the first time I have encountered it. '*Je suis très, très désolée*,' says Delphine. 'It's Didier's speciality but I didn't think he would be doing it today. Normally, word spreads around the village if *tête de veau* is on the menu. I was expecting coq au vin or something like that.'

'Oh, no need to apologise,' I say, trying to sound blasé. 'It will be fine.'

'Are you absolutely sure?' says Delphine. 'Me, I've eaten this all my life, so I'm quite used to it. But I understand if you don't want to eat it.'

I'm momentarily tempted to say I'll stick with bread but I don't want to make a fuss, to embarrass Delphine or offend Didier. In my head (ha!) I justify what I'm about to do as research into *la vraie vie rurale*. It helps enormously that the dish in front of us doesn't look like it should be attached to four legs and a torso. Instead, it looks like an innocuous stew – large pieces of greige meat, carrots, onions and leeks in a pale-coloured gravy – and it smells, dare I say it, delicious. Underneath the table, I see Biff's nostrils twitching.

I try to put to the back of my head (ha again!) what I know about *tête de veau*, which is, surprisingly, quite a lot. When I looked it up on the Internet recently – partly to see if it was a rural myth or if it actually existed – I was horrified to find that it offers numerous possibilities for the adventurous cook. You can for example, mash the brains, toss in a few breadcrumbs, add salt and pepper *et voilà* – you have a dish that is apparently 'delicious with a glass of port'.

Meanwhile, on another gastronomy website I discovered that the traditional dish of *tête de veau* 'includes the brain, tongue, cheeks and ears, cooked with onion, carrots, leeks and potatoes'. I also learned that you need to be a skilled chef to make it and that it takes from four to seven hours to prepare. The skin, hair and fat must be removed first, and if it isn't removed entirely, the resultant dish can taste 'disgusting'. You don't say? The same is true if it is not cooked completely. In the chat forum of another cookery site, I discovered several ghoulish pieces of information, including the fact that boiling the head 'gives off a lot of scum' and that you will need, in the words of one cook, 'a HUGE pot... and I mean HUGE'. The other alternative is that you saw the head into quarters first. (Delia Smith this isn't.) And finally, you must allow the head to cool properly, otherwise – *oh my God* – it might explode. Really, it sounded like the stuff of a horror movie – or something a serial killer might rustle up – rather than a culinary treat.

Fortunately, Didier's version looks quite tame in comparison to some of the pictures I've seen of this dish. There are no visible signs of ears or tongue and he appears to have been punctilious about removing any scum. 'It's best to eat it quickly, while it's still hot,' says Delphine. 'Otherwise, the sauce goes to... how do you say...? Like jelly.' I try to put the jelly to the back of my mind. 'And the tongue can become a little... *rubbery*, when it gets cold. Are you sure you are OK? You look a little... stressed.'

'Yes, fine,' I lie, helping myself to a decent-sized serving and bracing myself for the first forkful, while Delphine watches with concern.

The flavour is actually quite similar to Irish stew and nowhere near as... *challenging* as I had imagined, although I try not to think too much about what the various bits of meat represent. In particular, there are some clear, gelatinous pieces, that are very chewy and I suspect might be tongue. But otherwise, it is quite edible. Delphine looks relieved that I'm eating it, if not exactly with gusto, without visibly grimacing.

We talk about our plans for Christmas. Delphine will be spending it with her family – all five generations of it – in the little farming hamlet where they all have houses and where Delphine herself has returned since her divorce. Considering that the papers were only signed a few months ago, she seems remarkably cheerful – another of the personality traits that I love about Delphine. Whatever is going on in her life – and no matter what problems or disputes she is dealing with in her village – there is always a merry twinkle in her eye; a smile never far away from her Vermeer-red lips.

'And what about you, *Ka-renne*? What are you doing?'

'I'm spending it with Travis, who is coming out for Christmas, and Sarah and Steve and some other friends,' I say.

'You are not going back to your family in England?'

I explain that my parents are going to New York to see my youngest brother and their latest grandchild.

'And what is happening with those very noisy men who live next door to you?'

'Fortunately, they seem to have gone back to Portugal for Christmas.'

Halfway through our feast of offal, an odd grinding sound commences in the kitchen to the side of the dining room. Delphine and I look at each other. 'My goodness,' she says. 'What he is up to in there?' The noise is quite deafening and then suddenly it stops with a loud bang. Didier comes out of the kitchen looking more red-faced than ever and disappears up the wooden staircase at the back of the room, reappearing a few minutes later with a large box that appears to contain an industrial-sized food mixer. Delphine asks him what he's doing and he replies in rapid-fire French something about broken blades. 'He's grinding up a roe deer to make pâté,' she explains. 'The hunters caught it this morning. The other food mixer wasn't up to it so now he is using this one, which is much more powerful.'

The grinding commences again, even louder this time. It's like the French equivalent of the *Texas Chainsaw Massacre*, but with animals rather than humans. A creature that was running gracefully across fields this morning is now mincemeat in Didier's blender. Even I'm beginning to feel queasy as the sound of it being carved up in the kitchen continues. I'm glad that Biff, who is lying peacefully under the table, has no idea what is going on. It could be very upsetting for him. A vegetarian would likewise be traumatised if they were to venture in here now, hoping for an innocent omelette and *frites*. Only the live disembowelling of a pig could make it any worse.

Looking around at my fellow diners, I already feel like I'm complicit in some ghoulish act by eating *tête de veau*. Of course, I know all the arguments – for example, that young male cows would be slaughtered anyway as they don't produce milk or give birth to calves. And yet, since Biff entered my life, I've been more cognisant of the fact that animals have a spirit and a soul. Recently I found myself almost moved to tears by the sight of Gordon Ramsay shooting, skinning and cooking a young reindeer on TV, brutally depriving it of the opportunity to ever wear sleigh bells or appear on a Christmas card. And now, when I see a lamb gambolling happily in a field with its mother, I'm almost reduced to tears at the idea that it might soon end up on someone's plate. I've even had occasional thoughts about becoming a vegetarian but, if I'm honest, I'm too fond of the taste of a juicy, pink steak cooked *saignant*.

And so our pre-Christmas lunch passes in a blur of brandy, brains and gelatinous tongue. In the rosy light of this quirky little room, cosseted against the dull and darkening December afternoon outside, I eat my first calf's head, feeling like I am being initiated into a clandestine cult, unique to the deepest French countryside.

'So what did you think of Le Café de la Paix?' asks Delphine as we leave.

'I loved the decor. All those red lights – very bordello chic,' I reply.

'Hmm,' replies Delphine thoughtfully, as if I have made a very salient point. '*Bordello chic*. I see what you mean.'

Outside, in the cold damp air, I wish my friend *'un joyeux Noël'* and *'bon courage'* with the 'packets' for the elderly. While she heads back to her charming little *mairie*, I take Biff for a short walk around Puysoleil. Wrapped around the Christmas tree and old church like big gemstones are coloured fairy lights. Even in the murky light of a late December afternoon, Puysoleil looks pretty. I drive back to Villiers, thinking that there is no place I'd rather be for Christmas than rural France.

Chapter 13

The Gift

CHRISTMAS DAY DAWNS crisp and clear. I walk Biff under a milky blue sky and then rush to wrap presents and assemble prawn cocktails for six people – my contribution to Christmas lunch. Biff watches with interest as, dressed in my blue silk party dress, I de-vein prawns and shred iceberg lettuce. I still can't believe that this little creature is mine. I know that I did sort of help myself to somebody else's dog but I firmly believe that he is my four-legged soulmate and that we were destined to meet each other here in France and spend our lives together. I like to think that when he jumped (or was thrown) out of that van near Bergerac, he was taking the first step on his journey to me. And now that he has his paws firmly under the table in Maison Coquelicot, it looks like this is one love affair that might have a happy ending.

I tie a piece of blue tinsel around his collar (yes, we're colour coordinated, my beloved and I) and set off for Travis's house. The journey takes us through several small villages, where inflatable

Father Christmases climb up the sides of houses on ropes – a sight that always brings a smile to my face – and fake Christmas presents in metallic wrapping hang off lamp posts and trees. Rural France, with its quaint villages, old churches and roaring log fires, provides the perfect backdrop to Christmas.

When we arrive, Biff jumps out of the car and waits at Travis's front door, while I pick my way across the gravel carrying a tray of prawn cocktails, a straw basket of presents and a bottle of champagne. The smell of turkey, stuffing and roast potatoes pervades the air in his warm kitchen and the table is beautifully laid in shades of burgundy and gold. Steve, Sarah, Jill and Jocelyn are gathered around the woodburner in the *grand salon* with crystal flutes of champagne. 'We can always rely on Karen to be late,' says Jocelyn, looking very festive in a red lambswool sweater over a plaid shirt; while Jill looks more statuesque than ever in conker-brown knee-high boots and cords.

'Oh isn't he adorable,' she says, as Biff runs into the sitting room, a fizzy black ball of energy, making little barks of happiness.

'He does love an audience that dog,' says Sarah laughing, as he performs several laps of honour around the room.

And so begins a lovely Christmas Day. There are no dramas, no arguments and no one gets drunk – although Jocelyn does get a little tipsy and pink-cheeked on Côtes-du-Rhône. And because there are no children present (and Sarah and Steve have left Milou at home) my little dog is the centre of attention. Even Travis, who is very particular about his house, is very indulgent with Biff, giving him his own turkey lunch and laying a (pilfered) airline blanket on the sofa so that he can sit with the humans. And I'm touched to discover, when we hand out presents after lunch, that everyone has thought of Biff.

'You know, Biff was the best present I ever received,' I tell Sarah. 'And I don't know how I'll ever repay you for that.'

'It's a lovely thing to know that we've given someone their best present ever,' says Steve.

'He's certainly landed on his feet with you,' says Sarah. 'Haven't you Biffy?'

The only dissonant note is when I ask Jocelyn and Jill about their near-neighbour, Gloria, and immediately sense that I shouldn't have.

'She's gone back to the UK to spend Christmas with her children and grandchildren,' says Jill. 'Why do you ask?'

'Oh, no reason. I was just worried that she might be on her own. That's all. Given that this is her first Christmas without her husband.'

'She's an attractive woman. It probably won't be long before she finds another bloke,' says Sarah.

'That's true,' I say, while thinking that it's people in their fifties and sixties and beyond who seem to have the most dynamic love lives in France. They certainly seem to be having a more exciting time than those of us in our thirties and forties – myself, Travis, Delphine and the three Portuguese neighbours included.

After lunch, we sit around by the log fire and chat. I look at Jocelyn and Jill, sitting side by side, and think how wonderful it is to have been with someone for thirty years. (They met in their early twenties.) It's such an achievement, to keep a relationship alive and functioning for that long. And how nice it must be not to be going home alone on Christmas Day. For despite Delphine's saying that relationships are like boats – they always look better from afar than when you are in them – there are times when it would be very nice to be in a boat, particularly if you are flailing around in a choppy sea.

Christmas is, after all, for many people, the very definition of a choppy sea.

Driving home alone I remind myself that, at this time of year, it's easy to look around with selective sight and see only happy couples, but as Travis likes to point out, there are just as many single people in the world. I'm not sure if this is statistically correct, but his point is that there are millions of us in the same boat. Or not in a boat, if you use Delpine's analogy.

Back in Villiers that night, I take Biff out for his last walk before bed, and as we pass the silent house next door, I give thanks to the universe for my second-best present this Christmas, after Biff: the fact that my Portuguese neighbours have gone back to Portugal for the festive season – and hopefully for an extended stay.

New Year's Eve is a quiet affair, as the temperature has plummeted, and the roads are icy. Like most of my friends, I stay at home, spending the evening by the log fire with Biff and a good book, which proves far more enjoyable than most of the New Year's Eve celebrations that I've ever attended.

My Portuguese neighbours arrive back two weeks later but, instead of returning to work, they proceed to party like it's still New Year. I'm really alarmed. They can't possibly still be on holiday in the middle of January. Why, I wonder, are they at home during the day? Has Supodal, their employer, run out of work? Might they be at home for months? As usual, Monsieur Moreau, my French neighbour, is up to speed with the situation. 'It's too cold for concrete to set,' he tells me. 'They are supposed to be laying an industrial floor in La Rochelle – a big job that would normally keep them away for days – but it's not possible while the temperature falls below zero.'

In the mornings when I walk Biff around the square, I find myself monitoring the digital clock above the pharmacy with religious zeal. When the temperature drops a further degree or so below zero, my mood plummets with it. I'm supposed to be working on a beauty feature on how stress can cause wrinkles, but I'm too stressed to write it. If the wrinkle theory is true, and my Portuguese neighbours remain off work for much longer, I'll need a full facelift before January is over.

One Sunday morning, I walk Biff by the river, where the grass and trees are coated in a sparkling frost and the sky is a radiant blue. It's very invigorating to walk through the shimmering white landscape, which (hurrah!) is lit by a strong winter sun. Feeling hopeful that the freezing temperatures cannot last much longer, I stop off at the cafe on the square on the way back. The windows are steamed up and inside it's full, but one person stands out immediately from the crowd: The Lion. Drinking an espresso at the bar, and dressed in jeans and a thick black sweater, he is minus his Portuguese entourage, but looks like he owns the place.

I look around frantically for somewhere to sit but all the tables are taken. I can either leave or stand at the bar with my neighbour who, unfortunately, has already seen me. He pushes his hair back from his face and gives me a big grin. '*Ca va?*' he says, in his deep growl of a voice.

'*Oui, ça va,*' I reply, hoping I won't have to wait too long to get served. Fortunately, Marguerite, the wife of the cafe owner, turns to me immediately. I order *un petit crème*, or small white coffee, which I plan to drink as quickly as possible. I've got nothing to say to The Lion, who, vis-à-vis the recent noise, is still very much The Enemy as far as I'm concerned. But as Marguerite puts the little green cup down on the bar, The Lion reaches in his back pocket for his wallet and signals that he will pay. It is, I have to admit, a friendly gesture, but it's the last thing I want, as now I'll have to talk to him.

'*Merci.*'

'*De rien.*'

As a diversionary tactic, I turn to pat Biff, whose dark eyes are fixed on The Lion, staring at him with a hopeful expression.

'He's very good, your dog,' says The Lion in French, looking down at Biff and wiggling his big fingers in front of his nose in a playful gesture.

'Yes, it's true,' I say. I search in my coat pocket for one of the dog treats that I always carry around and offer it to my neighbour to give to Biff. To my surprise, he puts the beef chew stick in his pocket.

'*Merci,*' he says, finishing his coffee. 'I will save it for later.' Horrified, I realise that he thinks it is for him. Before I have time to tell him it is for the dog, he is distracted by one of the local hunters who slaps him on the shoulder, seemingly delighted to see him. (The Lion, I have noticed on several occasions, is very popular with the French locals in this bar.) The moment has gone and I don't want to interrupt the conversation, so I bolt down my coffee and slip guiltily out of the bar without saying anything.

February can be the bleakest month in France, but at least the Portuguese neighbours have gone back to work. Even better, the projects they are working on seem to be keeping them away for up to four days at a time. Some weeks, if I'm really lucky, they don't return until Saturday lunchtime.

Meanwhile, Travis has hatched a plan to cheer everyone up – a *disco d'hiver* ('winter disco' or 'disco diva' – get it?) in the *salle des fêtes* in St Hilaire. It's part of his ongoing mission to prove that glamour and *la vie rurale* are not mutually exclusive.

He and his friends – despite not living here full-time, he has many in St Hilaire, both French and English – are organising it; while the professional DJ who lives locally has volunteered to do the music. The idea is that we will all group ourselves into tables and each table will organise its own food and drink and decor. The added pull is the possibility that the elusive Andy Lawton – whom I haven't seen since the Halloween party back in October – might also be there, since the party is practically on his doorstep.

Travis spends the day of the *disco d'hiver* helping to decorate the *salle des fêtes*; and then drives over to my house to borrow an enormous white-linen antique tablecloth to dress our table. (I bought the giant tablecloth in one of my blonder moments, thinking it was a duvet cover, not realising that there is no such thing as an antique duvet cover).

Travis, who only flew in on Friday afternoon, has spent the last twenty-four hours slowly simmering a *boeuf bourguignon* for the main course. I'm doing a goat's cheese and onion tart with a green salad as the starter, while my French friends Mathilde and Sebastian have offered to do the cheese course, and two English friends Anita (who I met through line dancing) and her husband Kevin are making the desserts. Delphine, meanwhile, is planning to make an aperitif called *soupe de champagne*, which sounds quite marvellous. (It consists of a ladle each of an orange liqueur such as Cointreau or Grand Marnier, lemon juice and sugar syrup, chilled overnight in the fridge, and then topped up with a bottle of champagne just before serving.)

Having arranged to meet at Travis's house, which is just a few minutes' walk from the village hall, we all gather round in the kitchen as Delphine serves the aperitif with great ceremony from a vintage glass punchbowl, ladling it into champagne glasses. She has also made a platter of pale-pink salmon on bread with salted butter, which is the perfect accompaniment to her fabulous cocktail. All I can say is that champagne soup is just the thing to get the party started. Or as Travis put it, 'It's better than class-A drugs'. After just a few sips, we're all sitting around the roaring fire in Travis's salon with ridiculously big smiles on our faces.

It's cold outside and the sky is as black as Kalamata olives as we walk (or, in my case, wobble) over to the village hall. Clutching my foil-wrapped tart, I make my way along the country lane, wearing a ruffled chiffon dress beneath my coat and Prada heels with metal studs that are almost as lethal as Delphine's cocktail – especially when walking on gravel or in the countryside.

The *salle des fêtes* is packed and everyone has made an effort to glam up. The little village hall – normally lit to the sort of incandescent level that makes environmentalists throw up their hands in despair – has been transformed into the rural equivalent of a hip Paris *boîte de nuit*, with low lighting, candles on every table and big glitter balls hanging from the ceiling. The room is filled with a cordial mix of French and British, chatting, laughing, drinking and dancing.

The DJ, meanwhile, pitches the music perfectly, playing classic disco hits and a mix of French and British pop music earlier in the evening to appeal to the children and older revellers. Then after midnight, when most of them have gone home, the music gets more clubby, with dry ice and strobe lights thrown in for that authentic nightclub ambience. All that is missing is someone dealing drugs in the loo and a few Premier League footballers on the prowl. Oh and Andy Lawton, who is nowhere to be seen.

'It's odd,' says Travis. 'I did invite him and he was supposed to be organising a table of his own, but he cancelled at the last minute. It was quite a garbled message that he left – something about "unforeseen circumstances". I got the impression that someone had shown up in France unexpectedly and taken him by surprise.'

Typical, I think to myself. The one occasion when I'm looking quite good (i.e. not wearing a Stetson or stuffed into a white T-shirt like a *boudin blanc*), he isn't around to see it.

In truth, it doesn't really matter, as the evening is so much fun. It culminates in a surreal moment, with some of the older members of the gathering – including Jean-Claude, the silver-haired goat farmer – happily grooving away alongside the thirty- and fortysomethings on the dance floor to The Prodigy's 'Smack My Bitch Up'. This could only happen in rural France. As Travis and I limp back to his house a few hours before dawn, we both agree it has been a fantastic evening. Dancing, I've realised, is the one activity that really draws French and English together in the depths of the French countryside.

Much as I love *la vie rurale*, every now and then I need a big city fix. In February, Biff and I spend a few days in Paris, staying in five-star luxury at the Plaza Athénée as guests of a well-known couture house. The beauty division had invited me to a skincare launch, but I was forced to decline as Sarah and Steve were away on the relevant dates and I couldn't organise another dogsitter in time. When I explained the situation, the public relations director said that they were happy to invite Biff too, and that the Plaza Athénée would even supply a dog bed, bowls and someone to walk him. And so my little dog accompanies me to Paris, lying peacefully under his allocated seat in the first-class carriage of the TGV for the entire journey. (I had no idea that dogs were allowed on the TGV, having never seen one on a train.) The people working on their laptops around me couldn't be nicer when I ask, out of courtesy, if they are *'deranged'* by his presence. (Although in reality, they have no choice as he has his own fully flexible, adult-priced ticket.) The French, bless them, love little dogs as much as the British do, and the woman next to me strikes up a conversation about her own dog that lasts all the way to Paris.

Biff, as usual, is very blasé about the experience, but for me it feels like a real adventure, not least because it is the first time that I have taken my little country bumpkin (a) on a train, and (b) to a big city. He barks briefly at the pigeons in Montparnasse station before climbing into a chauffeur-driven car for the journey to the Plaza Athénée. Casting his eyes around the palatial, chandeliered lobby for the first time, he wags his tail and trots over to the concierge desk, as if entirely used to such luxury. Honestly, you can take that dog *anywhere*. When I ask the concierge if he would prefer us to use an alternative entrance, he looks at me as if I'm a little mad and tells me that Biff is welcome to use the main entrance, just like all the other guests. That's what I call a first-class establishment.

But the majority of the hotel's canine clientele, I realise, must be chihuahua-sized, because the velvet dog bed (actually more of a chaise longue with wooden legs) in our room is perfect for a miniature dog to recline in but Biff can only fit in it if he sits upright. And frankly, he looks a little ridiculous. Not that he minds. He is just happy to be there. I leave him in the five-star room alone, watching President Sarkozy on the television, while I attend the beauty presentation. Afterwards, as a reward for his good behaviour, and before going out to dinner, I attach a little safety light to his collar – it's hard to see a little black dog in the dark – and walk him along the Champs-Elysées, with his light patriotically flashing the colours of the tricolore. He happily browses in a branch of Zara with me, unfazed by the crowds and the loud music. Then we trot back down Avenue Montaigne – Paris's equivalent of Bond Street or Fifth Avenue – to the hotel, narrowly missing the sixty-million-pound jewellery heist taking place at the Harry Winston boutique next door. That would certainly have given him something to boast about to his four-pawed friends back in the Charente.

That evening I leave him alone again – warning him not to help himself to the snacks and vintage champagne in the minibar – while I go out to dinner with the other beauty journalists. Christine, the public relations director, takes us to the Buddha Bar, a fashionable restaurant and nightclub, which is so dark that we have to grope our way to the tables and hold the menus to our noses in order to read them. It's a sharp contrast to the over-illuminated restaurants and community halls of rural France, which are usually so bright as to kill any ambience.

Much as I love my life in the country, I have to admit that I really appreciate the stylish surroundings, the Parisian standards of service and the company of my fellow journalists, who are always a mine of information and gossip. The conversation turns to 'slebs' (celebrities) and everyone swaps tales of difficult people they have worked with – celebrities who've failed to show up for cover shoots, refused to model the clothes, stolen the clothes, thrown strops or been downright obnoxious. Libel laws forbid me from mentioning names but, I'm surprised when one beauty editor reveals that her worst-case scenario involved a pop star who is always portrayed as having a sweet and unassuming personality.

Back in my luxe beige hotel room, Travis sends me a text saying, 'Is there any connection between the fact that millions of pounds of diamonds have gone missing in Paris and you and your hairy mate just happen to be there?'

'None whatsoever,' I text back. 'But Biff is now wearing a diamond collar and we're heading for the Côte d'Azur.'

Towards the end of February, I have an interesting encounter with The Lion. I spot him leaning against the wall outside the cafe having a cigarette as I walk by with Biff one Saturday afternoon. He beckons me over and bends down to pat Biff. (Is he undergoing a personality makeover, I wonder? He seems to be making an effort to be friendly – even if it is mostly to my dog.)

'*Écoute!*' he says, after the usual '*Bonjour*' and '*Ça va?*'. 'That chewing gum, where did you get it from?'

'Chewing gum?' I repeat, looking at him blankly and thinking I have misunderstood his French.

'Yes. The chewing gum that you gave me in the cafe. Where can I get some more?'

I realise that he is talking about the dog chew and have to fight back the laughter. He takes a drag of his cigarette and fixes me with those dark, penetrating eyes.

'You ate it?' I ask, eyebrows raised.

'I didn't, but Piedro did. And now he wants to know where he can buy some more.'

I toy with the idea of telling him that it is a very special chewing gum that I brought back from the UK. It would be excellent revenge for all the noise they have made. I could even give them some more. But then I can't help it. I start to laugh and the game is up.

'You find it funny?' he says, narrowing his eyes.

'Yes,' I say when I finally stop laughing. 'The gum I gave you was meant for the dog.'

'*C'est vrai?*' he says, a slow smile appearing on his lips.

I nod. 'I'm sorry. I did try to tell you.'

'*Merde,*' he says and starts to laugh too – a deep, sonorous laugh that I can still hear as I walk away.

March arrives, cold and grey, and with it an email from Jon. He's been in the UK he says, and is coming back to France. He's really missing me, thinks he has made a 'terrible mistake' and wants to know if we can meet up. It's difficult as I do eventually want to be friends with him – I like to stay on good terms with former boyfriends – but not yet. I don't think it would be fair to give him the wrong idea. But on several occasions I bump into him in the Liberty Bookshop, where he is taking French lessons. It's a little awkward, to say the least. Then one day, towards the end of March, he arrives at my door carrying a peony bush. 'I bought it in the *foire*,' he says. 'I saw it and thought of you as I know you like peonies.'

It's a very nice gesture, but I think we both know that it's too late.

'I really miss you and Biff,' he says. 'Maybe we can go for a walk sometime?'

I nod. But I think that moment is still quite far into the future. As he walks towards his car, Biff, who is very fond of Jon, stands by the door, making sad little barks after him.

Coralie from the Douhe class and her glamorous friends on the front row are organising '*Une Soirée Stomp*'. It will consist of country dancing, a *casse-croûte* (a snack), a 'best-dressed cowboy competition' (yes, really!) and a disco. All for €10. I'm feeling much more comfortable about my clandestine dancing activities now that the cowgirl look has become a hot fashion trend. I am *so* vindicated. And I am even more vindicated now that the countryside has just been taken as the theme of a much-publicised Chanel fashion show in Paris. The catwalk was decorated with hay bales and singer Lily Allen gave a live performance surrounded by models romping around in rustic get-ups. Through no fault of my own, I'm ahead of the curve on this trend. Finally, I can come out of the country dancing closet and stop pretending that I'm doing it under duress, when the truth is that I *LOVE IT*! I'm a line dancer and proud of it.

The village hall in Douhe, in fact, looks way better than the Chanel catwalk. The French have pulled out all the stops for this barn dance, decorating the room with real hay bales, antique-looking pitchforks and even an old cartwheel. This is the real rural deal. There are also – bizarrely, for a small village hall in rural France – lots of American flags hanging from the walls. It looks fantastic – as do Coralie and her friends, who are all dressed identically in outfits that are hybrids of cowgirl meets medieval wench, with frilly white skirts, brown cowboy boots and hats, and tight white tops that tie with ribbons and give an impressive upthrust to the cleavage. It's not dissimilar to the look currently being promoted on the Paris catwalks.

The Douhe line dancers have also brought along their husbands, boyfriends and children – and in some cases, their grandparents. Astonishingly, none of them look embarrassed to be there, and they don't appear to have been dragged along under duress. In France, country dancing is a family affair and there is no shame attached to it. I embark on the usual round of kissing, which takes a good half an hour, before sitting down at a table opposite Gloria, Jill and Jocelyn. The three of them are wearing matching scarlet cowboy hats this evening, and look like they are really enjoying themselves.

For some people, life in France is a series of long lunches. Me, I've come to realise that I could map out my life here in terms of long tables and *pamplemousse rosé* – a mix of grapefruit juice and rosé wine. It's surprising how many events in rural France culminate in this and a *casse-croûte*, which, according to the dictionary, is a 'snack', but in reality usually means a three-course meal, seated at long trestle tables. The format is nearly always the same, commencing with a pink aperitif – either *pamplemousse rosé* or a kir. This is typically followed by bowls of crisps, baguettes, a selection of charcuterie and pâté, possibly quiche, then cheese and dessert.

I have attended night markets in the summer, Halloween parties, music festivals and other events too numerous to mention, all of which culminated in a variation of the above. Sometimes, a *casse-croûte* can take you by surprise. At the end of a night walk organised by the *mairie* of a nearby village last summer, for example, we were ushered into the *salle des fêtes* for a four-course meal prepared by the lady mayor and her helpers at midnight. (This, having stopped twice during the walk itself to enjoy refreshments served at trestle tables hastily assembled in the dark.)

These *casse-croûtes* are never very fancy but they're usually put together with an enormous amount of goodwill. And so it is this evening. Coralie and the French line dancing group have made a huge effort to ensure that the evening is a success. As the best-dressed cowboy competition commences, I can't help thinking of the disparity between this and my former life. This evening a very glamorous Fendi party is taking place on the Avenue Montaigne in Paris, to which I was invited. I could have been there, Prada'd and baubled up to the nines, sipping champagne and nibbling posh canapés. But much as I love a little fix of glamour every now and again, I have opted instead for the *Soirée Stomp* and the overly lit *salle des fêtes*. Listening to Dolly Parton and sipping *pamplemousse rosé* from a plastic cup, while surrounded by familiar faces, I realise that there is nowhere in the world that I would rather be at this moment than here.

And so the months fly by in a whirl of country dancing, dog walking, work trips and trying to avoid my Portuguese neighbours. From March onwards, the slow slog through the winter months evolves into a fast, light-footed sprint towards summer. In April I start to notice wildflowers – bluebells, buttercups, dandelions and daisies – popping up in the hedgerows and in the grass verges again. Thanks to Biff I experience the evolving seasons with a new intensity, noticing the subtle changes and stirrings of new life on our daily walks. The mottled grey-and-white winter sky evolves into a palette of blues, from a pale wash of colour to a full-bodied azure.

When I step out of the door in the morning, a soft scent of wisteria and lilacs from a neighbouring garden trails sweetly in the air. And walking Biff along isolated farm tracks, the smell of mould and mulched leaves has been replaced by a cucumber-like greenness – the clean, sweet smell of spring.

The rape crops are already knee-high and brightening up the landscape with their small yellow flowers, while the corn has been sewn in neat rows. The countryside is coming alive again. It even sounds different. The wintery silence – broken only by the pop of a gun or the plaintive crying of hunt dogs left outside in the cold – is replaced by the buzz of insects and the rustle of birds and other small creatures hopping around in the hedges.

The farm tracks around my village no longer consist of large puddles and sticky troughs of mud that suck boots and paws into the ground. In April I get my bike out of the garage for the first time in months and, looping Biff's lead over my handlebars, cycle to a grassy track, where he runs alongside my bike for over an hour. When I return, The Lion is firing up the barbecue for the first time this year and nods *'Bonjour'* as I put the bike back in the garage.

May arrives – my favourite month of the year, as it always seems so full of promise – and with it, the peonies, my favourite flower. I seize the moment and fill the house with big, fluffy, globular blooms of pale pink and a purple-red that I find in the market in Poitiers. Meanwhile, in the mornings I notice that the birds sing and the pigeons coo much more vigorously. Unfortunately, the surfeit of testosterone cooped up next door also manifests itself in higher noise levels. As the nights get lighter, and the days warmer, my neighbours get progressively louder. If only they could find girlfriends, I think, they might calm down.

Biff is not bothered by the loud music and voices next door. If anything, he often looks as if he'd like to go and join them – especially when they are barbecuing food. He watches their activities from his perch on top of the sofa in the *petit salon* with interest and seems magnetically drawn to their house. Many times I have to drag him away from their kitchen door.

One Saturday morning in May, I wake up to particularly loud music next door. It's early and I'm tired, having been to a raucous expat dinner party the night before, so I decide to retaliate with a tactic that Jon once suggested. I find a hard-core rap CD – one that I must have been given at a press launch as I don't remember buying it – and put it on at full volume in my bedroom, as close as possible to the thin wall that divides us. I then take Biff out for a short walk, feeling very pleased with myself. Unfortunately, my guerrilla tactics backfire spectacularly. When I get back, the Lion is polishing his car and singing along to an Eminem track. He's actually enjoying it. At one point, he even gyrates his hips. It's extremely annoying. Worse, Monsieur Moreau suddenly appears in the street outside, shaking his fist and shouting at The Lion. The Lion stops polishing his paintwork and then politely points his finger towards my house. I run inside and turn the music off. My big mistake, I realise, was to choose a rap compilation rather than a medley of country dancing classics. A touch of Dolly Parton would probably have had the desired effect.

Later that month, I march up to the shoe shop on the square to complain again to Fernando about the noise his workers are making. He listens patiently while I rant for five minutes, and then says: 'Don't worry, Madame Willer. They are moving out soon.'

'They are?' I say, unable to suppress a smile of joy.

'Yes.'

'When?'

'Very soon, Madame Willer.'

By the end of May, at least one of my wishes has come true and two of my Portuguese neighbours have acquired girlfriends. Piedro's *copine* is a little on the plump side and usually has a brush or a duster in her hand and a big smile on her face. The Brad Pitt lookalike, who is in his early twenties, has gone for an older woman – a bespectacled blonde with a secretarial bob. Only The Lion remains without a mate, which is a pity, as he is the one I'd most like to see disappear from the street outside – even for just a few hours. Anything to stop him laying in wait on the doorstep, annoying me with his loud laugh and his oppressive *Bonjours*. But as May slides into June, with news of a heatwave on the way and the best months of the year yet to come, I start to feel optimistic that something wonderful is waiting just around the corner.

I'm wrong. What waits around the corner is a disappointing discovery. At the end of May, lured by the rising temperatures, Travis flies out for the weekend and invites me over to his house for aperitifs, along with Jocelyn, Jill and some other friends. Everyone is sitting around the table in the garden when I arrive, drinking rosé and looking pink from the sun. While Biff runs around the garden emitting little barks of happiness, Travis indicates for me to follow him into the kitchen.

'I've got some interesting news for you,' he says, adding a dash of crème fraiche to some home-made guacamole.

'What?' I ask, helping myself to a cheese straw.

'I dropped by Andy Lawton's house yesterday to invite him over this evening.'

'And?' I say, eager to know the response.

'Well, it seems like he's not on his own any more. His ex-girlfriend has booked herself indefinitely into Annabel's gîte.'

'What?'

'I guess she wants to be near him,' says Travis.

'And is he happy about that?' I ask.

'I don't know,' says Travis.

'I shouldn't think so,' says Jocelyn, coming into the kitchen and overhearing the conversation. 'He's been seeing a French woman from our line dancing group for the past few months.'

'No way,' I say. 'Who?'

'Coralie,' says Jocelyn.

'Oh my God,' I say, trying to hide the fact that I am really disappointed by this news. 'I suppose that would explain why he came to line dancing events.'

'Well, you didn't think he actually enjoyed it, did you?' says Travis, raising his eyes theatrically.

'But Coralie is married,' I say.

'Yup,' says Jocelyn with a shrug.

Typical, I think to myself. Many of us can't even find one man, while some greedy married people have two.

'I was actually starting to think he might be gay, as most times I saw him, he had another guy with him,' I say.

'Oh no, that's James,' says Jocelyn. 'They know each other from the army. James is on leave at the moment but is planning to buy a house out here.'

'God, I hope it's in my hamlet,' says Travis. 'I'd love to see that six-pack in action everyday.'

'Andy most definitely isn't gay,' says Jocelyn. 'Far from it. It seems like he's got quite a few women stashed away in the French countryside. His nickname locally is *le dragueur anglais*.'

'Oh dear,' I say, even more disappointed.

The French verb *draguer,* means to chat up – literally 'to dredge' – and a *dragueur* is someone who chats up or 'dredges'. It's a word that has no equivalent in English and normally it makes me smile. But not in this instance.

Still, at least we now know why he always seemed so busy, rushing off to see his various 'friends'. And I guess, if I think about it, it's not that surprising. A guy like him was never going to remain single for long.

'Blimey,' says Travis, echoing my thoughts. 'I suppose it's to be expected. He's a good-looking bloke.'

'Well, you can see why he didn't have time to play tennis,' I say.

'Yeah. He was playing the field instead,' says Travis. 'But it'll be interesting to see how long the girlfriend lasts in Annabel's gîte.'

'Let's just hope she doesn't leave the gates open,' I say.

I try to pretend that I'm not bothered by this news and go back into the garden to throw a stick around for Biff. But driving home later that night, windows wound down to release the heat that's built up in my car, I feel very deflated by this discovery. It all seemed so promising when Andy stopped to replace my tyre on that deserted country lane last spring. But now my one remaining romantic possibility has bottomed out.

Chapter 14

The Lion

JUNE ARRIVES IN a blaze of colour and sunshine, and with it, the summer solstice. In France, 21 June is also known as *la fête de la musique*, with outdoor concerts and festivals taking place across the country. We're in the middle of a punishing heatwave so I take Biff out early. But by 9.00 a.m., the sun is already burning up the countryside; the sky an undiluted blue and the sunflowers, which are now at shoulder height, an extravagant yellow. It's like cycling through fields of sunshine, with butterflies beating an elegant path in front of my bike, and birds hopping around in the hedgerows. Biff couldn't be happier, bounding and bunny-hopping along in front of me, occasionally darting off into the avenues of sunflowers on the scent of something interesting. Then he reappears on the dusty earth track ahead, his black coat standing out dramatically against the landscape of primary yellow and green. We pass a field of recently born lambs – Biff stops for a good stare at those – and later, a deer darts unexpectedly across a field of blonde barley. The Poitevin countryside is throbbing with colour and life.

So too is the village square when I head to L'Épicerie to buy a lettuce later that morning. Félix, the local artist, has set out his psychedelic deckchairs and there is a dreadlocked band playing bongo drums on *'la plage'* outside his atelier. Céline, the owner of L'Épicerie, meanwhile, has created a makeshift bar outside her little shop, where her husband is serving fruit punch. Félix calls me over, which is a little odd, as he normally just nods a curt *Bonjour*. He admires the yellow-and-white skirt that I'm wearing and tells me that I am looking *'très jolie'* today before clasping me to his chest in a bear-like hug and planting two bristly kisses on my cheeks. Biff gives a little proprietorial bark as if to warn him off.

'He's lucky that dog,' says Félix, with real feeling. 'I wish I could swap places with him.'

It's a flattering exchange but, I think, less inspired by my charms than the heat, the fruit punch and possibly the persistent throb of the bongo drums.

I spend most of the day at my desk, the curtains semi-drawn to block out the aggressive sunlight that renders my computer screen unreadable. Even though I'm dressed in a thin cotton dress, arms and legs bare and my hair clipped up, the heat is unbearable. It's going to be impossible to sleep tonight, I think to myself as my desk fan whirs ineffectively in the background, not much use against the mantle of warm air that hangs in every room. There is no respite anywhere. Biff lies dozing in his bed as if drugged by the heat, and the only sound is the buzz of a fly that has slipped in through the open windows. The Portuguese neighbours seem to have been tranquilised by the 40 degree temperature. For a Saturday, they are unusually quiet. In the late afternoon, I take Biff out for his second walk. As I push my bike downhill towards the river – I'm hoping it might be cooler there – I hear someone call out in French behind me: 'Wait!'

I turn around. I'm surprised to see that it is The Lion. What on earth does he want? I hesitate for a second before stopping. He walks up to me, and stands very close. He is wearing flip-flops, baggy shorts and a red T-shirt. In one swift movement he scoops Biff up from the ground into his muscular arms. I'm about to protest, tell him to put my dog down before I call the gendarmes (a threat that won't exactly have him quaking in his flip-flops) but he is smiling, rather than looking fierce as he usually does. Biff, annoyingly, seems quite content in his strong, brown arms, making no attempt to wriggle away.

'He's pretty, your dog, like his mistress,' he says, stroking Biff's ears. As chat-up lines go, it's not bad and I allow myself to be flattered, which is foolish, as (a) he is most likely doing this as a bet; (b) he has probably been drinking; and (c) it is very hot and the summer solstice and everyone's thoughts seem to have turned to lust, as evidenced by my encounter with Félix earlier in the day.

The Lion is standing close enough for me to know that he smells of lemons mixed with green ferns and a hint of freshly smoked nicotine – a strangely alluring combination. It is the first time I have looked at the neighbour at close-quarters and in this proximity, the impression of power and elemental strength is even more pronounced. His skin is smooth and very brown, and his eyes and hair as black as Biff's. 'My name is Luis,' he says, his black eyes drilling into mine. He might just as easily have said, 'My name is Tarzan.'

'Why are you following me?' I ask, convinced that his friends have put him up to it. We have been at war for over a year. He is, as far as I am concerned, The Enemy. And vice versa. After all the shouting out of my window, the angry scowls that I have flashed him in the street and the various incidents of marching off to report him to the gendarmes, he cannot possibly want to befriend me now.

'Because I want to invite you to have a glass of port with me this evening,' he says. Or at least that's what I think he says, as he speaks French with a very thick accent.

'It's not possible. I'm going out.'

He holds his ground, standing very close, his intense black eyes looking beyond the words I am speaking. Annoyingly, Biff's eyes roll backwards in his head with pleasure as The Lion strokes his ears.

'Where to?'

'Puysoleil.'

'Where is that?'

'It's a little village about ten kilometres from here.'

'What's happening there?' he demands.

'Celtic music and a big pig,' I say.

He looks at me, uncomprehendingly.

'A big outdoor concert,' I explain. 'And a barbecue. A roasted pig.'

'Ah, *un barbecue*,' he says, as if this was a major breakthrough. Gently, he puts Biff back down on the ground and, after demonstrating his powers of mastery over my dog, he places his large brown hands on the handlebars of my bike, which is wobbling precariously as Biff pulls on his lead. It's hard enough coping with a dog and a bike, without the added complication of The Lion in our path.

'What time do you return?' he persists.

'I don't know. Probably very late.'

'It doesn't matter,' he says. 'I will be waiting for you.'

I am still not sure if he is making fun of me, if he is doing this to win a bet with his friends. Biff, I notice, has positioned himself so that he is practically sitting on the The Lion's big brown feet. Such a betrayal! I just wish he'd stop gazing up at The Enemy with such longing in his eyes. 'It's not possible,' I say, shaking my head and trying to regain control of my bike and Biff. 'And now I am going to make a tour on my bike.'

He nods. '*D'accord*. Have an aperitif with me later. It doesn't matter how late.'

He makes it sound like an order rather than a request. Then he stands aside to let me pass. I ride off, shaken (and stirred) and wondering what to make of this. What is my neighbour up to? I cycle for about an hour, to the point of exhaustion, in the oppressive heat. At one point the track by the river slopes downwards. Freewheeling downhill delivers a blast of hot air to my face, like opening an oven door, rather than a pleasant breeze. When I arrive back in rue St Benoit, my hair is damp with sweat and clinging to the back of my neck, my face a rosy pink. Even Biff looks a bit limp. Fortunately, the neighbours are not outside to witness our return, though I can hear salsa music and laughter emanating from their kitchen.

For tonight's *fête* in Delphine's village, I pull out all the stops in a sundress printed with big splashy roses and red-velvet wedge shoes. As I'm leaving, The Lion appears on his doorstep, and without even looking in his direction, I can feel his dark, all-seeing eyes following me as I walk over to my car and open the door for Biff. He jumps in readily (the dog, not The Lion) even though it's so hot it's like opening the door of a blazing woodburner. (I swear to God, that dog would blindly follow me into an erupting volcano if he thought there might be a good walk at the end of it.) Despite the fact it's past 8.00 p.m. and all the windows are wound down, the car is still hotter than a fire pit as we drive to Delphine's village.

'I know it's hot, but don't worry, it's not far,' I say to Biff as we drive past fields of sunflowers and champagne-coloured barley crops. The French countryside is at its best-dressed and prettiest on a summer evening, the blonde grass verges at the side of the road liberally sprinkled with wildflowers. The long-armed irrigators, meanwhile, are pumping soaring arcs of water over the maize and rapeseed crops, drawing white ribbons across the smooth blue sky.

The first glimpse of Puysoleil is a riot of crimson roses, climbing up an old stone wall. It is, as Delphine once told me, a past winner of the *Village Fleuri* or 'flowered village' award – the horticultural equivalent of a Michelin star as far as French villages are concerned. Sadly, it hasn't won this award for a while, though I'm sure that Delphine will do something about that. The centre of the village, and the green plastic tables and chairs outside Le Café de la Paix, are deserted tonight, as everyone is down by the river for the concert, which is in full swing when we arrive. The jaunty violins of a Celtic jig and the smell of roasting pig and woodsmoke fill the warm evening air. Long trestle tables have been set up on the bank of the river, with an expanse of grassy space for dancing in front of the stage, which has been framed in multi-coloured lights. Didier, the pink-faced, bouffant-haired owner of Le Café de la Paix is in charge of tonight's catering. He and what Delphine calls 'his special team' (a trio of three elderly ladies who apparently have a crush on him) have set up a bar area and, to the left of the stage, the catering area, where an enormous cognac-coloured pig is roasting on a spit.

'*Ka-renne!*' shouts Delphine, getting up from a crowded table and waving. She looks fantastic tonight in a tangerine-coloured gypsy skirt, black cardigan and a rope of beads, the size and colour of apricots, around her neck.

'Wow, this is amazing,' I say. The idea that this sleepy, backwater village has organised such an event is impressive, for it is far better than anything happening in Villiers, which is practically a metropolis by comparison.

'Yes,' says Delphine. 'This band is very good, don't you think? Here, I have saved you a seat.' We squeeze in, Biff happily assuming his default position under the table – he knows there are rich pickings to be had from a large-scale al fresco meal – while Delphine introduces me to a fiftysomething British couple sitting opposite, who have just bought a holiday home nearby.

'Bob is a councillor in London,' explains Delphine. 'And Helen is a doctor.'

'Generally, when in France we aim to avoid our fellow countrymen,' says Bob, with a pomposity crying out to be pricked. 'But Delphine speaks very highly of you and tells us that you are almost French, so I suppose we can make an exception.'

'Oh,' I say, wondering how many of the fellow countrymen that they are referring to would probably avoid them too. I've met this kind of person before. Playing at being Perfect Expat, they boast about the fact that they never plan to set foot in the UK again, while desperately trying to love *andouillette* and acquiring French friends as if they were trophies.

'So what made you buy a house here?' I ask.

Bob looks at me, with an expression of displeasure.

'*Nous preferer* [sic] *parler en francais quand nous sommes en France, c'est plus poli*,' he says, in wooden and incorrect French, nodding towards Delphine, 'We prefer to talk in French when we are in France. It's more polite.'

'OK, but I think you'll find that Delphine speaks perfect English. And she won't think it impolite,' I reply, avoiding stating the obvious, which is that Delphine is not even part of this conversation as she is talking to one of her villagers.

'*Mais les autres gens,*' says his wife, nodding to the other people on our table who are also engaged in their own conversations and couldn't be less interested in ours.

So I ask Bob, in French, which council he sits on and am surprised that he seems so smug about it, given that it is generally acknowledged to be one of the worst-run boroughs in the UK. He asks me what I do and I tell him I'm a journalist and this time, looks of displeasure flash across both their faces – probably because his council has had more than a few run-ins with investigative journalists over the past few years. (Obviously, I don't tell them that my specialist subject is handbags.)

'And who do you write for?' Helen asks, suddenly reverting to English, which is a relief as it feels ridiculous conversing to fellow Brits in bad French.

I name one of the publications for whom I occasionally write. 'Oh, we don't read that kind of newspaper,' says Bob. 'We like to be able to believe the things we read, don't we Helen?'

'It's got some top-notch, award-winning journalists though,' I can't resist saying. 'In fact, I think they've exposed quite a lot of incompetence and corruption in your borough over the years.'

'You can't believe everything you read in the newspapers,' says Helen tartly.

'Quite true,' says Bob. 'Journalists actually waste an awful lot of valuable council time, constantly bombarding us with requests under the Freedom of Information Act.'

'Yes, that must be inconvenient,' I say.

Helen and Bob, I quickly realise, have robust views on almost everything – the sort of people who make you feel that you are wrong about most things and that their intellect and insight are vastly superior to yours. I signal to Delphine – who has no idea of the battle lines being drawn across the table – to ask if she would like a drink.

'I'll come with you,' she says, getting up. 'Maybe we can do a little tour.'

Biff, who has been lying patiently under the table, perks up at the prospect of a walk and a sniff-around. It's fun walking around with Delphine, as she is very popular. We are constantly stopped by residents of Puysoleil wanting to greet their mayor. 'You should be so proud,' I say, as we join the throng at the bar. 'This is an incredible turnout.'

'Do you think so?' says Delphine. She manages to make everything look effortless, but I know that a lot of hard work has gone into organising this evening. 'What shall we have to drink?' she asks. The choice is red, white, beer, water or cola at the impromptu bar that has been set up in a large wooden shack by the river. We decide on a bottle of red and are served immediately, as one of the men behind the bar turns out to be a cousin of Delphine's. We walk over to where Didier and his crew are working flat out, despite the heat, to prepare the buffet.

'Regarde ça,' says Delphine with a wink. I am not sure if she is pointing me in the direction of Didier – who is dressed in a white chef's jacket, his bouffant hair looking like it has been glued into position this evening, his face pinker than ever thanks to the heat from the barbecue – or the long-haired tattooed man who is vigorously and expertly carving up the pig. Wearing a white vest – all the better to show off his glistening muscles – the tattooed man is the highlight of the evening as far as I'm concerned. 'Thanks gods [sic] he's on good form tonight,' says Delphine, referring to Didier. 'Sometimes we never know with him whether he will show up or not. He threw a tantrum this afternoon and threatened that he might not do it. I don't know what is going on with him at the moment but he is very temperamental. And there are some very peculiar gossips [sic] about his cafe.'

'Really?'

'Yes. Some people in the village are saying that there have been… strange activities late at night.'

'Like what?'

'Well, it sounds crazy but women dancing naked on top of the tables.'

'That sounds a bit unlikely,' I say, unable to imagine such raucous behaviour in a quiet village like Puysoleil. Then again, as I've thought many times since moving to France, you never know what is going on behind closed shutters.

'Well, I have no evidence of this, so I am not paying any attention for the moment.'

'Who has he got helping him?' I ask, nodding towards the tattooed man. 'That man has got very good carving skills.'

'Ah yes,' says Delphine, 'that's Jean-Luc, the butcher. He also leads the local hunt.'

There is, I think to myself, no place more alluring than rural France in the summer. You can keep St Tropez with its chi-chi boutiques and champagne bars. The men who stroll the boulevards of the Côte d'Azur wouldn't know how to get the better of a wild boar or expertly carve up a pig. What matters here in the French countryside is not the label in your shirt or the size of your car engine, but something more elemental. Give me a man in a vest with the knife skills to feed a mass gathering over a rich playboy with a wallet full of credit cards and a cashmere sweater over his shoulders any day.

I look at the children dancing in front of the stage, Didier's 'special team' laying out the buffet and the men in animated conversation at the bar, and realise how timeless this scene is. This kind of event has been going on in this village for centuries. Many of the children running around on this midsummer's eve will probably one day be watching their own children, and grandchildren, doing the same thing, in exactly this spot.

The meal that Didier and his team have prepared – roast pork with coleslaw and a delicious potato salad – is excellent for a large-scale al fresco dinner. Afterwards, Delphine takes to the stage to thank everyone for coming and to welcome the main band. As the sound of pipes and soaring violins starts up, people move from the long trestle tables to the grassy dance floor. Grandmothers twirl around with toddlers, teenage girls giggle in little huddles and couples of all ages dance in each other's arms. At one point, the crowd forms a big circle to dance a simple jig, the steps of which everyone seems to know. The men gathered by the bar become more exuberant as the night wears on, and by the river a young couple kiss passionately against a tree.

It's 2.00 a.m. when I leave, after successfully dodging Helen and Bob for most of the evening (although, in truth, they were probably also dodging me). The Celtic band is still going strong under the starry night sky and so is Delphine who will stay until the very end to help with the clean-up operation. Like many mayors in small, rural communes, she is very hands-on and considers it her duty to pitch in and help out.

I drive back under the lush, velvet embrace of a midsummer's night. The sky is a violet-blue, dotted with stars, like a scene from *Arabian Nights*. I'm hoping that The Lion will have gone to bed. But no, as I pull up in rue St Benoit, I see that he is waiting on his doorstep with a hopeful expression on his face. I can hear his compatriots, laughing and talking, in the kitchen.

'I'll come straight away with a bottle,' he says, when he sees me.

'*Non. Non, c'est pas possible,*' I say, closing the downstairs shutters. 'I'm too tired and it's too late.' I wonder how it would play with my French neighbours if I were to allow The Enemy into my house in the middle of the night.

He is persistent but I manage to fob him off with the vague promise of an aperitif another time. I close the front door, surprised at this sudden turnaround. The Lion has revealed a much friendlier side to his personality today.

It's even hotter inside my house than out. For a second, I'm tempted to join him on the pavement for a nightcap and a little conversation. But instead, I go upstairs to bed. I leave the curtains and the casement windows open, so that I can see the stars glittering like sequins in the sky. Tonight, the low-level laughter and murmur of conversation from the Portuguese house feels reassuring, rather than irritating, but I can't sleep. It's too hot. The heat lingers in my bedroom, like a warm lagoon. I toss and turn and lie awake most of the night. Looking out at the stars in the early hours of the morning, I wonder if Luis – a nice name, I think – is also lying sleepless on the other side of the wall.

The next day, which arrives in another thick blanket of heat, the neighbours are up early, laughing and playing salsa music again, but the noise levels are bearable. In the mid afternoon, they have a barbecue outside, joined by the two girlfriends and Fernando and his wife.

Early evening, I take Biff out for a long walk. The maize in the fields is now taller than me. Biff and I have a new game – dodging the long-armed irrigators that send giant arcs of water soaring across the green and blue horizon in the early morning and evening. On one of our favourite walks, the farmer has positioned the irrigator on the narrow grass track close to the edge of the field. This means we have to judge the moment and then run swiftly past it to avoid a drenching should the rotating pipe suddenly swing in our direction. Sometimes, we wait for a good few minutes watching the white water soar across the blue horizon before being able to pass by.

On our return Luis is hanging out of his window, bare-chested and smoking a cigarette, looking subdued by the heat.

'*Ça va?*' he says with a lazy smile.

'*Ça va bien, merci,*' I reply, avoiding eye contact, as I don't want to encourage him. At least I think that's the reason.

'When are we going to have that aperitif?' he asks, in a voice that suggests the invitation is for more than a neighbourly chat.

'I'm very busy at the moment,' I reply.

Ten minutes later, I'm grilling a venison burger for Biff's dinner when the doorbell rings. It's Luis, now wearing an orange T-shirt, denim cut-offs and flip-flops. His arms and legs look browner than ever.

'*Bonsoir,*' he says, in his deep, macho voice. 'I am sorry to bother you.'

'Yes?' I say, a little impatient, as I don't want to burn Biff's burger.

He speaks French with a very thick accent but it seems that he wants to borrow some tomatoes to make a bolognese sauce. 'Come in,' I say, thinking it will be easier to figure this out in the kitchen, though it feels like a big step allowing The Lion into my house.

As Luis walks into *le petit salon*, Biff is beside himself with excitement, barking, jumping up and down on the sofa, and hurling himself against our neighbour's legs. That dog is an embarrassment, I think to myself. Must he really make it so obvious that he's so eager for company? Luis follows me confidently through to the kitchen, his flip-flops squeaking as he walks (or rather struts) across the wooden floor. Biff drags out his favourite toy – a threadbare bunny rabbit that squeaks – and drops it at the neighbour's feet. Now, he's really showing off. The neighbour laughs and bends down to pat him on the head. Biff looks up at him with awe.

I pull a can of tomatoes out of the cupboard and Luis nods his head. But he wants something else. After a while, I figure out it is tomato purée but I don't have any. I offer him an ancient bottle of tomato ketchup instead. 'Please don't forget to bring it back,' I say sternly, as I hand over the almost empty bottle.

'*Bien sur*,' he says, with another languid smile. '*Et bon appétit.*'

The following evening, a Monday, I'm sitting in front of my computer when the doorbell rings, sending Biff into berserk mode downstairs. I throw open the bedroom window and see The Lion below.

'*C'est moi. Luis.*'

'Wait!' I say, annoyed at being disturbed. I'm wearing my glasses and because Biff has hidden my hairbrush, my hair looks a little on the wild side. But I go downstairs and open the door. My neighbour, by contrast, is looking very clean and neatly pressed in jeans and a T-shirt the colour of my rhododendron, while his skin looks freshly-shaven. He is holding a new bottle of ketchup and a large jar of chopped tomatoes in his big brown hands.

I'm both impressed that he bothered to replace the stuff I gave him and humbled, since there was hardly any ketchup left. And suddenly, I can see the potential in this new neighbourly arrangement, popping next door to borrow an onion or a couple of cloves of garlic if necessary. I much prefer it to all-out war. 'That's really very nice of you,' I say, noticing that the elderly French neighbour opposite is staring over, with an expression of disapproval, as she pretends to close her shutters.

'*De rien,*' he says, before returning next door. I am surprisingly disappointed that he did not ask me again to have an aperitif with him. Biff looks strangely disappointed too. He sits in the hallway, long after The Lion has gone, as if hoping that he will reappear. It's a shame, I think, that The Enemy and I could not have reached a more cordial understanding before.

Chapter 15

Scent of a Man

SHORTLY BEFORE I moved to France, I went to Paris for the weekend to visit my Canadian friend Lauren. Her mother, an energetic sixtysomething, who had been married four times, was also visiting and over dinner at Brasserie Lipp one night, she gave us a piece of advice that I'll never forget. 'Do you know the best way to find a man?' she asked, as the waiter served espressos.

Lauren and I both looked at her agog, as if she was about to reveal the whereabouts of the Holy Grail. 'Girls, forget the high heels, the make-up and hanging out in bars and restaurants…' she said. (Not that I was doing any of the aforementioned at the time, as, following the break-up with Eric, my French boyfriend, I was too depressed to get out of my pyjamas most days, let alone don a pair of high heels or drag myself to a bar.)

'What is it?' I asked impatiently, so eager to learn the secret that I would have grappled her to the ground to get it.

She paused for effect. 'Get a dog.'

'Get a dog?' I repeated incredulously. 'And how does that work exactly?'

'Well, firstly, you have to walk it several times a day, which gets you out and about. And secondly, it's a really easy way to meet people. *Everyone* talks to you when you've got a dog.'

'Unless it's a pit bull,' said Lauren.

'Trust me,' said Lauren's mother. 'A dog is a man magnet.' She made a canine pal sound like a must-have accessory, but one that, unlike the latest handbag, was guaranteed to attract admiring glances from the opposite sex rather than your own. I was doubtful. And yet this technique had worked for her – four times. It also worked for Lauren. Within a few months of her mother's visit, she had acquired a black Labrador, and a year later she was married with a baby on the way.

The dog strategy, I could see, had its advantages (assuming that you liked dogs). For a start, you wouldn't have to spend a fortune on high heels and designer clothes to attract admirers. Instead, if Lauren's mother was to be believed, a good pair of trainers and a Gore-Tex jacket would be your best pulling kit. Secondly, rather than sitting around in bars and restaurants, imbibing vast quantities of alcohol and empty calories, you'd at least be getting some exercise, which could only be a good thing, regardless of the effect on your love life. And thirdly, this method seemed a vastly preferable way of looking for love than say, the Internet, because the other piece of advice that I really believe in is that the more you look, the less you find.

I base this on personal experience, though admittedly of trying to find my glasses, rather than a man. Whenever I lose them, which is often, rarely do I find them while searching in (literally) a blind panic. Usually, it's while hunting for my car keys or something else I've misplaced. And Delphine recently reinforced the message further, when we were talking of the best way to meet someone in the French countryside. 'No, *Karenne*,' she said with conviction. 'You don't go looking and they will come to you, I am sure of it.'

'Well they'd have to knock on my door or drop through the bathroom skylight,' I replied, 'since I'm nearly always at home working.'

How could I ever have guessed that both pieces of advice – both Delphine's and Lauren's mother's – would come to fruition at exactly the same moment? But one stifling Saturday afternoon in early July, I am sitting at my desk surrounded by bottles of cologne, working on a male fragrance feature, called 'Scent of a Man', when the doorbell rings. I throw open the upstairs window and see Luis. He's wearing a clementine-coloured T-shirt and in his arms he is holding a familiar little bundle of black fur. *'Boeuf était sur la route,'* he says in his thickly accented French. ('Beef was on the road.')

He places a sheepish-looking Biff in my arms. As he leans towards me, I detect a subtle smell of citron cologne. 'He's called Biff, not *Boeuf*,' I say, with an involuntary smile. 'But thanks all the same.'

'Beef,' says my neighbour. 'He's very funny.'

Then it occurs to me that my neighbour might have reached in through the casement windows, which were left slightly ajar, and taken Biff from his favourite perch on top of the sofa, in order to have an excuse to knock on my door. (It's just over a week since he came to borrow tomato sauce.)

But then I notice the sheepish expression on Biff's face and the open windows in the sitting room, confirming the truth of Luis's story. I also remember the stories that Sarah told me about Biff's Houdini-like escapes, and how he had even figured out how to stand on his hind legs and slip the catch on the garden gate. She and Steve had a constant battle to prevent Biff from taking himself off for three-hour walks or hopping next door to torment the neighbour's Great Dane. Briefly, it occurs to me that Biff might have done this intentionally, that being brought home by our handsome neighbour was part of the plan. He certainly looks very happy in Luis's arms and in no hurry to wriggle out of them. As for me, I'm completely disarmed by the sight of my big, macho neighbour, holding my little dog. And I'm extremely grateful to him. 'Thank you for bringing him back,' I say. 'It's very kind of you.'

'He's got a lot of character,' says Luis, stroking the top of his head.

'He's very naughty to have jumped out of the window like that,' I say, trying to sound cross.

'It could have been dangerous, it's true.'

'I'm very grateful to you,' I say. 'He could have been killed by a car.'

'*De rien*,' he says, with a disarming smile. 'But still I don't know your name.'

'It's Karen.'

'*Ka-renne*,' he repeats. '*Voilà*.' Gently, he places the dog in my arms and goes to walk away.

'Wait!' I say. 'That aperitif. We could have it tomorrow evening if you like?'

He stops and turns around. '*Pas ce soir?*' he says, suddenly encouraged.

'No, not this evening. I'm going out to dinner with friends. But tomorrow evening at seven.'

'*Ça va?*' he says, looking at me in disbelief.

'*Ça va*,' I say.

'*À demain. Ciao*,' he says, in his deep growl of a voice, and he walks away looking very pleased.

I'm also pleased. Maybe it's the heat, but I'm really starting to warm to him – and not just because he brought my dog back. The Lion has seemed much friendlier of late. He has dropped the fierce demeanour and seems a little more approachable. Maybe it was the recent sight of his tanned, muscled torso leaning out of the window, but grudgingly, I have to admit that there is something quite compelling about The Lion cooped up next door.

'Très bien,' I say to Biff, who has played his part in making it happen. I didn't even have to take him out for a walk. And as Delphine predicted, it happened when I wasn't looking and when I least expected it. I go back to my desk and try to concentrate on my feature, 'Scent of a Man'.

The following afternoon, I water the profusion of plants in the courtyard. I've gone big on evergreens this summer, including a rhododendron, as they seem to be less easy to kill. Having done the rounds of the various terracotta tubs, the peony shrub with its voluptuous pink blooms and my hollyhocks, which have shot up out of the ground and are almost as high as the house, I fill a bowl with nuts – and wait. I'm really looking forward to drinks with Luis but by 7.30 p.m. there is still no sign of him and I'm beginning to wonder if he misunderstood. But just as I'm about to give up, the doorbell rings.

Luis is standing on my doorstep, looking freshly shaven and smelling faintly of lemon cologne. He's wearing red surfer shorts and a black T-shirt, stretched tight across his broad torso. It's hard to reconcile my new suitor with The Enemy that has been living next door for the past twelve months. He hands me a bottle of port. 'Super,' I say (or 'sooo-pair' as it is pronounced in French), thinking of the bottle I already have, given to me by his boss and lying unopened in the cupboard.

'I'm sorry I'm late,' he says, in French. 'Fernando, *le patron*, called a meeting at the depot. It was very annoying.'

'A meeting on a Sunday evening?' I say.

'Yes, it's usual. He tells us where we are going to be going and what jobs we are doing next week.'

'You work very hard,' I say.

'It's normal,' he shrugs. Then, lowering his voice, says 'But all I've been thinking about all day was coming to have an aperitif with you.'

'Oh,' I say, trying not to look too delighted at this revelation. I don't tell him that I've been thinking exactly the same. I invite him through to the private *terrasse* at the back of the house. Biff follows us with little barks and hops of excitement, his tail rotating like a wind turbine. 'This is very nice,' says Luis, taking in the courtyard, with its colourful abundance of red flora and thick green shrubs. He nods at the coral-pink geraniums on my windowsill, at my thriving purple hibiscus and the bell-shaped blooms of my rhododendrons, and looks impressed by the hollyhocks thrusting up towards the sky. 'Very nice flowers,' he says. 'And this *petite terrasse* is very private.'

'Actually, I was wondering about that,' I reply, pointing to the opaque window at the side of their house that overlooks my courtyard. 'Can you see through that glass?'

'No,' he says, with a cheeky grin. 'I swear, I tried many, many times.' He shakes his head from side to side to emphasise the word 'many'.

I laugh. 'Well, you wouldn't have seen anything interesting anyway.'

'Are you sure?' he asks, narrowing his eyes playfully.

'Very sure. Nothing interesting happens here. I'm mostly working.'

He narrows his eyes again, as if to suggest that he doesn't believe me.

'Do you mind if I smoke?' he asks.

'No problem,' I say, although normally I can't bear cigarette smoke. Biff, I notice, is trying to wrap his body around Luis's bare brown legs. As I look at my neighbour's magnificent muscles and lean physique, I wonder how I could possibly have overlooked the enormous potential of the man living next door to me for the past year.

I drag Biff off of our neighbour and shut him in the sitting room until he has calmed down. In fact, I feel like running around and making little barks of excitement myself. I bring glasses from the kitchen and Luis pours the port with one hand, his other holding his cigarette down by his side so as to keep the smoke away from me. Everything he does is so movie-star masculine, that it's almost a cliché. His presence entirely fills my little courtyard.

From behind the sitting room door, Biff is complaining loudly at being excluded from the romance, but I know if I let him out to join us, he'll be all over Luis as if he were a juicy bone. I signal for my neighbour to sit down and I go back into the kitchen for the nuts.

Even, though it is nearly eight in the evening, the sky is still an unbroken sweep of blue and it's warm enough to be wearing a bikini (though obviously I'm not that forward). The narcotic scent of the night-blooming jasmine in my flowerbed – what a survivor that plant has turned out to be – fills the evening air and above us, pigeons are cooing and birds call to each other. I pray we don't get bombed by their droppings, as it would ruin the moment, although there are so many birds hanging out on the high stone walls, watching the spectacle unfolding below, that's it's more than possible. Otherwise, it's the perfect setting for neighbourly drinks – and dare I say it, seduction.

'It's all very nice, this,' he says. 'Thank you.'

'My pleasure,' I say. 'The least I could do after you brought my dog back to me.'

'What do you do all day here?' he asks, his flip-flopped feet planted firmly on the ground, leaning slightly forward on his delicate wrought-iron chair, which only serves to emphasise his masculine physique.

'I'm a journalist. I write about fashion.'

'*C'est vrai?*' he says, looking interested.

'Yes,' I say. 'I write for newspapers in the UK. And you? Why do you get up so early in the morning?'

He explains that they work for a building company. They do everything – from laying concrete floors and building partition walls to tiling, painting and decorating. And they work not just in the Poitiers region, but in locations up to 200 kilometres away – in Cognac, Niort, La Rochelle and Tours. Often, he says, they start at 5.00 a.m. and don't get home until midnight. He doesn't mind the long hours, he says, because he and his compatriots enjoy it and the boss pays them well. 'What happened with your boyfriend?' he asks, changing the subject suddenly. 'The one with the fast car.'

'Oh, we're not together any more. He's a friend now,' I say.

'But he was your boyfriend?'

'Yes. You know that because you were always watching him.'

'Yes, it's true,' he says, with a laugh. 'I was.'

Funny, I think, how his laugh used to irritate me when I considered him The Enemy next door. But not any more. He laughs hard and loud and sincerely at even the littlest of jokes. And as daylight glides into dusk and then darkness, he makes me feel as if I'm glittering like a Baccarat-crystal champagne glass. I love the fact that he is so full of life and that he talks and laughs so much and so enthusiastically. I was worried, given that we are both speaking in a second language, the conversation would be stilted and difficult. In fact, it flies along. His French vocabulary is better than mine – he uses lots of colloquial phrases that he has obviously picked up from his workmates – and even though his French is laced with a Portuguese accent, I find it gets easier to understand him as the evening progresses.

We talk about our French neighbours – the ones that he likes and the ones that he doesn't – and what he misses about Portugal (lots of things but primarily the fact that there are places open there after 7.00 p.m.). We both agree that Villiers is not exactly rocking, although for me, the peace and quiet of the countryside is part of the charm. *'Moi aussi,'* he says. 'But it could do with a *little* more life.'

I learn that he loves music (not exactly a surprise), that he used to box (Jon was right about that) and that sometimes, he likes to go out dancing in Poitiers. I also discover that he is fiercely proud of his native country; that he comes from a small fishing village about an hour's drive from Lisbon; that he is close to his mother but not his father, who abandoned them when he was a small boy. He tells me that his boss, Fernando, is more like a friend: they knew each other in Portugal, and when Fernando's construction business took off in France, he asked Luis and his friend Piedro to join him. All of this I find out over several hours, a bowl of nuts and one too many glasses of port.

It's close to midnight before there is a pause in the conversation. Luis takes control of the situation, and among the candle-lit flowers, he leans forward on his delicate wrought-iron chair and kisses me. Long and hard and with a passion that takes me completely by surprise. Suddenly, I want him to go home.

'OK,' I say, pulling away. 'Thank you for an excellent evening.'

I want him to leave now so that the evening can finish on a high, so that I can replay it endlessly in my mind, and look forward to seeing him again tomorrow. Suddenly, just stepping out of my front door – with the possibility that he might be barbecuing fish in the street – is going to be exciting.

'*D'accord,*' he says, standing up. 'It's time to go. It is a half past four start tomorrow morning.'

And so, in the warm clasp of my sweetly scented *jardin*, I have finally got to know my neighbour (not, I hasten to add, in the biblical sense). '*Merci, huh, pour une soirée excellente,*' he says, and as he slips next door in the warm night air, I think it's fair to say that the war is over. And I cannot wait for the *entente cordiale* to begin.

Chapter 16

The Builder's Arms

OH, DEAR GOD, what have I done? I wake up wrapped in the big brown arms of The Enemy. Obviously, I know exactly what I've done. It's the inevitable conclusion of seven nights of *porto* and conversation in my scented courtyard. At some point last night, he pulled me up from my delicate wrought-iron chair and carried me upstairs in those beautiful, strong arms.

And now, through the open bedroom window, I can hear birds singing and pigeons cooing outside. It's light but early as there are no cars or voices in the street below. I reach for my mobile phone and see that it is 5.00 a.m. Luis will have to get up soon and go to work. On cue, the alarm on his mobile phone kicks into life with a burst of salsa. He puts his hands around my hips and pulls me even closer to his warm, solid body, just as a van pulls up in the street outside and beeps its horn. I'd recognise the sound of that van anywhere.

'*Merde. C'est José,*' he says, rushing to pull on his clothes. 'He is early this morning.' He bends over towards the pillow and kisses me one more time. 'See you later,' he says.

After he has gone, I lie in bed for another couple of hours, looking through the open curtains at the intensely blue sky and terracotta roof tiles, wondering if life can get any better than this. Then the patter of small paws on the staircase tells me that is time to slide out of my crumpled bed, which I'm loath to leave as it smells of lemon and Luis.

I open the bedroom door and find Biff sitting on the landing, his dark eyes full of recrimination as if he has been cruelly neglected – which, by my normal standards, he probably has. Over the past week, he's been just as excited to see Luis as I have (actually, that's an understatement: he's hurled himself around the sitting room and practically performed back flips on the sofa to get his attention), but he is not so pleased with this latest development. Last night, he looked visibly miffed as his beanbag was relocated from the end of my bed to *le petit salon*. '*Dans ton lit, maintenant,*' Luis ordered him in such a masterful way that I would have climbed obediently into my bed too, had he been talking to me. Amazingly, Biff did what he was told, albeit reluctantly.

Despite his accusatory eyes this morning, I decide on the lazy walk option, which means taking him over to the grounds of the old chateau, rather than the usual circuit of a nearby lake. I pull on a sundress scattered with little blue sequins the colour of the sky and my scarlet flip-flops and, in the voluptuous heat of a July morning, walk him across the square towards the chateau. I pass Monsieur Moreau on rue St Benoit and bid him a guilty '*Bonjour*' wondering if he can guess what I've been up to. (My slightly wild-looking hair probably provides a little bit of a clue.) But I don't care if people know that I'm sleeping with The Enemy. Everything about this morning is magical. I feel like I'm walking on a ribbon of fairy dust and glitter and billowing chiffon. In my head, Goldfrapp's 'Little Bird' is playing. The lyrics – about dancing in a land of blue and gold, and the soaring 'July-ly-ly' refrain – seem to sum up the moment perfectly.

When we reach the secluded patch of grass by the chateau I let Biff off his lead. I sit on the little white bench under a lime-blossom tree, with its view of the sloping allotments and the river below, feeling as though I am living life in soft focus. Everything has slowed down. My 'Scent of a Man' feature is due in today and only half-written but it seems so insignificant compared to the real thing. I can still smell Luis in my hair. All I want to do is lie around in the torpid heat and think of him. What, I wonder, will happen next? Maybe this will be the end of our nightly chats in the courtyard, or perhaps – I almost dare not think it – just the start.

I don't have to wait long to find out. That evening, under an electric blue sky, Luis returns. He knocks on the door and tells me he is going next door for a shower and will be back straight away. When he reappears, hair still wet, he sweeps me up in his arms, carries me upstairs and removes my clothes, stopping to hold my cardigan to his nose and breathe in its scent. '*J'adore ce parfum*,' he tells me (it's actually not perfume at all but the scent of Jo Malone's Vitamin E Body Oil, which smells a little like marzipan). And so begins a summer to remember.

Lying beneath him later that night, I look up into his dark eyes and behind him, through the open window, I can see a mesmerising full moon in the tanzanite sky. The summer becomes a series of erotic and unforgettable snapshots, stored forever in my mind. Luis, as I always suspected, turns out to be a lion in the bedroom... and in *le petit salon*, under the skylight, in the pale-green mosaic shower, on the staircase and the kitchen table. And even the little wrought-iron table in the courtyard. (A use for it that never crossed my mind when I bought it from Jardiland.)

Suddenly, I'm leading the sort of life I could never have imagined. I no longer fall asleep reading tranquil memoirs of life in France. I am living my own memoir. Each day unravels slowly, memorably, in a languid fug of lust. Luis knocks on the door early evening or, if he's been working somewhere far away, late at night, and slips quietly into my house. (Ironically, given that I used to dread the arrival of the Supodal red or white van each evening, now I cannot wait for it to draw up outside my window.) Usually I have made dinner, but it's never the first thing on his mind when he arrives in the evening. Sometimes, we don't get round to eating until midnight, nearly always *sur la petite terrasse*, surrounded by flowers.

In the mornings he leaves early, just after the sun has come up. I lie in bed for a voluptuous few hours after he's gone. Then I walk Biff and sit on the bench under the lime-blossom tree by the chateau feeling sedated by sex. Work deadlines, bills that need to be paid – none of that seems to matter very much. Life takes on an easy, almost liquid quality. I could live like this forever. Pulsating with life, always laughing, Luis is not like anyone I have ever known. Everything about him is magnificent. But it's not just the raw physical attraction. I love the fact he works so hard yet has so much energy – he never complains about the ridiculous hours that he and his compatriots work – and that he laughs so much and lives life to the full. He is also, I realise, very intelligent – not in a Kafka-reading, PhD kind of way – but a deeper, more elemental intelligence. And when I look into those dark, magnetic eyes, I somehow feel that for the first time, I have met my equal. I love talking to him in the candle-lit courtyard, and falling asleep with him, his solid, muscular body pressed against mine. I've always been a restless sleeper, unable to sleep easily in someone else's arms (it makes me feel like I'm being suffocated). But with Luis it is different.

I have no idea how long this will last but, at this moment in time, my life is perfect. I live in a place of great beauty, I have lovely friends, my adoring dog, and at night I sleep in the arms of my Portuguese lover. It is one of those rare interludes in my life where I can say that I am completely happy. And to think, it only took nearly forty years to find this.

Biff is not so happy about it. One morning, while Luis is in the shower, he pads softly up the stairs and into the bathroom and steals his T-shirt. He slinks into the bedroom with his prize then tries to shake it to death as if it were a rabbit. I almost fall out of bed laughing. (Biff is probably sending Luis a coded message, as he has come to regard him as a rival for my affections.)

'*C'est quoi, chérie?*' says Luis, naked and dripping from the shower.

'*Regarde ça,*' I say, pointing to Biff, who is trying to kill his T-shirt.

Luis smiles, narrows his eyes in mock anger and raises his finger. '*Eh Beef, viens-là,*' he says, trying to retrieve the piece of clothing, but Biff does a victory parade with it, his tail wagging triumphantly, before sliding under the bed with his trophy. I am almost in pain laughing, as I watch this powerful man running naked around the bedroom in pursuit of a little black dog. And so begins a new daily ritual of Biff sneaking up the staircase in the morning to steal Luis's clothes.

Travis, who I still speak to most afternoons on the phone, is delighted by this unexpected love affair. 'It sounds as though there is something very pure and honest about it,' he says, by which I think he means that it is based on animal attraction. Another of my friends in London (married with three children) is less enthusiastic. 'It will end in tears,' she says, her tone disapproving. But so what? Even if this thing with Luis only lasts a couple of weeks, it will be worth it; and it will be forever fixed in my mind as a summer perfumed with jasmine, Jo Malone oil, lemon cologne and lime blossom. And of course, Luis.

I can't help feeling I've lived my life the wrong way round. In my twenties, when I should have been having a wild time with men like Luis, I was as good as married to and settled down with my successful, BMW-driving, public-school boyfriend, who is today the head of a big financial company. And now, at an age when most people are cosily embedded in family life, organising playdates and making costumes for the school production, I am enjoying passionate nightly trysts with a Portuguese builder. Sometimes I ask myself if, given the choice, I would take this passion over a more conventional life of a husband and children? I don't know the answer to that but if this is my consolation prize for not having those things, I'm not complaining.

'Are you kidding me?' says Travis, when I raise the subject with him. 'Do you know how many women would kill to be in your situation?'

'Really?'

'Yes,' he says with absolute conviction. 'There are loads of women – even those bloody irritating yummy mummies, who are stuck in boring, loveless marriages – who would love to be in your shoes, enjoying nights of passion with a hot builder.'

'Well there are probably just as many of them who are happily married and have that kind of passion with their husbands. And they have security.'

'Hmm,' says Travis. 'Maybe. But security involves sacrifice – and not just of freedom but usually passion.'

'But this is not exactly a *conventional* life that I'm leading. And I can't exactly see Luis and I growing old together.'

'Why not?'

'I could be wrong but I don't think he is the sort of man that you tame forever, and sit by the fire with in your dotage.'

'Would you want that?' says Travis. 'Look at Newland Archer and Ellen Olenska.' He is referring to my favourite novel, *The Age of Innocence* by Edith Wharton, in which Newland Archer falls for the bohemian, Countess Ellen Olenska, but rather than being with her, spends his life trapped in a loveless marriage. When he is much older, there is the possibility of being reunited with Ellen, but he decides against it since the dream and memory of her are better, and more real, than anything else that has happened in his life.

'But Luis and I are not exactly Newland and Ellen,' I say. 'For a start, they didn't consummate their relationship.'

'The point is that they didn't grow old together, and that's what preserved the magic. And quite frankly my girl, I would kill for your lifestyle and a hot Latin lover right now,' says Travis.

The truth is that life with Luis is very unpredictable. I never know what time he will arrive home – if at all. Rarely is it earlier than 9.00 p.m. and often it is midnight or later. Sometimes he phones to say they are leaving the '*chantier*' or building site, in Cognac or Saintes or wherever they are working that day, and that he'll be with me in an hour or so. I love hearing his gruff, macho voice on the other end of the phone. But usually, I will hear nothing at all from him (his mobile is ancient and the battery often flat) until a Supodal van draws up outside and three exhausted workers spill out. And sometimes – if he and his compatriots are working '*en déplacement*', or far away – he doesn't come home at all for three or four nights. How ironic that I used to dread the sound of next door's van drawing up, but now I spend the day waiting for it to arrive.

At weekends, I get to spend more time with him. But Portuguese culture, I realise, is very macho, and despite spending up to twelve hours together most days, Luis and his compatriots – there are about eight of them working for Supodal – also like to socialise at weekends. As I know from experience, they gather around the kitchen table at 7 rue St Benoit or on the pavement. Fernando, *le patron*, will often join them. But wives and girlfriends are usually conspicuously absent. Of course, I no longer mind the noise next door. I love knowing that Luis and his friends are on the other side of the wall.

Many women would want more than Luis is offering – sometimes just a few snatched hours at night before he sets off for work again – and would not be able to cope with the unpredictable nature of his lifestyle. But in many ways, this is the perfect relationship for me, as I also work unconventional hours, and I like to have time on my own. It suits me fine if we spend the daylight hours apart and the nights interlaced. In between, I walk the dog, go to line dancing (something I keep secret from Luis) and go to dinners or barbecues at friends' houses. Occasionally, I even manage to do some work. Unlike Jon, who was around a little too much, Luis is hardly around at all and so I treasure the hours, the languid Saturday afternoons and Sunday mornings, that I spend with him.

One hot Saturday afternoon in early August, Delphine knocks on my door unexpectedly. 'I'll be right down,' I shout from the bedroom window, before quickly pulling on some clothes.

'Is everything OK? I'm not disturbing anything, am I?' she asks, pretending not to notice that someone is moving around upstairs. 'I was just wondering if you would like to go for a coffee.'

'Well, actually, there is something I've been meaning to tell you,' I say, just as Luis comes down the staircase, barefoot, still pulling his T-shirt over his chest and then running his hands through his long jet hair. Delphine's eyes widen and her lips, red as a Rothko painting, break into a smile.

'Ah, bonjour,' she says.

'Bonjour,' says Luis, politely stepping forward to shake her hand. He then puts his arm around me proprietorially, while Delphine makes some small talk about how hot it is. I mention that Delphine and I are going to the Liberty Bookshop for a coffee, and he says that he is meeting Piedro in the cafe on the square for a beer. 'See you later, *chérie*,' he says, planting a kiss on my lips and then politely saying goodbye to Delphine.

'Mon Dieu,' says Delphine, after he's gone, fanning her face theatrically with a limp hand. 'Is that the man living next to you? The noisy one?'

'Yes,' I say. 'It's quite a long story.'

'Oh la, la. He's very 'andsome up close.'

'Yes, he is.'

'You make a very beautiful couple,' she says. 'You look like you belong together. The way he had his arm around you and everything. He looks so in love with you. In France, we would say *"Il est très amoureux"*.'

'Yes, he's definitely that,' I say. 'I will tell you everything over a coffee.'

We speak quietly and in French in the Liberty Bookshop, so as not to scandalise the trio of elderly *Anglaises*, enjoying PG Tips and lemon drizzle cake and seeking refuge from the

273

afternoon sun. I tell Delphine how Luis knocked on my door with Biff in his arms, and how this led to a summer of love (well, over a month so far, and counting). 'So you were right,' I conclude. 'As you predicted, I didn't have to look far for a new boyfriend; he came to me.'

'I knew it,' says Delphine, clasping her hands in front of her magnificent embonpoint. 'This is smashing news.'

'Fortunately, he knocked on the door, rather than coming through the skylight,' I say, referring to the joke I once made, that any potential suitor would have to drop from the sky.

'Well, I am very pleased for you my friend,' says Delphine, beaming. 'I really am. Do you know his birthday? If so, I could do his chart.'

Delphine, I recently discovered, knows a lot about astrology and has a big, mysterious book full of tables and symbols and figures, from which she works out the planetary alignments at the moment of birth. Quite often she is to be seen in the Liberty Bookshop, pouring over this tome and doing friends' birth charts, 'Like an old witch,' she jokes, though 'witch' is the very last word I would associate with her.

'I don't know his birthday but I can ask him later,' I say.

'And do you know how old 'e is?' asks Delphine.

'Thirty-five,' I say. 'Five years younger than me. A toy boy.'

'No big deal,' says Delphine. 'And anyway, when I saw you together just now, you looked very well matched. He looks very... electrical.'

'Well, it might not last forever,' I say, smiling at Delphine's description of Luis. 'But it is making me very happy right now.'

'I can see this,' says Delphine. 'And I am very 'appy for you.'

Delphine has to leave to go to *un cocktail* at a gathering of mayors in Douhe, and after that she has a meeting with the gendarmes, following complaints that naked dancing was taking place in Le Café de la Paix in her village. (Something that neither of us can quite believe.)

Walking back down rue St Benoit, I see Monsieur Moreau coming towards me and keep my head down, trying to pretend I haven't seen him but it's too late. *'Écoute!'* he says, in a conspiratorial way. 'Listen! I have some very good news.' He points to the Portuguese house. 'The mayor has noted our complaints about the noise,' he says.

I immediately feel very guilty. I am, after all, sleeping with The Enemy.

'Yes,' continues Monsieur Moreau. 'There have been *seventeen* different complaints about the noise lodged at the *mairie*. Imagine!' He shakes his head. 'But finally, the mayor has decided to take action. They are moving out at the end of the month.'

'Oh,' I say, surprised, as Luis hasn't mentioned his impending eviction.

'Where are they moving to?'

'I don't know exactly. But that doesn't concern us. The important thing is that they are going.' He pats me on the arm. 'It must be very distressing for you.'

'Yes,' I say, struggling to look distressed, when in fact, thanks to The Lion, I have been walking around with a permanent smile on my face.

'But it is excellent news, *non?*' persists Monsieur Moreau.

'Yes, it's very good news,' I say, doing my best to look happy about it.

'With a bit of luck they should be gone by the end of August,' says Monsieur Moreau. 'So only a few more weeks to go.'

I return home unsettled by this news. It's true that I've wished my neighbours would move out, since... well, since they moved in, over a year ago. But that was before The Lion became my lover. It now feels like serendipity rather than a torment to have him living next door (though, in fact he is pretty much living with me now.) The last thing I want is for him to leave.

When Luis returns that afternoon, he is carrying a bag of shopping from Intermarché and announces that he is going to make a fruit salad, 'Portuguese style'. He unpacks a carton of strawberries, along with bananas, oranges, a large bag of kiwis and, bizarrely, a bottle of 7UP onto the kitchen table. He then rolls up the sleeves of his vibrant green T-shirt and sets to work. I fetch him a glass dish and slide onto the bench opposite to watch. One of the surprising things about Luis is that he is really into healthy food and loves fruit and vegetables. The biggest cause of arguments between him and Piedro, he told me in one of our early courtyard conversations, is that when it is Piedro's turn to make dinner, he often fails to make a salad to accompany it. 'And that really gets on my nerves,' he said, shaking his head gravely.

'*Chéri*,' I ask, casually, as he chops bananas into the bowl, showing off those powerful brown forearms to stunning effect. (Who knew that watching someone slice up a banana could be such an aphrodisiac?)

'*Oui?*'

'When is your birthday?'

'3 *Novembre, chérie,*' he replies. 'Why?' He pulls his wallet out of the back of his jeans and flicks it open to reveal his identity card. I look at it, make a quick calculation and then, shocked, look again, hoping that I've made a mistake. I must have misheard when Luis told me his age, because according to his *carte d'identité*, he was born in 1979, which means that he is thirty-one, not thirty-five, and oh God… nearly a decade younger than me.

'What is it, *chérie*?' he asks, seeing the look of horror on my face.

'Nothing darling,' I lie, thinking I must choose carefully the moment to tell him.

'And now for my magic ingredient,' he says, unscrewing the bottle of 7UP and adding a slug of it to the salad.

I pull a face, not convinced by the idea of adding a fizzy drink to fruit salad. 'Trust me,' he says. 'This will make it taste superb.' I'm forced to admit that Luis's fruit salad, *à la portugais*, is very good. But not anywhere near as good as watching him prepare it. Delphine was right. He really is 'electrical'. I ask him if it's true that he has to move out and he tells me that yes, they must go soon and have started to look at other places to rent in the village.

'Why didn't you tell me?' I ask.

'It's not for you to worry about *chérie*,' he replies. 'It is my problem.' Luis, I realise, comes from a very macho culture, in which such matters as his impending relocation are probably not considered my business.

'*Chéri*,' I say, when we are lying in bed later. 'Do you realise that I am much older than you?' (Luis, bless him, has never asked my age.)

'Really?' he says, not looking at all bothered.

'I will be forty this year, *chéri*. Much older than you,' I say, looking directly into his dark eyes. To my surprise, he doesn't even blink.

'It's not important *chérie*,' is all he says, pulling my head onto his chest and stroking my hair. '*Tu es ma femme, je t'aime, et ça c'est tout.*' ('You are my woman, I love you and that's all that matters.') The word '*femme*', incidentally, can mean either 'woman' or 'wife' in French. Either way, I love the idea. And I can't help thinking that Luis is a class act.

When I tell Delphine that Luis was born on 3 November, she laughs and says 'Oh la la. He is a scorpion [sic]. I thought so.' I don't know a great deal about astrology but intrigued by the accuracy of Delphine's comments – Scorpios, she says, are 'very spicy, very magnetic, very passionate' – I look up Cancer (my sign) and Scorpio on the website www.astrologyzone.com, and I find that we are, according to astrology doyenne, Susan Miller, a perfect match. It's not all great. Scorpios, it seems, are possessive, moody, egotistical, and determined to have ultimate control. 'But in the end, who cares?' Miller concludes. 'This lover adores you, and is one in a million. Grab your Scorpio with two hands and don't let it go.'

Unfortunately, Luis and Piedro do have to go. The following Saturday, the white Supodal van pulls up outside their house in the afternoon, and assisted by two or three friends, Luis and Piedro proceed to fill it with their possessions. I watch as they throw clothes, duvets, shoes, a straw hat and a Portuguese flag out of the first floor windows into the arms of one of their strapping friends below. The soundtrack to their departure – as with their arrival – is relentlessly happy salsa music. 'See you later, *chérie*,' says Luis. Then they all jump into the van and drive off. And suddenly, there is an unnerving silence at 7 rue St Benoit.

As I stand on the doorstep watching the van depart, I realise that I have no idea where they have gone. Luis has not gone into great detail about the new living arrangements. I hear nothing from him for the rest of the evening and when I call his mobile it clicks straight into the answering service. I tell myself not to panic as Luis's mobile is very old and the battery is often dead.

But the following morning, Sunday, it is disconcerting to wake up to silence. I eat my *pain au chocolat* and drink my coffee in silence. And I spend a couple of hours reading the Sunday newspapers online. In silence. By mid afternoon I am really starting to miss the sound of my Portuguese neighbours firing up the barbecue on the pavement outside, laughing, chatting and popping open cans of beer. I walk Biff around the sleepy village in the afternoon sunshine, listening for the telltale signs of music, loud macho voices and laughter. But all is quiet in the square. I start to panic that Luis and Piedro have left the village for good. Back home, I try to focus my mind on a feature on 'boudoir dressing' but can't. Where is Luis? And why isn't he answering his mobile?

But early evening, the smell of barbecued fish drifts in through my open window. Strangely, Sergio, the Brad Pitt lookalike and the quietest of the Portuguese neighbours, seems not to have moved out. And then I hear a very familiar, loud and deep laugh – a laugh I would recognise anywhere – and the doorbell rings. I almost cry with joy to see Luis is standing on the doorstep, dressed in jeans and a bright checked shirt. I race downstairs and throw my arms around him.

'Where were you?'

'I was getting myself organised in my new apartment before I invited you over, *chérie*,' he says.

'But why didn't you call?'

'I was busy tidying and doing laundry. I was going to call you but I left my mobile in José's van.'

'How is your new flat?'

'*Très agréable.*'

'Have you moved far?'

'Just across the square,' he says with a grin. 'Come with me and see.'

As we walk across the sunlit square towards his apartment, my hand in his giant paw, Biff trotting alongside us, I feel ridiculously happy. Luis has not moved far at all. He and Piedro have moved into the building with the pale-green shutters opposite the pharmacy. He leads me proudly up the staircase and into the first-floor apartment, which is large and airy, with old-style casement windows and narrow-parquet flooring. It is minimally furnished, with a pimento-coloured sofa in the sitting room and a round table with a floral plastic cover in the immaculate kitchen, which is remarkably free of clutter. Only a bottle of whisky and a jar of ground coffee are visible on the white worktops.

It is the first time he has shown me inside his den. When he lived at rue St Benoit, I never ventured further than the kitchen, as he preferred to spend most of his time at my house. So it is a surprise to see that Luis's bedroom is also very tidy. It, too, is minimally furnished, with a low, futon-style bed and – surprisingly – hot pink bed linen, which makes me smile. Somehow, his vibrant Schiaparelli pink duvet and clashing violet pillowcases reflect his personality perfectly.

'Look!' he says, proudly. 'I made everything very clean and tidy for you.'

'*C'est très bien, chéri,*' I say, looking at his giant flip-flops, trainers and other shoes lined up neatly against the wall. His apartment is very neat and clean but at the same time – with the exception of his pink bed linen – very masculine. This environment, I realise, is much more suited to him than my Laura Ashley-filled domain. Suddenly, for the first time, I am struck by the comical vision of The Lion sleeping in my delicate wrought-iron bed, surrounded by handbags and perfume bottles. Invited into his lair, I see his real character – he seems even more powerful here – and I love him all the more.

Over a coffee in the kitchen, he tells me that Sergio has taken over the lease and is going to remain at 7 rue St Benoit with another worker, called Ruigi, who has just arrived from Portugal. 'But don't worry, *chérie*, they are both very quiet, so there will be no complaints from the neighbours. And more, *le patron* has warned them that they must be on their best behaviour. It will be very different at 7 rue St Benoit now that Piedro and I have gone.'

I am sure it will. It feels like the end of an era to no longer have Luis living next door and watching my every move with his penetrating eyes. But, as I lie in his vibrant bed later that night – the bright pink duvet is the perfect counterpoint to his tanned skin and dark hair – I am thrilled to have finally entered The Lion's den.

Chapter 17

Out of Line

DELPHINE PHONES TO say that she is in the Liberty Bookshop and needs to talk to me about something urgently. I retrieve my sun hat from between Biff's teeth – the Poitevin sun is so strong that just the 100 metre walk to the square is almost enough to give you sunstroke – and go immediately to meet her. 'Are you OK?' I ask, seeing immediately that Delphine is not looking her usual jolly self. She's not even wearing her red lipstick, so things must be bad.

'Have you seen today's newspapers?' she asks.

'Why what's happened?'

'Well, I am a little flaggerbastard [sic]. For some time now there have been some gossips [sic] in my village that Didier is running the cafe as a brothel.'

'What?'

'Yes. As you know, there has been some talk of people dancing naked on the table tops. I ignored these gossips thinking they couldn't be true but the gendarmes, they have been watching 'im and on Saturday night, they carried out a raid, with three vans.'

'Three vans? In such a tiny village?'

'Yes, they came from all the communes around. It is said that they found some prostitutes in the rooms upstairs, above the cafe. It's in all the newspapers – even the national ones – so I'm not saying anything that's not already talked about.'

'Oh my goodness,' I say, thinking back to how I once described the rosily lit interior of Le Café de la Paix as 'very bordello chic', not imagining for a second how accurate this assessment might be. It's hard to imagine Delphine's sleepy, backwater village suddenly becoming a centre of vice; or Didier, the bouffant-haired, slightly effete cafe proprietor acting as the pimp-in-chief.

'But how can there be prostitutes in Puysoleil without you knowing about it?' I ask. 'Puysoleil is tiny.'

'Well, it is claimed that he was bringing them from Poitiers.'

'But who are the customers?'

'I don't know,' says Delphine. 'But it seems that they are coming from miles around. I am sorry to bother you with this, *Ka-renne*. But now I have journalists and even a TV crew turning up at the *mairie* in Puysoleil.'

'*Mon Dieu.*'

'Yes. Because it is August and nothing else is happening, everyone is very interested in this story. It's a disaster for my village. We have had to close down the bar while the gendarmes investigate and no one will want to rent it now.'

'Well, I'm not sure that's true,' I say. 'This could put Puysoleil on the map.'

'Well, my commune is now on the map for the wrong reasons,' says Delphine, glumly. 'But what shall I say to these journalists? I was hoping that you might be able to give me some advice.'

'Well, if I were you, I'd just say "no comment" and that the matter is in the hands of the gendarmes.'

'Yes, this is what I was thinking,' says Delphine. 'They are asking very 'orrible questions, such as 'ow could I not know about this.'

'Just give them your big smile, like everything is under control,' I say. 'And make sure you are wearing your red lipstick. That way people will at least think, "Oh this village has a very glamorous mayor". And you never know who might want to rent the cafe after that.'

'*Bonne idée*,' says Delphine. 'Thank you my friend. This is what I will do.'

I give her a hug and walk home, thinking, not for the first time, that you never know what is happening behind closed shutters in a quiet French village. That evening, Delphine appears on national TV, issuing a cheerful 'no comment' outside her rose-covered *mairie*, with a big red-lipsticked smile.

Towards the end of August, only a week or so after he moved house, Luis's company closes down for *le congé annuel* (the annual vacation). He returns to Portugal to see his mother and sister, driving down with Piedro and Fernando. It's too early in the relationship to go with him, and to be honest I could do with two weeks to regroup and catch up on my deadlines and sleep. But Luis calls every evening to ask where I am and tell me that he is missing me and thinking about me a lot.

I'm usually at home, sometimes walking Biff or visiting friends for dinner or a barbecue. Several times I have bumped into Jon in the Liberty Bookshop and he always asks after Biff, but I avoid making any plans to go for walks or cycle rides with him, as I get the impression that he would still like to be more than just friends. And on Monday evenings of course, I am to be found jumping and skipping around a community hall in Douhe, where the ante has been considerably upped of late. Coralie and her clique have taken to wearing fully coordinated outfits. One week, eight of them show up in identical brown ruffled skirts with white cowboy boots and fringed belts. This divides the class into two distinct groups: those wearing this ensemble (who take themselves very seriously) and those who aren't (who just want to dance and have a bit of fun).

Unfortunately, many people have stopped coming altogether, intimidated by the 'hard core' element. Even Jill is conspicuously absent on Monday nights. Whenever I ask Jocelyn where she is, she invariably gives a vague reply such as, 'Oh, she just didn't feel like it this evening.' Meanwhile, Vivienne, the Entente Cordiale's social secretary, has made a full recovery from her ankle injury, and in addition to starting a new children's class, has taken control of the Douhe group, assisted by Jocelyn and Gloria. Rather than resenting this, Jocelyn seems mightily relieved, as the pressure to teach new routines every week has become relentless. (Coralie and her friends get very upset if they are not taught at least three new dances at each class.)

Gloria, meanwhile, is blooming. Each passing week, she looks a little slimmer and blonder, her gap-toothed grin noticeably wider, while her collection of cowboy boots gets ever more impressive. Sitting at home and playing the tragic widow is not for her. Instead, she is out in her rhinestone jeans, shimmying and strutting her stuff at every opportunity. Meanwhile, another '*Soirée Stomp*' is scheduled for the end of September. Although officially it is being run by the Entente Cordiale, with Vivienne in charge, Coralie and her friends have pretty much taken over. In particular, a formidable-looking woman called Sandrine, with short paprika-coloured hair and severe, rectangular glasses seems to think that she is running the show.

(And who would argue with her? I, for one, am terrified of Sandrine, who always looks like she has been sucking lemons.)

Ostensibly, *le Soirée Stomp* is in aid of a local charity, and in addition to the Civray Stetsons, other line dancing groups in the region – there are now many – have been invited to take part, including the much-revered Adnaks. The Stetsons are now almost entirely French, since many of the Brits, including Colin, dropped out long ago, unable to keep up with the complexity of the routines. As for me, I've lost my exalted status as a 'helper teacher' and now lag behind the fearsome front row when it comes to learning new dances.

The question of what dances the Stetsons will perform at *le Stomp* gives rise to a vigorous discussion. Sandrine, brandishing a list and a clipboard, seems to have already decided the matter and no one argues. Vivienne then delicately raises an issue that is apparently even more contentious – our outfit for public performances. Having missed a few classes in the past month (mainly because Luis proved more alluring than line dancing) I wasn't even aware that there were plans to change our uniform, let alone that it was a cause of discord. Personally, I was quite happy with the existing arrangement: blue jeans, white T-shirt, brown boots and whatever Western accessories you wanted (if any). So I watch in horror as the more enthusiastic members of our group unfurl a frightening succession of Western shirts including a particularly hideous design in cream and brown. *Ewww!* I hang around on the sidelines, traumatised at the idea of wearing such kit, even more so the thought of having to buy it.

A very heated discussion takes place between Coralie (backed by sour-faced Sandrine) and a pale, androgynous French girl. Jocelyn, Gloria and I can only stand and watch as a vigorous conversation ensues, with lots of pointing, finger-stabbing and head-shaking. Vivienne steps in to moderate and then there is a vote, from which Coralie and Sandrine clearly emerge victorious. It then falls to Vivienne to announce that from now on we will wear a white Western shirt with, wait for it... brown jeans. I am gutted.

Seven For All Mankind – the only jeans I look good in – do not, as far as I know, do brown. Just what is it about the French and the colour brown? Why, I wonder, do they love *marron* so much?

I know I won't look good in this outfit, which incidentally, also includes a long white-fringed leatherette belt/skirt to go over the brown jeans, which has the unfortunate effect of making everyone's bottom look twice as big. Where possible, we are to wear white cowboy boots. It gets worse. The one hundred per cent polyester shirt with fringing has to be ordered from a catalogue at a cost of €25 each. I say nothing but there is no way that I'm going to wear a fringed polyester shirt, let alone pay for it. I've got to draw the line (ha!) somewhere. I suppose it could have been much worse: namely, the beige shirt with brown fringing, But I'm still not sure I can bring myself to wear mud-coloured jeans.

In mid September Luis returns from Portugal, looking as brown as the autumn leaves. His return coincides with the start of a glorious Indian summer. The evenings are drawing in, but during the day the fields around our village are bathed in radiant sunshine and the sky is an unblemished blue. The Café du Commerce even has its red parasols up, so strong is the afternoon sun.

The evening that Luis returns, I run down to answer the door in a blue-and-white sarong, which has a very unexpected effect. 'Oh, I love it when my woman answers the door in a sarong,' he says, scooping me up in his arms and carrying me upstairs caveman style.

'*Chérie*, you did tell me you were Catholic, didn't you?' he asks me later, when we are sitting at the kitchen table.

'Um, yes, I went to a Catholic school,' I say, not sure what the French is for 'lapsed Catholic'.

'*Ah bon,*' he says, presenting me with a bag containing something heavy. 'Because I spent a long time thinking about a gift for you.'

'I'm sure whatever you've chosen for me is lovely,' I say, disarmed that he thought to buy me a present and determined to love it whatever it is. I throw my arms around him and then open the bag to find a bottle of port and... a large statue of the Madonna.

I'm stunned but I do an impressive display of being delighted. I haven't the heart to tell him that port gives me a headache (that I will now have two unopened bottles in the cupboard) and that, after a strict Catholic upbringing, I'm not a lover of religious ornaments. Instead, I (reluctantly) put the statue on display on a side table in *le petit salon*.

'It's very nice of you, *chéri*,' I say. After all, it is the thought that counts. Though who knows what he was thinking? Later, Travis laughs for a good ten minutes when I tell him about the gift. 'Psychologists would have a field day working out the subliminal message in that,' he says.

But I'm delighted that he is back and that his enormous green flip-flops are once again lined up against my beaded Miu Miu sandals in the bedroom (which look tiny by comparison). I've given Luis a set of keys to Maison Coquelicot, so that when he gets back from work late, he can let himself in. But often I spend the night in his apartment. He calls to say that he is home and after kissing Biff goodnight, I cross the square to the building with the pale-green shutters where he lives. The next morning, I leave at the same time as Luis (usually about 5.30 a.m.) and do the walk of shame back across the square in the darkness, his scent lingering in my hair. When I arrive back at Maison Coquelicot Biff sniffs my ankles suspiciously and looks me up and down with resentful eyes, unimpressed I've stayed out all night (or part of it, as I'm never gone longer than six hours).

The evening of *le Soirée Stomp* arrives. I know that line dancing is nothing to be ashamed of (despite what Travis says), but I tell Luis that I'm going to visit some friends and will call him later, as I really don't want him to see me (a) dressed as a cowboy, and (b) wearing brown jeans. (I've managed to keep the Monday night class a secret from him, since I'm normally back from Douhe before Luis has made it home from work.) I've actually interpreted the new uniform very liberally: plum-coloured cords by Seven For All Mankind – which in the right light could be interpreted as brown(ish) – and a plain, fitted shirt, which lacks the mandatory fringing but is at least white. I've also taken a firm stand against the white-fringed leatherette belt, and white cowboy boots. Perhaps as a punishment for breaching the new dress code, when we come to line up on the dance floor to perform our first dance, 'Party for Two' by Shania Twain, I am peremptorily removed from my position in the front row and ordered to the back by Sandrine. She tells me that at the last rehearsal (which, as she correctly points out, I didn't attend) they reorganised the lines. *Et voilà*, I am at the back *'avec les enfants'*.

Yes, that's right, I'm the sole adult dancing in a line of children – I hadn't even realised that Vivienne's junior dancers would be performing with us this evening – and I look ridiculous. It is an indication of how far my status has fallen. It is *malséant*, unseemly. Even Jocelyn and Gloria – who have both adhered to the new uniform, right down to the hideous fringed belt – have been bumped to the second row. Only Vivienne, who, as social secretary of the Entente Cordiale, is nominally in charge of the event, remains in the front line. Under the discerning eyes of the Adnaks – who, dressed in their arresting red and black uniforms, are nothing short of line dancing royalty – we perform three out of our six scheduled routines. And then we come to an abrupt stop. Vivienne, having halted the music, takes the microphone and, to a round of applause, introduces the Adnaks.

But the Stetsons refuse to relinquish the dance floor. Coralie and the front row clique gather in an outraged huddle, while Sandrine looks as if she would like to throw a lasso around Vivienne's neck and slowly tighten it. As the Adnaks stream onto the dance floor, it feels like the *danse country* equivalent of the Battle of the Little Bighorn, with Sandrine as Sitting Bull. But as it slowly dawns on the Douhe group that they will not get to perform 'Backtrack' or the 'Boot Scootin' Boogie', they make a slow and reluctant withdrawal.

As the Adnaks launch into their first routine, at least half of our number leave the hall looking petulant. I follow out of curiosity and find them regrouped in an angry huddle outside, furiously smoking cigarettes. Once again, it's *tres malséant*, as the Adnaks politely (if a little disdainfully) watched our performance, and they are also our guests, so we should at least return the courtesy. I go back into the hall and find Vivienne. 'What's going on?' I ask. 'It's like the Wild West out there. Everyone is really angry.'

'I know,' says Vivienne. 'I told them all along that they couldn't perform six dances, that it was too many, but Sandrine and Coralie wouldn't take no for an answer. There are four other line dancing troupes who've travelled across the region to come here this evening and we have to be fair and let them dance too.'

'Well, of course,' I say.

'I told them they can dance again later,' says Vivienne. 'They'll just have to wait.'

Guessing I won't be welcome on the French table, which looks like a council of war, I sit with Gloria and Jocelyn, for the *casse-croûte*. They, at least, look like they are having a good time. 'So where's Jill this evening?' I ask, as I pour *pamplemousse rosés* all around. There is an embarrassed silence and then Jocelyn says:

'Have you not heard?'

'Heard what?'

'Jill and I are no longer together,' she says, looking shame-faced. 'You must have heard the rumours?'

'*What?*' I say, almost choking on my *pamplemousse rosé*.

'And before you say anything, yes, I do feel absolutely terrible about it. And I completely understand why no one is talking to me and everyone thinks I'm a complete shit.'

'Oh God! But you've been together thirty years,' I say, noticing for the first time the beatific expression on Gloria's face, which tells me everything about what has been going on.

'I know, I know. Since we were both twenty. But I honestly couldn't help myself. I swear. I've always been faithful to Jill but then Gloria came along and before I knew it, I was knocked off my feet.'

Well, I suppose if you're going to be knocked off your feet, better by Gloria than Button I think to myself.

'This is the first time we've been out together in public,' says Jocelyn. 'We don't want to run the risk of bumping into Jill and upsetting her more than is necessary. And no one is speaking to me because of what's happened.'

'We mostly stay at home anyway,' says Gloria, with a grin. 'Last night we drank a bottle of champagne in the Jacuzzi in the garden. Naked.'

'Oh,' I say, trying not to imagine it. 'So where are you living?'

Jocelyn nods at her new girlfriend – mother of four, grandmother and recently bereaved widow – sitting next to her in a sequined cowboy hat. 'I've moved in with Gloria.'

I gasp. 'But that's just a few doors down from Jill.'

'I know,' says Jocelyn. 'It's far from ideal. And I don't really know what to do about it. I feel absolutely terrible.'

Later that evening, I drive home from *le Stomp* feeling terrible for Jill, and not for the first time, marvelling at what is going on behind closed shutters (or in this case garden hedges) in the French countryside.

A couple of days later I receive a group email from Vivienne. It is an invitation to a meeting in Douhe and it sounds ominous. 'Everyone will have a chance to air their views,' it says. 'The grievances of ALL dancers will be heard and NOT just those who shout the loudest.'

I'm not quite sure what the grievances are but it sounds like we're going to be discussing more than the colour of our uniform this time. And so I arrive in the harshly lit community hall on a Monday evening in late September for the line dancing equivalent of Agincourt. I can't help noticing that the lines have already been drawn: *l'anglais* (Vivienne, Jocelyn and Gloria and another recent recruit, Deirdre) are sitting at one end of the long trestle table; a posse of angry-looking French ladies at the other, led by Coralie and Sandrine.

Sandrine is scary at the best of times, but arms folded and red hair teased into angry spikes, she looks positively terrifying tonight. She fires the opening salvo with: 'We were very angry that we were only allowed to perform three dances at *le Stomp*.'

'And our husbands were also very angry,' says Coralie. (I doubt this very much: a little line dancing goes a long way as far as most men are concerned.) There are angry murmurs of support, then someone else complains that we are not learning enough new dances. Yet another person jumps in with another grievance – this one has something to do with the cakes served at *le Stomp* – and suddenly the meeting degenerates into a shouting match. It's impossible to follow all the different complaints but there appear to be many. Vivienne listens calmly but the meeting culminates in Sandrine, Coralie and six of their friends storming out. Those of us left behind – there are about twenty of us in the silent majority – vote to carry on with the Monday night class but at a slower pace, to give people a chance to catch up with the various dances. But as I drive home in the darkness, through swirling pockets of fog, I can't help feeling that something wonderful, that brought many of us together and provided a great deal of fun, has come to an end.

Sure enough, the following week, only two French ladies show up to class and one of them – the keeper of the key to the community hall – announces that she won't be able to come any more. Coralie and her posse, it seems, got to them in the intervening week. Oh dear. *La danse country* was the fastest way that I've found to integrate in rural France, but who would have guessed it could also evoke such passion and end in disharmony? Vivienne announces that the Douhe class will be discontinued. Looking on the bright side, at least I won't have to buy that hideous fringed shirt.

Chapter 18

Broken

EARLY IN OCTOBER, I receive a nasty shock. I haven't seen or heard from Luis for several days. I've called his mobile several times, sent him a few texts to see where he is – '*Chéri, où es-tu?*' – but heard nothing. I don't worry too much. I know that he works crazy hours and I know that his mobile belongs to the Palaeolithic age and that more often than not, the battery is dead. I figure that he and his compatriots are working in a *chantier* away from home and will show up late on Friday evening as usual. But he doesn't. On Saturday I wake up with a feeling of foreboding. Something isn't right, I know it. I put Biff in the car and we drive to one of our favourite walks, around a remote reservoir. The autumn sunshine fails to make me feel better and even Biff picks up on my mood. At one point he finds an enormous tree branch and prances along with it in his mouth, in an attempt to make me smile.

Driving back into the square I notice a large group of people sitting outside the cafe in the autumn sunshine. There are seven men and three women – in addition to the girlfriends of Piedro and Sergio there is a dark-haired girl that I haven't seen before – and sitting opposite the dark-haired girl, larger than life and looking very pleased with himself is... Luis. Feeling viscerally shocked, I park the car on the other side of the square and walk back towards the cafe to get a better look. I go into the newsagents next to the bar and see that Luis is talking to the dark-haired girl and she is laughing. In the few seconds that I have to take in the scene, I see that the girl is in her mid thirties – a little younger than me – and has dark eyes, a fringe and olive skin. She looks a little like Penelope Cruz but not as pretty. She is wearing a black quilted jacket and very tight jeans. I'm wearing tracksuit bottoms and a bobble hat.

Inside the newsagents I stare blankly at the wall of the magazines, heart thumping, wondering what to do next. I'm pretty sure Luis has seen me. I'm tempted to march back out and confront him but I'm not feeling calm enough for that. I stare at the magazines for a while longer, until my heart has resumed normal service, and as I leave the shop, I look directly over at Luis. Immediately he looks sheepish, guilty, averting his eyes and confirming my worst fears. I don't know how I muster up the courage, but almost without thinking, I approach to get a look at even closer quarters.

'*Bonjour,*' I say as coolly as possible, though inside I am a foaming whirlpool of emotion. '*Ça va?*'

'*Bonjour,*' he replies, looking uncomfortable. I scan that table, taking in as much as possible. At least Sergio and Ruigi, my neighbours at 7 rue St Benoit have the decency to look embarrassed. Sergio tries to stroke Biff who has sat down at my feet, his jet eyes fixed on Luis with an accusatory stare.

'What's going on here?' I ask in French, scanning Luis's

compatriots, sitting around the three tables that have been pulled together. 'Is it a party?'

'Kind of,' says Luis, looking away, not daring to meet my eyes. 'But I can explain.'

'*Très bien,*' I say, voice noticeably quivering now. '*Bonne continuation.*'

I walk away from the cafe, back across the square, under the gaze of ten pairs of Portuguese eyes. How I wish I wasn't wearing my glasses and looking such a mess. At least Biff manages to hold his head high, assuming the fancy walk, or rather prance, that he does when he knows he is being watched. I feel absolutely devastated. True, Luis and I have been together for less than four months but that's precisely why I'm so shocked. Only last weekend I was his *copine*, lying between his pink and violet sheets with him while he told me how much he loved me, and suddenly I am not. I certainly didn't see this coming. Back home, I sit down on the sofa too shocked even to cry. Biff climbs up beside me and puts his head on my knees in a gesture of consolation.

'You don't know for sure that she's his girlfriend,' says Travis, when I call him. 'Or even that she was with him.'

'Oh come on!' I say. 'It would explain why I haven't heard anything from him for nearly a week.'

'But he's always been like that,' says Travis. 'You told me you often didn't hear from him for days if he was away working and the battery of his phone was flat.'

'Well, if she isn't his girlfriend why hasn't he hauled his ass around here to explain?'

'Well, how long ago was it that you saw him?'

'A couple of hours.'

'Look it could be his sister or a relative or a friend of the family. The point is that you just don't know. When I saw you together in the summer, it was like a scene from *West Side Story*, with him smouldering against the wall and barely able to keep his hands off you.' I smile at the memory. Travis, like Delphine, thought the chemistry between us was borderline indecent.

I call Delphine and tell her what's happened. 'The divil,' she says (meaning devil and making him sound almost endearing). I decide that's what I'm doing to call him from now on: The Devil. With his dark hair and black penetrating eyes, the description suits him. 'But are you sure it's his girlfriend?' says Delphine, echoing Travis's thoughts. 'It could be a relative or a friend of the family. This sort of thing is very important to the Portuguese. And only last week, when I saw you together, he looked very in love with you. This is very strange.'

My French friend Mathilde, however, is more forthright when I meet her for a coffee in the Liberty Bookshop that afternoon. '*Mon œil,*' she says (meaning 'my eye') when I tell her Delphine's 'friend of the family' theory. Still, it's helpful to talk to her. Like Delphine, she is very savvy when it comes to men. 'Luis was very good for you and you seemed very happy with him,' she says. 'But some adventures in life are not meant to last forever. You have to take them for what they are and then move on to the next.'

Walking back down rue St Benoit with Biff, I see that Sergio and Ruigi are at home. Sergio says '*Bonjour,*' as I am putting the key in the door and looks over sympathetically. 'So did you all know that Luis had a girlfriend in Portugal?' I ask.

'It's not his girlfriend,' he says, looking uncomfortable.

'What is she then?'

'She's a friend, a colleague.'

'*Mon œil,*' I reply.

The following morning, a Sunday, I wake up at 5.00 a.m., unable to sleep and feeling utterly miserable. Last night, there was no sign of Luis visiting his friends at 7 rue St Benoit – where he spends most of his time when not with me at weekends – so of course my imagination tortured me with a number of graphic scenarios. I just can't bear the idea that someone else's head is on his violet pillow. The thing that's really killing me is not knowing how long it's been going on. How foolish I was to think that I could invite The Lion into my home and tame it, when in fact, Luis will probably never be tamed or owned.

As soon as it is light, I pull on my boots and take Biff out for a walk, wondering why these things only seem to happen to me? Why must my love life always be such boom and bust? My heart is starting to feel like a centuries-old Ming vase, broken so many times, that it's impossible to glue it back together.

The Indian summer – that brief, beautiful interlude of unexpected sunshine – is over. Where once there was blue sky and coppery light, now there is mist and greyness, and an expanse of dull brown brittle earth. At least it matches my mood. The sunflowers, meanwhile, are finally dying and if not already dead, their heads are drooping downwards, as if suicidally depressed. The countryside, once a source of joy, feels miserable, brooding and hostile. Suddenly Biff starts barking and stops dead just in front of me, refusing to go any further. It always unnerves me when he does this. A couple of gunshots ring out in the still air, I hear dogs barking and I remember it's the hunting season and a Sunday (a day I would not normally take Biff on this particular walk during *la saison de la chasse*). We turn around immediately and head back, defeated.

Back home not even the thought of watching *The Andrew Marr Show* on satellite can cheer me up. Pre-Luis, watching the jug-eared but endearing presenter killing politicians with his trademark politeness was a highlight of Sunday mornings. But now, I can't find peace anywhere. I put the coffee on and wonder how I'm going to fill the void that is Sunday in the French countryside. If I was in London I'd take myself off to Selfridges for some consolation retail therapy or meet a friend for a 'misery lunch' dissecting the previous day's discovery. But here in France, only Intermarché is open and only until 12 p.m. This reminds me that I need washing-up liquid. I'm about to throw my old Barbour and bobble hat back on, but suddenly I remember the ignominy of yesterday. As a point of pride, I cannot leave the house like this. I go upstairs and get changed into a brightly coloured dress and high heels, apply full make-up and an ironic dab of Annick Goutal's Grand Amour. Because it's nippy outside I throw on the tailored navy coat that I normally only wear in London, causing Biff to eye me up and down curiously. I cross the square – noting to my chagrin that Luis's pale green shutters are still closed – and make it into the supermarket with just ten minutes to spare.

'*Fuck you, fuck you.*' The cheery voice of Lily Allen singing 'Fuck You (Very Much)' is piped over the sound system, without the f-word being beeped out as it would be in the UK. It's quite surreal. Several people, including the cashiers, eye me suspiciously as I march in wearing full make-up and heels. Most people look more than a little dishevelled as they do the last-minute Sunday morning trolley dash before the store closes. I grab my washing-up liquid and am looking at some avocados, when I see them: Luis and the dark-haired girl pushing a large trolley towards the drinks aisle. I drop the avocados and watch from a distance. He is pushing the trolley leaning over it while she – looking very pleased with herself – is choosing a bottle of wine. They look very cosy, very tender together. I can't bear it.

'*Fuck you, fuck you,*' sings Lily as I march towards them. I have to know.

'*Ah bonjour Luis, ça va?*' I say in a loud cheery voice (and this time to my surprise it doesn't crack or quiver). He looks surprised, shocked and more importantly, is speechless. He also looks like he hasn't had much sleep, which causes me another stab of pain. I turn to the girl, whom I can now see close up. She is not as pretty as I first thought. She is small with dark hair but plain without make-up. She is wearing tracksuit bottoms (ha! I think to myself: the situation at least on that front is reversed today).

'*Bonjour!*' I say, In French, with a big smile. '*Vous êtes la copine de Luis?*' ('Are you Luis's girlfriend?')

'*Oui*', she says with an affectionate look in his direction.

'*Depuis longtemps?*' ('Since a long time?') She looks at him shyly and nods, telling me everything I need to know. His face is a fixed grimace. Then he says something to her in Portuguese. As I guessed from her skin and hair colouring, she is not French

'*Ah bon, il est charmant n'est-ce pas?*' I say with a big grin. ('He's charming isn't he?') I'm not sure she understands but she looks at him with pride and another soppy expression.

'*Oui,*' she replies, practically melting with love.

'*Fuck you, fuck you,*' goes the soundtrack.

'*Alors, bonne dimanche,*' ('Have a good Sunday'), I say and march off.

Knowledge is power, I tell myself as I head towards the exit, abandoning the washing-up liquid in a basket at the tills. I now know everything I need to. She's his girlfriend, she's Portuguese and judging by how comfortable they look together, she preceded me probably by several years. It is me who is the 'other woman', not her. Marching back across the square, I regret just one thing: that I didn't look in their trolley to see what they had bought.

I spend a miserable Sunday afternoon at home surfing the net and reading my horoscope. Jupiter 'the planet of gifts and surprises' is apparently touring my love sector. I call Delphine to tell her about the latest development. She pronounces herself 'flaggerbastard' by the news.

'*Mon Dieu!* He really is a divil,' she says 'but I'm sure this is not the whole story.'

'The annoying thing was that he looked really attractive when I saw him.'

'That's the problem with Scorpios,' says Delphine. 'They are very magnetic, very electrical and very hard to resist.'

Later in the day I walk Biff round the square and down to the river. As we pass Luis's building, it's distressing to see that his bedroom shutters are *still* closed. I can well imagine what is going on behind them. I tell myself that we were only together for four months, and that I shouldn't feel as devastated as I do. But, fraught with the knowledge that less than 100 metres away my (former) Portuguese boyfriend is now wrapping his big arms around someone else, the village suddenly seems like a different, very hostile, place. In a big town or city, I could avoid Luis and his girlfriend. Here, in a small village in rural France, I will be forced to confront the betrayal every single day. And worse, two of his best friends are living next door to me.

I call Jill to see how she is doing. Our situations are not dissimilar, since she too is dealing with infidelity on her doorstep. How much worse must it be in a tiny hamlet – knowing that your former partner is enjoying frisky whirlpool baths with her new lover, a few doors down? And how much more painful must it be when you have thirty years of memories to torture yourself with, rather than just four months? Despite all of this, kind, gentle Jill is behaving in a very dignified way, refusing to indulge in any self-pity or say anything negative about either Jocelyn or Gloria. The good thing is that she is hugely popular and buffered by many friends, so she is never short of invitations to dinner. When I ask how she is coping, she tells me that she has decided to go and backpack around New Zealand for a couple of months and will be leaving in less than week. 'I have to get away from here,' she says, in a particularly candid moment. 'It's unbearable.'

I can't help thinking that she is doing the right thing, in putting some distance (in this case, the maximum possible) between herself and her former girlfriend. 'When will you be back?' I ask.

'I don't know,' she says. 'But we've put the house up for sale.'

As I put the phone down, I find myself thinking along similar lines. There is a lot to be said for removing yourself from the scene of a failed love affair. I've been thinking of doing the same. The problem is: where do I go? I feel doubly trapped, because not only do I have to look at The Devil's girlfriend everyday, but the little house that I love so much is now horribly associated with Luis.

Late on Sunday evening my phone rings. Stupidly, I dare to hope that it's Luis with some plausible explanation. But in fact it's Jon. I can hear his favourite song, Eric Clapton's 'Wonderful Tonight', playing softly in the background. 'I can't do this,' he says.

'What?'

'Just be friends with you,' he says, sounding very down.

Oh,' I say, ignoring the fact that we haven't actually been behaving like friends. Although we agreed in principle that we would remain on amicable terms and occasionally go for walks or cycle rides together, in practice I've been avoiding him.

'It's too difficult,' he says.

'I understand,' I say, thinking of how cruel life can be. How many sad love triangles must there be in the world, where someone madly desires a person who desires someone else. Jon wants me but despite everything; I want Luis. And if I can't have him, I don't want to live here any more. It will just be too painful. And suddenly I feel unbearably sad.

As I expected, Luis's infidelity tortures me on a daily basis, in the form of his girlfriend wandering around the village with a big smile on her face. It also forces me to raise my game. No more throwing my coat over jeans and muddy boots to take Biff out. *Oh no!* Whereas before I often didn't even bother to brush my hair in the morning, now it's full *maquillage* and high heels even just to go and buy a newspaper. Frankly, it's exhausting.

And, when I walk Biff past his apartment each day, en route to the river, I find myself obsessed by the positioning of his shutters: debating the significance of their being closed, open or slightly ajar. One day, I notice that there is a new red organza curtain in the sitting room window – the new girlfriend is obviously making her mark on his living space – and find it strangely upsetting. But not half as upsetting as the Monday morning I see the pink duvet hanging out of the bedroom window, being given an airing (something which several of my French neighbours do).

I take some satisfaction from the fact that his girlfriend spends most of the day alone – wandering around the village or frittering away the hours in the local cafe while Luis works long shifts. Often she hangs around with the guys next door. I always smile and try to look happy when I see her. The last thing I want is for her to think I am bitter because she has escaped with the big prize. I like to think that when I walk around the village, head held high (and immaculately groomed) the message I am conveying is 'You're welcome to him!' Not, of course, that he is mine to give.

And when I see Luis – which unfortunately, is several times a week – I cut him dead, while attempting to look like I've just won the lottery, when the reality is that I feel like I've lost the winning ticket. Even when I don't see him, I can hear him, as he visits his friends next door on an almost nightly basis, and I would know his loud laugh anywhere. Is this situation better or worse, I wonder, than not knowing what your ex and his new girlfriend are up to? In some ways, it is comforting to know that they are just sitting at the kitchen table next door, chatting to Ruigi and Sergio rather than enjoying a love-fest under Luis's brightly coloured duvet. But seeing the two of them speeding off in Luis's Renault Clio, on the other hand, is very painful.

One evening, I return from visiting friends, to find the door open next door, and Luis sitting in the kitchen with Ruigi, Sergio and Fernando, the boss. There is no sign of the girlfriend and I can't resist confronting him. '*Ah bonsoir, Luis,*' I say. '*Ça va?*' I motion with my finger for him to come outside, which he does, looking sheepish (and annoyingly attractive). He stands against the wall, cornered by me, a half smile of grudging respect across his rugged face. And in that moment I somehow know that he is still attracted to me. '*Alors,*' I demand in French, 'why did you tell me "I love you darling, I love you very much"?' I say this very loudly – in fact, I shout it – so that his boss and his friends can hear.

He takes a slow drag of his cigarette and narrows his eyes, looking at me intently.

'I can explain,' he says.

'I'm listening,' I say.

'It's not a good moment,' he says.

'*Je t'aime, chérie. Je t'aime beaucoup*,' I repeat sarcastically, and just at that moment, the girlfriend appears out of the shadows. I don't know how much she has heard but she looks upset. '*Bonne nuit*, Luis,' I say and go into my house. Through the open window in my bedroom, I hear raised voices, shouting and an upset female voice next door, just as my telephone rings. It's Delphine. I tell her what has happened. 'Oh la la!' she says. 'Trust me, it is not all over with that big divil yet.'

This makes me laugh. Loudly enough, I hope, for Luis and his entourage next door to hear. It seems to have the desired effect. The raised voices escalate into a full-blown argument, and then suddenly, I hear doors slam and the Clio drive off at speed. It's a satisfactory conclusion – Luis underestimated me if he thought I'd behave like a typical jilted girlfriend and fall apart – but then I realise that at some point this evening they will probably kiss and make up. A very sobering thought. For although I am doing my best to pretend otherwise, the truth is that I am devastated by what has happened. During the day everything feels sad and forlorn as I walk Biff along muddy tracks under a colourless sky; while the long, dark evenings have lost their allure, without Luis to look forward to. And all around me, things seem to be coming to an end. Even René Matout has finally sold the *boulangerie* and is about to move on.

And so I start to think about leaving Villiers for good, rather than just running away for a while. I've had many wonderful experiences in the four years that I've lived in France, but maybe it's time to return to London. And as I start to think these thoughts about going back, out of nowhere, an opportunity arises. One of my friends is about to relocate to New York for three months with her advertising agency, and, for a nominal rent offers to let me have her apartment, which is round the corner from where I used to live. She doesn't mind Biff staying either but warns me that it is a top-floor flat and I'll have to schlep down three flights of stairs whenever I want to take him out. 'No problem,' I say, thinking it can only be good for the thighs and glutes.

Before I leave for London, I ask Marie-Claude, the estate agent on the square, to value Maison Coquelicot with a view to a quick sale. The suggested selling price is €85,000, which means that, allowing for the money I've spent on renovations, I'd break even. Marie-Claude tells me that I will have no trouble selling it. And that's my worry: if it sells really quickly, where will I go? I'm responsible for a little dog now and I don't want to make him homeless. I'm hoping my forthcoming trip to London will help me to decide, and perhaps give me a sign as to what I should do or where I should go next. I téll Marie-Claude that I need some time to think and will call her as soon as I've made a decision.

And so, towards the end of October, I start to pack up my life in France and prepare to move back to London. Ostensibly, it's only for three months. But deep down, I know that this is a trial run, to see if there is any possibility of going back, of resuming my old lifestyle after my interlude in the French countryside. Plus, it's exhausting having to look my best every time I step out of the front door in case I bump into Luis. I could do with a break.

Preparing to go back is also a welcome diversion from monitoring the situation next door – listening out for Luis's laugh or looking to see if his car is parked in the street outside. It is also Biff's first trip abroad, so it feels like a big adventure booking him in at the vet's for his worm and tick treatments, which have to be done no less than twenty-four hours before departure and no more than forty-eight. Madame Beaupain, the beautiful vet, checks him over, stamps his passport and sends us on our way with a cheery, *'Bon voyage, Beef!'*

Biff has, in fact, started misbehaving since Luis's departure. Rather than sleeping downstairs on his beanbag, as Luis trained him to do, he sneaks up the stairs and into my bedroom while I'm brushing my teeth and hides under the bed until I switch the lights off. Then out he pads, launching himself onto the bed, with a surprising sense of entitlement. I know that I should carry him back downstairs to the sitting room, but I don't. There he remains, curled up against my feet at the foot of the bed. And some mornings I wake up to find his little bottom wedged against mine, on the other side of the duvet. If I'm honest I find this quite cute. But Travis, who has been reading dog training books on my behalf, is shocked at this development. 'Oh my God,' he says. 'This is just about the WORST thing you can do. By jumping on your bed, you're letting him think he's the leader of the pack. No wonder he's out of control.' Well, I tell myself, there is a big difference between a small black terrier that's taking liberties and a Rottweiler that is out of control.

But he's not just taking liberties. Sometimes he takes my dinner too. One evening, I look under the grill to check on the chicken breast I'm cooking for dinner, only to find that it's not there. I search around the kitchen for a good ten minutes, wondering if I've put it back in the fridge or absent-mindedly thrown it in the bin. (According to a newspaper article that I recently read, one of the consequences of living on your own for a long time is that you are more prone to Alzheimer's later on in life. Maybe this is an early sign.) But then I notice Biff lying on the sofa… licking his lips, with an unmistakable look of guilt on his face. 'B-I-F-F,' I shout. 'YOU ARE A NAUGHTY BOY!' He rolls over on his back (a sure sign of guilt) to reveal his soft pink belly, head and eyes rolling to the side. He's so manipulative. When he does this, I just can't be cross with him for long. 'There is always a cleverness to his naughtiness,' says Delphine, who is his biggest advocate. When people come to visit us, I watch, half horrified, half amused by his show-off antics, which include standing on top of the kitchen table so that he is closer to human height (another sign of dominance according to Travis). Sometimes he even tries to climb on top of people's heads when they are sitting on the sofa. Fortunately, most guests take it in the friendly spirit that it is intended (though Travis continues to warn me darkly about 'dominance issues'). The problem is that I find almost everything he does so adorable that I can't tell him off. It's a good job I don't have children, as I'd be one of those liberal parents who allow their teenage offspring to stay out all night and take drugs. If Biff was a human teenager as opposed to the canine equivalent, he'd probably be smoking crack cocaine in his bedroom by now. But maybe a visit to London and a new routine will be good for him too.

Departure day arrives. The last weekend in October, I pack up the car with Biff's stuff first – his beanbag, bowls and toys – followed by my clothes, my computer and some work files. I close the blue-grey shutters of Maison Cocquelicot and we set off under a dappled grey sky, for the ferry port at Caen. As we drive through the drab countryside towards the motorway, it looks as depressed and sapped of life as I feel. But I take comfort in the thought of the small black creature curled up in his usual position under the driver's seat. Every so often I reach round to pat his warm fur, to reassure myself that he is still there. At least when I make these long road trips I'm no longer alone. Biff, I know, will be loyal to the end.

Tellingly, the further I drive from Villiers and Luis, the happier I feel. Biff remains curled up behind my seat for the entire 350-kilometre trip, emerging from the car, tail wagging, eyes alert, to sniff his way around the L'Air de la Dentelle d'Alençon, the service station, at roughly the halfway point, where we stop for a break. We arrive at the little port of Ouistreham mid afternoon. *Hors de saison*, half the cafes and shops are closed, and it doesn't look like there are many people on the 5.00 p.m. crossing. I head to one of the seafood restaurants around the port in the hope of a late lunch and the waiter tells me it is 'no problem' to bring Biff into the restaurant. I order *moules frites* and feed little morsels to Biff, who is impeccably behaved at my feet. I notice a smartly dressed elderly couple sitting at a table nearby smiling at us. 'Isn't he lovely,' says the woman. 'What breed is he?' A conversation ensues about Biff's parentage and how I came to own him. Normally, people tend to ignore those dining alone in a restaurant. But Biff is my little furry ice-breaker, a weapon of mass approval.

As boarding time approaches I start to feel worried about him. Will he be OK for the seven-hour journey or will he get seasick? I'm nervous as we go through passport control and I present his papers and passport. I know how much the French love their paperwork and I'm worried that they'll find a reason why he can't travel. But all is in order. I'm given a big pink sticker with a paw print on it, and waved through to the boarding lanes. I spend the last half-hour before boarding nervously walking him up and down the lines of parked cars. But Biff is his usual laid-back self, sniffing around with enthusiasm, as if he knows we are headed for a new adventure.

Once we've boarded, I stay with him for as long as possible. Then I hug him one more time and head up into the boat, where I spend the next six and a half hours feeling guilty that I didn't drive up to Calais, where the crossing would have been much shorter. But when I go down to check on him, accompanied by a steward a few hours later, he's sitting at the steering wheel looking (a) very perky, and (b) as if he's about to drive off.

As we approach Portsmouth in the brooding darkness, I receive a text from Delphine. 'Bon voyage, my friend. And come back soon. We will miss you. *Bisous*, Delphine.' She doesn't know that when I go back it might be to pack up Maison Coquelicot for good. How weird it feels to be doing the same journey, car packed to the rafters – duvet, clothes and work stuff – as I did four years ago but in reverse. And what is waiting for me now? I still have friends in London but they are mostly married and settled down. Yes, they'll be pleased to see me but life has moved on. Still, I'm hoping that three months in the metropolis will take my mind off Luis and the fact that I played with a lion and got very badly bitten.

Back in my car on deck six, Biff greets me like I've been gone for a decade. After a short stop for him to stretch his legs, we follow the dark, meandering road back to London.

Chapter 19

Re-bonjour Kensington

I WAKE UP in Rachel's elegant, pale-coloured flat to a view of blue sky and autumn sunshine through the top-floor window. I feel liberated to be back in London, happy to escape the claustrophobic round of Luis-watching that French village life had become. Biff also seems delighted to be here and is unfazed by his slick, new urban surroundings. Last night he climbed happily onto his beanbag, which I placed at the end of the bed in Rachel's spare room, and fell asleep immediately. This morning he's in high spirits and raring to go, running round with one of my socks, his tail bobbing madly, thoroughly pleased with his prize. (Honestly, it doesn't take much to make a dog happy.)

It's so kind of Rachel to have entrusted her flat – all pale grey walls and Camembert-coloured furnishings – to me and my hairy mate. But I trust Biff completely. He is on his best behaviour and seems to know intuitively that he can't sit on the white sofas or stretch out on the bed, paws in the air, as he would do at home. I decide to induct him into my former routine, starting the day with a walk to Prêt A Manger on Kensington High Street for a cappuccino. The journey takes me past my old apartment and as I turn into my former road I am accosted by a familiar voice shouting 'CAROLINE!'

It's Trevor, one of the refuse collectors that I used to chat to when I lived here – a friendly chap and always a rich source of information as to what was going on in the street. I'm touched that he remembers me but I never did have the heart to tell him that I'm not called Caroline. (Corinne, Caroline, Madame Willer: everyone, it seems, wants to call me by something other than my real name.) 'HOW ARE YOU CAROLINE?' he shouts. 'HOW'S FRANCE? ARE YOU BACK FOR GOOD?'

'That's the million-dollar question,' I think to myself, stopping to talk to him.

'You've got a dog!' says Trevor, patting Biff on the head. 'Where did you get him from?'

'France,' I say, proudly. 'He's a French dog.'

'Are you still happy in France then?' asks Trevor, cutting straight to the chase.

'Well, I'm beginning to miss London,' I say, not wanting to explain the real reason why France has lost its allure. 'And what's been happening here?'

'Oh, the usual stuff,' he replies, before giving me an update on my former neighbours: the girl at seventy-three put all her boyfriend's clothes out with the refuse after discovering he'd been cheating on her; the banker at number eight is having problems with his builder; and Ricky, the blonde, angelic-looking teenager who is responsible for nearly all crime in the area – everything from car mirror theft to daylight muggings and break-ins – has been sent to the south coast on a two-week 'victim awareness' course. (Presumably aimed at making young villains more aware of the effect of their crimes, rather than how to spot a potential victim.)

'Nice to have you back, anyway,' says Trevor, throwing three black bin bags into a pile on the pavement. 'You take care now, Caroline.'

It's amazing how little has changed in the four years I've been away. I see many familiar faces marching down the long road towards the tube station, smartly dressed, ready for the cut and thrust of office life. I admire them for having the discipline and the drive to hold down full-time jobs, to get themselves to an office for a 9.00 a.m. deadline every day – something I'm not sure I'd be capable of any more. Ironically, given that many of my friends tell me I have the perfect life, I feel a little jealous of these smartly dressed Londoners, with a structure to their day, meetings to go to and colleagues with whom to go to lunch. But then I remember the reality of office life – the backstabbing, the bitchiness, the assistant who seemed so sweet and unassuming when I hired her, but turned out to be the Rosa Klebb of the beauty world, in hipsters and high heels.

I was so unsuited to office life that for the year or so before I moved to France, I worked from home as a freelancer. It was then that I got to know many of my neighbours. To avoid spending quality time with my iMac, I was always looking for an excuse to pop out and buy something – everything from printer cartridges to Kit Kats – which created lots of opportunities for neighbourly encounters. Several of the people in my street, on the outer borders of Kensington, were on 'care in the community' programmes and always keen for a chat. And, unless I was on a tight deadline, I nearly always obliged in order to be polite.

I spot one of them – Jeff, a friendly man with learning difficulties – crossing the road to speak to me. Like Trevor, he seems delighted that I'm back. 'And who's this little chap?' he asks, pointing at Biff, who is sitting politely, looking up at him.

'That's my dog, Biff.'

'Isn't he lovely,' says Jeff, looking charmed. 'Ahh, look at him! He's got a nice attitude that dog has.'

I laugh, and after a ten-minute chat, I continue on my way, touched by the little exchange with Jeff and his heart-warming assessment of Biff's personality.

We cut through Holland Park and I let Biff off his lead when we reach the main path around the playing field. As he springs over damp, caramel-coloured leaves to say hello to a Jack Russell, many people turn their heads to admire him. This dog gets way more attention than an It-bag. 'What breed is he?' asks a glamorous woman in Ugg boots and tight jeans. It's the first of many such enquiries. Everyone wants to know what breed Biff is and most are amazed when I tell them that he is of mixed parentage.

'But he holds himself like a show dog,' the sturdily built owner of an English bull terrier says. 'The way he stands, everything about him suggests that he is a thoroughbred.'

'Well, he does have a lot of self-esteem,' I reply.

As we walk through the park, Biff approaches every dog that we meet for a quick sniff, like an over-friendly guest at a cocktail party. He is thrilled to encounter so many other dogs and he particularly enjoys chasing the pigeons near the entrance. It's with great difficulty, and after an unseemly skirmish in some bushes, that I manage to clip him back on his lead for the walk along the high street. I am nervous that, after the huge open spaces and calm of the countryside, Biff might be overwhelmed by the crowds, the traffic and the pace of urban life. But it soon becomes obvious that there is no need to worry. This dog, I realise, is equally at home in town and country. And I love him all the more for it.

He trots along the high street entirely at ease, as if he has been a Kensington resident all his life. He is delighted by the new smells and the bountiful feast that the pavements of West London have to offer – everything from burger wrappings to bits of old croissant and half a chocolate bar. The most he ever found in Villiers was an old chicken bone. For a dog, such rich and varied pickings must be the equivalent of dining at The Ivy. Many people, I notice, are smiling at us. Biff seems to have noticed too, that he's attracting a lot of attention, because he's added a little bounce and swagger to his step, as if the pavement were a catwalk.

We head to Prêt A Manger, where the staff greet me like a long-lost member of the family. 'Great to see you again,' one of them says, and I marvel again at how little changes in four years and how many of the faces behind the counter are exactly the same. It's all very reassuring – and flattering that so many people remember me. Perhaps, I think to myself, it wasn't necessary to move to a small village in France to feel part of a community, after all.

We can't stay because dogs aren't allowed in Prêt, so, clutching my cappuccino, I go and buy the newspapers from the stand outside M&S, where the ruddy-faced seller greets me with a cheery, 'Hello love, I haven't seen you in ages. Where have you been?'

'France,' I reply.

'What's France got that we haven't?' he asks, producing a box of dog biscuits.

'I'm starting to wonder that myself,' I say.

Biff immediately sits bolt upright, like a solider, as he always does when food is a possibility. He's having the time of his life, with all these new experiences, unexpected treats and lavish compliments from strangers.

Walking home through the park, I feel happier than I have done in ages. It's so great to be away from the Luis situation that I start to figure out ways that I could move back to Blighty. I've loved living in France but maybe the abrupt ending with Luis is a sign that the time has come to move on again. It's not going to be easy. First, I will need to find somewhere for us to live. Perhaps I could speak to Rachel about renting her spare room on a long-term basis. And I will have to work harder if I move back – that thought really doesn't appeal – as it's a lot more expensive living in London than rural France. But I'm surprised at how quickly I've slotted back into my old lifestyle and impressed that Biff has made the transition to urban life with such ease.

That afternoon, aware that Biff's lead is looking a bit chewed and that his standard of grooming is not quite up to that of the thoroughbreds in the park, I take him to a pet shop in Notting Hill called The Dogs Frolics. It's so posh you have to ring a doorbell to get in, as if entering a Bond Street jewellers. This shop caters for a superior class of canine, offering an extensive collection of cashmere dog sweaters and £200-plus leads in sumptuous chocolate-brown plaited leather by Italian label Bottega Veneta, more usually known for its super-expensive handbags. While I'm browsing in the dog Barbour section – yes, I know clothes for dogs are *so* wrong, but there's no harm in looking – a woman in a green Range Rover pulls up on double yellow lines outside, and charges into the shop, holding the exact Bottega Veneta lead I'd been looking at, but bearing the intricate work of canine incisors. 'I need another,' she says, brusquely. 'Betty has eaten it.' As she hands over her credit card, I look out of the window and see one *very* pampered cockerpoodle – easily the most fashionable breed in the London parks – sitting in the passenger seat.

Unlike Betty, Biff won't be sporting what is obviously this season's must-have accessory for four-legged folk. I buy him a nice new lead but made from braided nylon rather than plaited Italian leather. And because his beanbag – the one printed with bones and 'woofs' – has lost its bounce, I splash out on a luxurious taupe-coloured doughnut for him. Its subtle colour and suede-like fabric is much more in keeping with the aesthetics of Rachel's flat. I also book him in for a grooming appointment (the first one available is in ten days time). As we drive home, I wonder if he will like his new bed or whether he will prefer the comforting, familiar smell of his old one. Again, I need not have worried. That night, he climbs into his plush new doughnut without so much as a look back at his old beanbag. A new bed, I think, for his new London life.

Over the next couple of weeks I catch up with those of my friends who still live in London (many have moved out after having children). We nearly always meet in a pub, rather than the fashionable West End bars of my former life, as I don't like leaving Biff home alone. I've found one or two pubs in West London that are dog friendly, my favourite being the Ladbroke Arms, opposite Notting Hill police station, where the bar staff are friendly and offer Biff a bowl of water, while he helps himself to any stray crisps on the floor.

It's not just Biff who is enjoying life in the metropolis. I'm delighted to be within walking distance of an M&S food hall again; to resume twice-weekly Pilates classes; and to be able to buy British newspapers, particularly the Saturday and Sunday ones with all their supplements intact. Most wonderful of all is the fact that there is life after 7.00 p.m., that it is possible to pick up the phone and have an Indian takeaway delivered to your door, and that the day is no longer sliced into two halves, as it is in rural France, with everything grinding to a halt from 12.00 p.m. to 2.00 p.m. And I love the customer service – the friendly checkout staff in Waitrose and the M&S food hall, and the idea that the customer is to be cherished, not treated like a shoplifter – that is taken for granted in London. I really appreciate not having to open my bag at the till – as is required in France – to prove that I haven't stolen anything.

It takes a few days to acclimatise to this newfound freedom and to get used to the idea of shops being open at a time that is actually convenient. It's hard to drop the habits I've acquired in France: on more than one occasion, I find myself walking into a restaurant or the local corner shop, flashing everyone a big smile and wishing them a friendly *'Bonjour'* – required etiquette in the French countryside but deviant behaviour in West London, where people respond by averting their eyes and backing away.

Biff, meanwhile, rapidly becomes one of the most popular dogs in the park, thanks to his handsome features and his friendly, non-dominant nature. His life becomes a social whirl and he befriends even the scariest pets, including Carver the pit bull, whose arrival in the park causes other owners to clip their dogs on their leads and walk swiftly away. Endearingly, on the few occasions when Biff's friendly overtures are met with a growl or a cantankerous snarl, he merely rolls onto his back with his paws in the air – the canine equivalent of waving the white flag.

He's never really in any danger, as thanks to his fitness levels – the result of all those long hikes and fruitless pursuits of rabbits in the French countryside – I am confident that he can outrun most of the urban dogs that we meet. In Holland Park and Kensington Gardens, Filipina maids with ball-firing devices watch aghast as he dashes out of nowhere to retrieve the balls they have fired for their charges. I then have to begin an embarrassing chase around the park to try and retrieve the ball that he has stolen.

Standing in the rain one morning while Biff sniffs around a park bench, I get talking to a fashionably dressed man in a dark overcoat. 'What kind of dog is that?' I ask, pointing to the mink-coloured, anorexic-looking creature that is trying to mount Biff.

'It's an Italian greyhound,' he informs me. 'The fastest dog in the park.' As if to prove it, he fires a tennis ball into the distance and the greyhound streaks across the park in pursuit. And so does Biff.

'That's my boy,' I think, as he beats the greyhound to the ball and turns nimbly on his large paws, in full control of it, like the Cristiano Ronaldo of the dog world. He gives a playful little bark, inviting the greyhound to tackle him. I'm so proud of him. This Italian greyhound might have an expensive pedigree but it's my little French rescue dog that got the ball.

'Blimey,' says the greyhound owner, visibly taken aback. 'What kind of dog is that?'

'He's a mix,' I say proudly, before launching into my spiel about his unknown parentage and the fact that he came from a rescue centre in Bergerac.

Basking in all the attention that Biff attracts, I almost forget about Luis. Compliments rain down on us wherever we go. 'What form!' cries one man, the owner of a listless Weimaraner, as Biff charges past on Hampstead Heath one Sunday morning.

'Oh, isn't he *magnificent*,' says a woman with a Pekingese in Kensington Gardens. 'Is he a Tibetan terrier?'

'I don't know what he is,' I reply and before I know it a little crowd of dog walkers has assembled and we are discussing whether or not he might be a Tibetan terrier, a schnauzer, or a Dandie Dinmont.

'He's possibly got some Portuguese water dog in him,' says a man in omelette-coloured cords. The parks of West London certainly seem to be home to some very exotic-sounding breeds. It gives me great pleasure that my little mixed-race dog – my wild-haired country bumpkin – has integrated so well. And I absolutely adore the earnest small boy, who asks, 'Excuse me, is your dog magical?'

'Why do you think that?'

'Because he always seems to get the ball.'

On another occasion, checking my emails in the Internet cafe on Kensington High Street, the man sitting next to me startles me by saying, 'I think he loves you.' Strangers rarely talk to each other in London, so I'm a little taken aback.

'Sorry?'

'Your dog. I think he loves you.' He nods at Biff, who is sitting patiently at my feet, staring up at me with love-struck eyes, as if overwhelmed with gratitude that I've brought him to this wonderful place, London.

My favourite encounter, however, is with a man who looks like a rock star – shoulder-length hair, wealthy looking, dressed in jeans and a leather jacket – in Holland Park. I've seen him several times reading the *Financial Times* in the outdoor cafe. 'Bloody hell, your dog is fit,' he declares one day, as Biff enjoys a morning frolic with Walter the whippet. Dog walking acquires an extra frisson after that, and before I know it I am getting dressed up to go to the park, switching my trainers for high-heeled boots on a bench near the gates.

Unfortunately, the rock star eventually turns out to be *very* friendly with the lithe, velvet-tracksuit clad owner of Chloe, a rather showy cockerpoodle. But, there is no doubt about it: in London, as in France, a dog is social WD-40, oiling the wheels of human interaction.

I soon know most of the park regulars by name, although I can't always remember the names of their owners. There is Cherie, the vain poodle with a pink Goyard collar and orange Hermès lead; Hector the rare-breed bulldog whose owner proudly tells me that he is insured for £60,000; and Winston, the rather snooty-looking schnauzer. For some reason, most of the dogs in the London parks have human names, which makes me wonder if I should change Biff's name to 'Bill' or 'Bob'. But with his roguish features and cheeky demeanour, he is definitely more Biff in character.

Although I am supposed to be researching features while I'm here, my days become a social whirl of friendly encounters and conversations in the park. In the mornings, I join a group of dog walkers who meet for morning coffee in the outdoor cafe, where everyone is bonded in dislike of a community plod with a pathological hatred of dogs. He spends his days thinking up new ways to persecute dog owners, hiding behind trees in order to catch those who haven't cleared up after their pets – an unthinkable breach of urban dog etiquette – and posturing menacingly outside the cafe with his notebook.

Anne, a small, feisty Irish woman and owner of Benji, an equally feisty corgi, makes me laugh one morning when she confronts the policeman, who is standing, notebook poised, as if ready to book one of us should our dogs stray into a no-go zone such as the Japanese garden. 'I'm not being funny or anything but you're wasted in this park,' she tells the policeman. 'With your skills, you should be out on the streets catching criminals and muggers.'

As the weeks pass – and the novelty of introducing Biff to London begins to wear off – I realise that owning a dog in London is not all a walk in the park. Unlike my village in France where Biff is welcome almost everywhere – 'Where's

Biff?' I'm asked, accusingly, on the rare occasions I venture out without him – in London's shops and cafes he is about as welcome as a rodent infestation. I'm particularly offended by the reception we are given at Oxfam while attempting to drop off a bag of clothes. Hardly is Biff's paw in the door before a security guard comes rushing over to bar our entry. 'The dog is a health-and-safety risk,' he charmlessly informs me. In a shop full of old clothes? With a few notable exceptions – Waterstone's on Kensington High Street is one, the Conran Shop is another – Biff is just not welcome.

It's a problem, as I wouldn't dream of leaving Biff tied up outside a store, even for a few minutes, as my very real fear is that he wouldn't be there when I got back. If people can be bothered to steal car wing mirrors in my street, I'm not taking any risks with my dog. But it severely restricts my movements. No popping into a supermarket on the spur of the moment for a ready-made dinner for one. I have to plan ahead. And nor can I leave Biff at home. In France, he is happy to watch the world (OK, a handful of retired neighbours) go by from his perch on top of the old-fashioned radiator in *le petit salon*; but here in London, the windows are quite high and he can't see out of them, thus removing his favourite *divertissement*. On the one occasion I do leave him, there is no response when I open the door on my return and call his name. I find him perched on the high, narrow window ledge, looking very sheepish. I've no idea how he got up there, or for how long he's been stuck, but I feel very guilty as I scoop him off the ledge and place him gently back on the floor.

Living in a top-floor flat in London, I soon realise, is not ideal if you own a dog. Descending three flights of stairs to walk him four or five times a day becomes a bit of a chore – not least because, if it's been raining, I have to carry him up the stairs on my return to avoid muddy paw prints on the communal carpet. It's so much easier in rural France, where I just have to step out of my front door and there are open fields five minutes away. The most difficult walk is the last one of the day. Curled up watching television, with the rain beating against the window panes, I can never quite relax, knowing that at some point I must pull on my boots, descend three flights of stairs, walk Biff, carry him back up the staircase and clean his paws.

The over-vigilant policeman in Holland Park also starts to irritate me. Each morning he eyes me with suspicion as if I'd walked into the park with an AK-47. Surely he can find something more useful to do than harass dog walkers, I think to myself? As Biff starts to look a little listless – though he perks up when we run errands and always enjoys the lengthy half-hour wait in the local post office – I start to feel guilty. I'm sure that he's missing the long walks and wide open spaces on our doorstep in France and poking his head down rabbit holes. I am too (though not poking my head down rabbit holes, obviously).

As November turns into December, I start to doubt that I can live in London full-time again. Now that the initial euphoria of having Prêt A Manger cappuccinos and M&S food hall on my doorstep has worn off, I am starting to miss my life in France. I long for evenings curled up on the sofa by my woodburner in my cosy little cottage and I miss the daily hikes in the countryside. Walking along Kensington High Street one evening, past the shop windows twinkling with fairy lights and Christmas displays, and the busy restaurants and bars, I feel like an interloper, a mere visitor. Ditto when I meet up with my friends at former haunts in Notting Hill. Those places are part of my past; they belong to someone else now. Like Biff, I feel displaced. I will always love London, but in small doses. This is no longer my natural habitat.

The feeling is reinforced one evening while shopping without aim in Selfridges – something I often dreamed of being able to do in France – when I experience a powerful sense of disconnect. The sound of a brass band playing 'Silent Night' drifts up the escalator from the basement, and I survey the hordes of people, many of them still in their smart office clothes, negotiating the store with a sort of harassed determination, and suddenly I feel completely alienated from my surroundings – the beautiful handbags, the counters stacked with make-up and perfume and luxury bath oils. There is nothing I can buy in this store, lovely though it all is, that will bring me long-term happiness. I've tried that formula before. And I know it doesn't work. So what am I doing, mindlessly shopping at 9.00 p.m. on a Thursday evening, when most people are at home with loved ones? In France, I realise, I feel less like an outsider than I do here. In my coat pocket, I feel my phone beep with an incoming text. It's a message from Delphine. 'How are you my friend? When are you coming back?' It seems like a sign. The next morning I book a crossing back to France and late on Saturday afternoon, I load up the car again with Biff, his toys and his luxury doughnut, throw in a Christmas pudding, crackers and cranberry sauce, and set off for Portsmouth. Luis or not, I'm going back to France for Christmas.

Early on Sunday morning, I pull over in the little port of Ouistreham, to walk Biff. Emerging from under the passenger seat, he sniffs the air appreciatively, jumps out of the car and does a little bunny hop of happiness to be back on French soil again.

Chapter 20

Le Retour

EVEN THOUGH I can't escape from The Devil (or 'Divil' as Delphine calls him) – his loud laughter can be heard next door most evenings, and his car is often parked outside my house – it's good to be back. Biff seems to have a new spring in his paws as we resume our old routine of long morning walks followed by coffee and a chat with Dylan and his customers in the Liberty Bookshop, and evenings curled up by the log fire. Once again, it's the simplest things that make me happy: a hint of pink sunset in a white winter sky, the scent of wood smoke on a cold evening, or having friends round for a stew that's been simmering all day.

I'm also delighted to find that the *boulangerie* has been bought by a charming French couple in their late twenties, Amelie and Grégoire. A few times I've spotted René, the former owner, in the shop chatting to them, or in the kitchen at the back, explaining how the various pieces of bread-making equipment work, and he looks like a different person. It's not just because he's dressed in civilian clothes rather than his baker's uniform. He looks happy again, like several bags of flour have been lifted from his shoulders. He won't say what he is planning to do next but the rumour in the village is that he might be going to work as the *pâtissier* for a big bakery in Poitiers. His flair for a choux bun and *chocolat croustillant* is such that his skills will always be in demand.

Travis calls to tell me that he has made a snap decision to spend Christmas in France and would like to meet me for lunch. I suggest the Mad Hatter's Kitchen – a charming farmhouse restaurant hidden in the depths of the Poitevin countryside. It's owned by a British couple who, several times a week, open up their private, rustic-chic dining room to paying guests, so that it feels like a secret destination. Anita, one of my friends from line dancing, and her husband first discovered it when buying a free-range turkey at the farm shop last Christmas. Since then, news of the Hatters' home cooking – in particular, the three-course Sunday lunch – using fresh produce from their garden has spread rapidly through the region by word of mouth.

The decor in the rustic dining room is just delightful and straight out of a French country interiors book, with old flagstone floors, a big wooden staircase, antique mirrors, hangings and vases of fresh garden flowers thrown together in a seemingly effortless way (Charlotte and Glen, the owners, previously had an antiques business). It's all charmingly homespun with an atmosphere like a private house party. Since Delphine and I are regulars – my French friend absolutely adores it – we usually know many of the people at the adjoining wooden tables.

So two days before Christmas, I drive 40 kilometres to meet Travis there for a pre-Christmas lunch. I take the narrow back roads and unfortunately miss an important turn, so that I end up lost, driving down muddy farm tracks in the middle of nowhere. In the French countryside signs are very intermittent on the so-called 'white roads' – 'white' because that's how they appear on a map – and it's not like you can stop and ask a passing stranger. Even if I could, they'd probably be very alarmed at the sight of someone dressed in a short, thin cocktail dress and very high heels in the middle of a freezing winter afternoon. (Well, it is Christmas and I wanted to make an effort.) Fortunately, I can get a signal on my phone, so I call the Mad Hatter's Kitchen and Charlotte, the blonde proprietress – who actually does look a little like Alice in Wonderland – manages to figure out where I've gone wrong and give me directions.

Pulling up in the gravel driveway, I'm charmed, as always, by the big, ramshackle house, with its pale-blue shutters and multi-coloured lights strung haphazardly around the door. There are chickens of all colours and denominations wandering around outside as well as a field of horses, and sheep and a big, black hairy pig in a pen nearby. Inside the packed dining room, a string of twinkling white lights has been thrown casually around a Louis Philippe mirror, and a big vase of silver-painted twigs has been placed in the window.

Travis is sitting at a table near the woodburner. Dressed in jeans and a grey sweater with a stripy scarf wound around his neck, he is looking surprisingly relaxed. This despite the fact that his job, I know, has been super-stressful lately, culminating in a recent showdown with the newsreader, Kelly Drubber.

'So,' he says, after making a big fuss of Biff. 'You decided to come back?'

'Yes. A bit like you, I made a snap decision to return for Christmas. I don't really know what I'll do after that. But I've missed France a lot.'

'Any news from Luis?'

'No, but I'm philosophical about it,' I lie. 'He gave me a good... summer, so I can't complain.'

Travis raises an eyebrow. 'I thought for a moment that you were going to say something else then.'

'That too,' I say, with a smile that is way more cheery than I actually feel about the situation. The fact is that since I got back just over a week ago, it's felt like Luis and his larger-than-life presence have been following me around. Not only is there the sound of his macho laugh at 7 rue St Benoit to deal with nearly every night – he seems unable to keep away from his friends next door – but he seems to pop up everywhere. While filling my car with petrol a few days ago, for example, he pulled up in the white Supodal van at the opposite pump and jumped out with a big grin and a cheery *'Bonjour'*. I've mastered the art of blanking him completely, but it's a bit difficult when someone is standing mere feet away, on the other side of a petrol pump. Obviously, I opted for the minimum delivery (five litres) before driving off with an unintentional screech of tyres. The following day, I bumped into him in the vegetable section at Intermarché (he was minus the girlfriend this time). I quickly dropped the courgettes I was buying, and made straight for the checkout. Unfortunately, he followed me and a minute or so later, he was standing at the opposite till, staring directly over at me. He seems to think that it's all an amusing game. The girlfriend, meanwhile, is often to be seen sitting in cafes on her own or moping around the village looking glum.

'It's really strange, what happened,' says Travis. 'I still can't believe it. Especially having seen how he was with you.'

'Well at least I had four months of undiluted happiness before it went pear-shaped. And I guess nothing lasts forever.'

'On that note,' says Travis, with a big smile. 'I've got something to tell you.'

'What?'

'I'm moving to France full-time as from the New Year.'

'No way!'

'Yes, I got made redundant from my job three days ago in the latest cull of staff, which is why I've decided to come out for Christmas. The pay-off wasn't huge but if I'm careful I should be able to live out here for at least a year. So I'm going to go back to London after Christmas, rent my house out and move out here full time in early January.'

'Oh my God, that's BRILLIANT news.' (Redundancy, I know, is not usually something to celebrate but only a few days ago Travis was talking of quitting his job anyway, so to be paid to leave is an unexpected bonus.)

'Tell me about it,' says Travis, pouring himself another glass of wine. 'Finally, I'm going to get to live my own French dream, rather than doing it vicariously through phone calls to you.'

As usual, lunch is superb – turkey with all the trimmings and the most fantastic array of vegetable dishes including red cabbage, carrot and swede mash, roasted parsnips and courgettes as well as platters of crispy roast potatoes. And just as the main course is served, I look out of the window and see snowflakes falling outside. At first it's just a few but within minutes, it's as if a shimmering fibre optic curtain has descended on the countryside, as the snow falls down at a steady pace. It's quite magical. I honestly can't think of a better setting for a pre-Christmas lunch.

We talk about Travis's plans for his house and his new life in France. I'm a little worried that for someone who has held down a fast-paced TV job in London, life in rural France might be a little... lacking in excitement. But as Travis talks about his plans – he seems particularly excited by the idea of growing his own potatoes, which is odd for someone who views carbohydrates with horror – it's clear that he is really looking forward to it. He talks about his plans for a vegetable patch in the same feverish way that he might once have talked about owning a BMW convertible. His new goal in life, it seems, is not to be rich but to be self-sufficient for a year.

'But you do realise,' I say, 'that it won't be as easy for a gay guy, even a good-looking one like you, to find a boyfriend out here as it would be in the city.'

'Don't you believe it,' says Travis with a knowing wink. 'There are loads of us poofs hanging out in the French countryside. As a matter of fact, I've got a blind date arranged with someone in your village next week. A guy called René.'

'Well you didn't waste much time,' I say. 'What does he do, this René?'

'I don't know but I gather he just sold his own business. He sounds really nice.'

'I'm sure he will be,' I say, with an equally knowing wink. 'I have a good feeling about René.'

'Oh my God,' says Travis, as we tuck into Christmas pudding and the snow continues to fall outside. 'I forgot to tell you about Annabel and Charles.'

'What's happened?' I ask. 'Please don't tell me they've asked you to look after their dogs.'

'No, they've split up,' says Travis. 'Annabel had some huge fall-out with the girl staying in her gîte – Andy Lawton's girlfriend or ex-girlfriend, or whatever her current status is.'

'No surprises there,' I say. 'Did she let the dogs out by mistake?'

'No, the girlfriend said she was going shopping but came back early because she'd forgotten her wallet and found Annabel snooping through her stuff. She was furious, there was a big argument and rather than just apologising, Annabel retaliated by accusing her of all sorts of things.'

'Like what?'

'Breaking the washing machine, which was apparently ancient, and damaging stuff in the gîte. She also accused her of flirting with Charles.'

'That woman is crazy.'

'Tell me about it. Anyway, the girlfriend packed her bags and has had to move in with Andy, who is furious with Annabel. And it seems Annabel won't give the deposit back.'

'Oh dear.'

'Then Charles simply decided he'd had enough of falling out with people, so he's asked Annabel for a divorce and moved into the gîte himself while they try to sell the house.'

'Oh my word. And how do you know all this?'

'Charles phoned me. He's a nice guy.'

'Well, good for him.'

'Oh, I almost forgot. The main reason that he phoned me was to ask if there was any way I could arrange a proper introduction to "that nice lady mayor from Puysoleil".'

'You mean Delphine?'

'Yes. She is single isn't she?'

'Well, I could ask her,' I say. 'But I know she has many admirers, including several farmers in her commune, and I don't think she is looking for anyone at the moment. It's not that long since she got divorced.'

When we leave the restaurant in the late afternoon, snowflakes are still falling from the sky like sequins. All around us, fields, roads and sky appear to have merged into an opaque white blur. The drive home is quite difficult and at one point the car slides out of control and to the centre of the narrow road, as I negotiate a bend. Thankfully, nothing is coming in the opposite direction.

Shaken, I crawl along at 20 kilometres per hour for the remainder of the journey.

Even the lorries that normally fly around these back roads at reckless speeds have slowed to a crawl, although it doesn't make them any less menacing. Each time I see the headlights of a large truck coming towards me, I pray that its tyres have a good grip, the driver doesn't have a heart condition, his wife hasn't recently walked out on him, and that he hasn't drunk wine with lunch. Biff can probably feel the fear as he's very still in the back. I take comfort in the fact that at least he'll be OK if we break down, as he's wearing a fur coat. But I'm not dressed in the best clothes for navigating snowfall in the depths of rural France, and if we do have to get out and walk, I won't get very far in my Prada shoes. I silently berate myself for not keeping a pair of wellies or even a blanket in the car. The worst scenario is that I'll end up trapped in a ditch as happened a few winters ago, when my car slid off an icy road on the way to Limoges airport and I had to be pulled out by a tractor. Driving in snow and ice is not my favourite thing.

I am so focused on possible perils that I hardly even think of Luis, whom I'm pretty sure has gone back to Portugal with his girlfriend for Christmas. Two days ago I saw the girlfriend carrying a huge black nylon bag between their apartment and 7 rue St Benoit. (It gave me some solace to note that, even though it looked like they were preparing to go away together, she didn't look that happy about it.) I haven't seen either of them or Luis's car in the village since then, so I imagine they're on a warm beach somewhere drinking chilled sangria as I battle home through the freezing snow.

It's a huge relief to finally arrive back in rue St Benoit. I close the shutters against the blue-white afternoon light and get the woodburner going, feeling sorry for anyone who is still out on the icy roads. Safely inside my warm house, I monitor the snow from my bedroom window, as it continues to lighten the landscape outside. Close to midnight, I pull on some thick socks and wellies and throw a warm coat and a big purple scarf over my cocktail dress to take Biff out for his last walk before bedtime.

I trudge up rue St Benoit towards the square, walking on crisp, crunchy, unspoilt snow, enjoying the childish thrill of being the first to leave footprints. My French neighbours, who always take refuge behind closed shutters in extreme weather, be it hot or cold, have probably been indoors since the snow started to fall this afternoon. I don't blame them. If it wasn't for Biff, I certainly wouldn't be venturing out in this cold (minus 5 degrees according to the clock above the pharmacy). But I've never seen Villiers look so enchanting. The white duvet of snow is the perfect foil for the red and gold Christmas lights glittering in the window of the Liberty Bookshop; and the string of blue icicles dancing in the organic *épicerie*. It's a scene of glittering, Christmassy perfection.

Back home I watch the late-night news bulletin, which is dominated by scenes of snow and travel chaos, with flights cancelled and Eurostars stuck in tunnels. I'm so glad that I don't have to go anywhere tomorrow, Christmas Eve, other than the Café du Commerce for lunch with Delphine. I fall asleep grateful that I'm in my warm bed, rather than stuck in the Channel Tunnel, or travelling on treacherous roads on such a glacial night.

But in the early hours of Christmas Eve I am woken from a deep sleep by the sound of Biff barking. I figure he will settle down eventually, but he doesn't, so I drag myself out of bed and over to the window and standing in the snowy white street below, dressed entirely in black… is Luis. At first, I think I'm imagining it, that's it's not really him. But no, his little white Clio is parked opposite and he is standing there, under a new moon, looking up at my window. I look at my watch: it's 2.30 a.m. What on earth is he up to? Shocked and half asleep, I open the window without thinking of the hurt that he has inflicted or the anger that I feel. Suddenly, all of that dissolves like a globally warmed glacier. 'Luis?' I say, just to be sure it's him and not some Christmas apparition.

'*Oui chérie*, it's me.'

'What are you doing there?'

'I have just driven to Portugal and back,' he says, 'without stopping.'

'You've done what?'

'*Ka-renne*, I have come back to you. I've taken the other one back to Portugal. It's finished. It's you I want.'

It takes me a moment to piece together what he's saying. If I've understood his heavily accented French correctly, Luis is standing outside my window on Christmas Eve, having delivered his former girlfriend to Portugal for good. Not in my wildest dreams could I have imagined such a scenario. 'Are you awake?' he asks. 'Can I come in?'

I'm tempted to run downstairs and open the door, throw my arms around him and drag him upstairs to my bed but I don't. Even in the hazy hours of early morning, I know that I cannot just let him back into my life so easily.

'I haven't slept for nearly forty-eight hours,' he says.

'You bloody idiot,' I think. Instead, I reply, 'Well, that's very dangerous. In this weather, you could have killed yourself and others too.'

'I drank a lot of Red Bull,' he says. 'I wanted to make sure that she went back to Portugal this time so that I could come back to you. Please, *chérie*, open the door.'

'No, not now,' I say. 'I'm tired.' Which is a ridiculous thing to say to someone who has just driven to Portugal and back.

After more pleading, he says: '*OK chérie, je comprends. À demain,*' in that way he has of making things sound like an order.

'*Bonne nuit,*' I say.

'*Chérie,*' he says in a plaintive way. 'What are you doing for Christmas?'

'I have plans,' I say.

'Spend it with me, *chérie*, just the two of us together.'

'We'll see.'

He seems pleased with this response. '*OK, à demain, chérie,*' he says. He leaves his car parked outside my house and I watch as he walks up rue St Benoit towards the square and his apartment, almost staggering with fatigue, his footprints merging with mine in the snow. I go back to bed thinking about the unexpected twists and turns that life takes. Not even Delphine – who was always convinced that Luis would come back to me – could have predicted this. Driving home this afternoon I imagined him loved-up and lying on a warm(ish) beach somewhere. How ironic that he was in fact, battling home in the snow too.

On Christmas Eve, I wake early and elated and look out of the window to find that a new layer of snow has fallen, covering both mine and Luis's sets of footprints. Everything (myself included) feels new and invigorated, set against a glistening white backdrop. I walk Biff down to the partially frozen river, which looks like a shimmering grey ribbon in the early morning light. He runs around the picnic area like a mad thing, a blur of black fur, making little barks of excitement, his paws creating little clouds of white powder as he bounds around in this new white substance. It makes my heart sing to watch him.

The sky is unusually pretty – white with a beguiling hint of blush-pink light, reflected, to stunning effect, in the part of the river that hasn't frozen over. The trees meanwhile, look like they've been dipped in Swarovski crystals, with beads of snow glistening on their branches. It's as if nature is conspiring to create a spectacular backdrop to a possible reconciliation with Luis. But I really have some thinking to do. The brutal fact is that he has spent the last two months with those brown arms wrapped around another *chérie* at night.

By late morning, there is no sign of Luis, which makes me wonder if I dreamt last night's scenario. But I figure that after his two-day road trip he is probably sleeping. Shortly after midday, I crunch through the snow to the Café du Commerce to meet Delphine for lunch. She is looking very dressed up in a purple ruffled skirt, with violet beads around her neck. She is carrying a striking new bag in shiny purple leather – 'My Christmas present to me,' she says. Later this afternoon, she will do the rounds of her commune delivering 'the packets' to the elderly. This year, it's a really good bottle of red wine and *confit de canard*.

'I 'ave some very good news,' she tells me. 'I have now finished consulting with all the lawyers and we are going to re-open the bar in Puysoleil early in the New Year.' Didier, she goes on to tell me, is now in jail and since Delphine's little village hit the national news for all the wrong reasons, she has been inundated with people wanting to take over the lease to the bar. 'I am very astonished,' she says. 'I didn't think anyone would be interested in this.'

'But why wouldn't people be interested? Puysoleil is small but it's very pretty and if the new proprietor's food is good enough, Le Café de la Paix could become a destination restaurant, with people coming from miles around.'

'Just like they did for the prostitutes you mean?' says Delphine, with one of her mischievous smiles.

I laugh. 'Well why not? Except this time they would be coming for tarts of a different kind.' I always thought that the scandal of the summer would put Puysoleil on the map and that some good would come out of it.

The most likely candidates to take on the bar, it seems, are two sisters, one of whom is a very good cook. And once all the legal work is tied up, Delphine is planning a big re-opening party.

Once we've ordered, I tell Delphine about Luis pitching up on my doorstep last night. Gratifyingly, her eyes widen and she says 'Oh my goodness!' in all the right places.

'I told you that this story was not over yet,' she says, before sounding a note of caution. 'But do you think The Divil is telling the truth? Maybe he has just taken this girl back to her family for Christmas and she will be returning in the New Year.'

'Well, yes, I did think of that,' I say, deflated that Delphine, who is very wise in matters of human nature, has thought along similar lines. 'It struck me as a little odd that he would bother to run this girl all the way back to Portugal if he has split up with her.'

'Not necessarily,' says Delphine. 'Remember he is Portuguese and it is a different culture. Family ties are very important and if this girl was a friend of the family, he would have to be seen to do the right thing by her.'

'I guess.'

'Wait until you've heard what The Divil has to say,' says Delphine. 'But just be careful my friend.'

'I know,' I sigh. 'But it's going to be so difficult to resist. When I saw him standing beneath my window in the snow last night, I was just so happy.'

'I understand completely,' says Delphine. 'These scorpions [she means Scorpios] are very spicy and irresistible. They have the power to make you very miserable and very happy in just a short space of time.'

Through the window I watch the snow fluttering down softly on the square. Right at this very moment, I cannot deny that I feel very happy. And that the spicy Devil has a lot to do with it.

'Oh, by the way – you have an admirer,' I say, suddenly remembering my conversation with Travis.

'C'est vrai?' says Delphine, her eyes widening.

'Yes, do you remember Charles, the Englishman in the Liberty Bookshop with his wife Annabel? They needed someone to look after their dogs.'

'Yes, I do.'

'Well he is divorcing Annabel. And he's asked for a proper introduction to you.'

Delphine laughs. 'Oh la la,' she says, waving her hand limply in front of her chest, in that funny little gesture she does. 'Oh, 'e is a very 'andsome and charming man and I'm flattered,' she says. 'But I don't think this is a good idea.' I don't press her any further.

After lunch, we wish each other Joyeux Noël with a hug outside. Delphine's daughter and son-in-law are arriving from Nantes this afternoon and she will be spending Christmas in the warm embrace of her family, in the little farming hamlet where they all have houses. She wants to know what I am doing and I tell her I will be spending Christmas day with Travis and some other friends. I walk back down rue St Benoit in the snow, which is now slippery and iced over, willing Luis's car to be there. And, as if by magic, it is. His white Clio is parked nose to nose with my tatty old Golf, as if kissing it. To confirm it's his car, I check for the magic combination of numbers on the registration plate – the 9470 that always quickens my pulse – and yes, they're there. No sign of Luis though. As I open the front door, I see a note on the doormat. I pick it up and see that it has three hearts scrawled on it, along with a very simple message: '*J'aime cherri*. Luis.'

I'm smiling at the misspelling of *chérie* and the fact he has omitted the 't' from '*je t'aime*' – this means that what he has actually written is, 'I love (a male) darling' – when he appears silently in the doorway. He's wearing jeans and a long-sleeved navy T-shirt – no sweater or jacket, even though it's snowing outside. I quickly take off my bobble hat and scarf, sending a little flurry of snow over the hallway and Biff, who has bounced into the hallway to greet me.

'*C'est moi, Luis,* who did that,' says The Devil, moving towards me and standing so close that his chest is touching mine, and I am forced to look up at him.

'I missed you,' he says, pushing my hair back behind my ears, and making Biff bark (whether out of excitement or to warn him off, I don't know).

'*Dans ton lit, maintenant!*' I shout at Biff, who, surprisingly, does what he is told and climbs into his bed.

I indicate for Luis to go into *le petit salon* and, after throwing another log on the fire, I sit down on the opposite sofa. Biff surveys the scene from his position, in between the two of us, as if he were a relationship counsellor or adjudicator. He seems to understand that Luis is in the *merde* and has some explaining to do.

'*Alors*, an explanation please,' I say.

'It's you that I want,' he says. 'I love you. That's all there is to say.'

'*Arrêtes tes conneries*,' I reply, sharply. 'Stop the bullshit and give me an explanation. Start by telling me how and when you met her.'

Biff stares at Luis as if he's as keen to hear what he's got to say as I am.

'She was a friend of the family that I've known her for a long time,' he explains, looking sheepish. 'But only as a friend. She is the ex-wife of my cousin.' This is the sort of explanation I am hoping to hear. So Delphine was right about the family connection.

'I bumped into her when I was in Portugal with Piedro.'

'And you decided to bring her back here?'

'No. She followed me.'

'Tell me the truth.'

'It's the truth. I swear. She followed me back from Portugal by bus and train. It was a complete surprise. Piedro and his girlfriend Paula picked her up from the station in Poitiers. That Saturday, when you saw us in the square, she had just arrived.'

I think back to that Saturday morning in October and all the shock and anger returns. 'You expect me to believe that she followed you back from Portugal, with no encouragement at all?'

'It's the truth,' he nods. 'It really got on my nerves. Three times I tried to make her go back. I even drove her to the station in Poitiers, but when we got there she refused to go. This time, I took her back to Portugal myself to make sure that she went.'

'Hmm.' I eye him with scepticism. Biff is doing likewise, his black eyes boring into Luis as if to try and get at the truth.

'I swear. All the time she was here I was thinking of you. Then you went away and I didn't know where you had gone or for how long. When I saw that the shutters of your house were open again last week and that you were back, I was so happy.'

'Well, if all that is true, why didn't you come and see me and explain?'

'Because I know you very well, *chérie*. I knew you would be mad and that you wouldn't take me back while she was around. So I decided the best thing was to try and get her to go back to Portugal and then explain.'

'And it took you two months?' I say.

'Yes,' he says. 'I'm sorry. I did think of coming to see you many times but I thought you would make a big display. Like that night when I was next door with Ruigi and Sergio and you called me into the street. It's true or not?'

'Of course I would have made a big scene,' I say, remembering the night in question, when I tried to embarrass him in front of his boss and colleagues.

'And then you went soon after and were gone for nearly two months, so I couldn't come and see you and explain,' he continues. 'I know you very well, *chérie*. You are very intelligent and have a strong character. Like me. We are very well matched. *Je t'aime.*' He gets up from the sofa and comes towards me.

Biff, looking very wise and superior in his doughnut, fires off a single, sharp warning bark as if to say 'Not so fast, mister'.

'Stop right there,' I say, signalling for Luis to sit down again, as I suddenly remember the encounter in the supermarket. 'If what you are saying is true, why did she tell me that she was your girlfriend and had been for a long time.'

'It's not true,' he says. 'She wasn't my girlfriend, though she wanted to be…'

He says this as if it was perfectly normal for any girl to want to be his *copine*.

'But she told me she was your girlfriend, while you were standing there.'

'She probably didn't understand. Her French was not any good.'

'It seemed to me like she understood,' I say. 'Did you sleep with her?'

He says nothing, confirming the worst.

God, I know I should send him packing right now, preferably with a bucket of icy water over his lush black hair. While this is a better explanation than I had hoped for, it is still nowhere near good enough. If what he is saying is true, he should have sent the Portuguese girl packing the minute she arrived, family honour or not. And he should have come knocking on my door with an explanation much sooner. 'Look, I need time to think about this,' I say.

'OK, *chérie*,' he says, sounding contrite. 'I understand. I will be waiting for you across the square.'

Chapter 21

Waiting for Me

NEW YEAR'S EVE and 'my family' in France are gathered around the wooden refectory table in my small, geranium-pink kitchen. We've had oysters and champagne (well, I had champagne but not oysters as unfortunately they make me ill) followed by Delia Smith's shepherd's pie. Midnight has passed and we've drunk a toast (or ten) to the coming year. Several people at the table are also beginning a new chapter in their lives. Travis, for example, is soon to move here full-time and start his own French adventure, while Delphine, who was unhappily married twelve months ago, is starting this year as an exuberantly happy single person. She also brings with her the exciting news that Le Café de la Paix will re-open its doors again in mid January with two new lady proprietors. Meanwhile, Charles – a last minute addition to our party, after Travis discovered he was spending New Year's Eve alone – is embarking on life as a single man, having broken free of Annabel 'Bitch' (as she is commonly known among the expat community). Also present are Steve and Sarah, whom Biff is especially delighted to see – he has in fact, squeezed himself onto the bench between his two former owners – and Jocelyn and Jill. For, yes, they are back together.

I'm not privy to the details that led to reconciliation, but I do know that Jocelyn was waiting at Charles de Gaulle airport for Jill when she returned from New Zealand on Christmas Day. The news has cheered everyone who knows them, though it is hard not to spare a thought for Gloria, whose exciting new love affair has come to an end. For every triumphant pairing, it seems to me, there is often a third party lying in bed with a broken heart and a bottle of vodka, thinking 'Why not me?' Not that Gloria is lying in bed with a bottle of vodka. She is far too ebullient for that. It's far more likely that she'll wiggle into into her rhinestone jeans and go out dancing. The word is that she is already enjoying a frisson – though possibly not the naked whirlpool baths yet – with a member of another *danse country* group in the area. (Honestly, who knew that there was so much going on among those checked shirts and Stetsons.)

Over dessert, I think about some of the people who've been part of my French adventure over the past few years, but who are no longer here. I will never forget, for example, L'Auberge de Claviers or its resilient former landlady. The chaotic quiz nights and sunny Wednesday mornings that I spent dancing there will always evoke fond memories. When I wonder out loud what happened to Barbara, Jocelyn says, 'Oh, didn't you know? She's back in Yorkshire and has a new boyfriend.'

'Really?' I say, delighted by this news (garnered, apparently, on a Ryanair flight when Jocelyn bumped into an old friend of Barbara's). Her French adventure may have ended badly, but I am so happy to hear that, in her late fifties, this stoical

Yorkshire woman has managed to find happiness and a new start – not to mention a new man.

'But it's such a shame about the line dancing coming to an end,' I say. 'We had so much fun that summer. It was the golden era of *la danse country*.'

'Well, actually, we've got some news on the line dancing front too,' says Jill. 'Some of the French ladies in my village have asked Jocelyn to start another beginner's group. And we might even have found a venue. La Grande Galerie in Civray has a room that might be big enough and the owners have said that we could use it.'

'You know,' says Delphine. 'I think this is going to be a very good year for all of us.'

It's been a lovely New Year's Eve but it's not over yet. Once my guests have slipped out into the cold, navy night, I look at my mobile and see that Luis has called half a dozen times. He has kept up the momentum all week, phoning and turning up at my door, pleading to be let in. On Christmas night, he stood outside for nearly an hour, throwing stones at my closed shutters and calling my name. I merely turned up the Joni Mitchell song that I was playing.

I take Biff out for his last walk of the day. After a slippery circuit of the square, still glittering with festive lights, I go home and get ready for bed. Then I kiss Biff goodnight, tell him to be good, and, wearing high heels this time, slip back out into the crystalline night. I make my way across the square to Luis's apartment, carefully so as not to slip in the snow. It would be little embarrassing to end up in casualty in just a coat, black lace and high heels.

Standing outside his building in the snow, I ring the bell and he appears at the window with a devilish grin. (And he doesn't yet know what I'm wearing under my coat.) *'Chérie!'* he cries and throws down his keys for me to let myself in the front door. Fortunately, I manage to catch them without falling over in the snow. I climb the wooden staircase to his first-floor apartment. He is waiting with the doors open, barefoot, wearing jeans and a bright pink T-shirt and a big smile. '*Merci, chérie,*' he says, throwing his arms around me. 'Thank you for giving me another chance. I have been waiting for you.'

'Don't make any more blunders,' I say, wagging my finger.

He looks contrite. '*Ka-renne*, I'm sorry.'

'*Regarde ça,*' he says, pointing around the sitting room, which looks immaculate as always. 'All week I have kept it tidy, so that it would be ready for you. Would you like a drink?'

'Yes, please.' I follow him into the kitchen. 'Where is Piedro?'

'He's gone back to Portugal for Christmas. I've got the place to myself for a week. Would you like some whisky?'

'Why not?' I say, taking a seat at the small kitchen table, still wearing my coat. I don't really care for 'whis-keee', as he pronounces it, but it makes a change from port.

'We can sit and talk all night if you want to,' he says, which is not exactly what I had in mind. He doesn't seem to think it odd that I'm sitting at the table, all buttoned up in my little black coat. He tells me about his forty-eight-hour trip to Portugal and how relieved he was to come back to Villiers.

'But didn't you want to spend Christmas and New Year in Portugal?' I say, knowing how much he loves his country.

'No, *chérie,*' he says, with conviction. 'I wanted to come back. I was worried that you might have found someone else.'

I tell him how upset I was, how injured by what happened.

'I know. I am very sorry. I was completely stupid,' he says, lighting a cigarette. His face looks even more macho, as he takes a drag, his eyes narrowing but all the time looking directly at me.

After several hours of talking – about Portugal, about France, about London (a place he has never visited) – we move into his neat, sparsely furnished bedroom. 'I've made the bed especially,' he says pointing at new orange and purple bed linen.

'*C'est magnifique,*' I say, finally unbuttoning my coat. '*Chéri,* I have a surprise for you.' He smiles appreciatively and pulls me to him.

'*Merci chérie,*' he says, as he unwraps me like a Christmas present. '*Merci beaucoup.*' And so my day ends with the best festive gift to myself that I could have imagined.

I had wrestled all week with whether or not to forgive Luis. When I asked Jill if it was a difficult decision to take Jocelyn back, she replied that she didn't have to think twice about it. 'It was what I'd been praying for,' she said. 'And doesn't everyone deserve a second chance?' I agreed wholeheartedly with that sentiment. But ultimately, for me, it all came down to one question: is my life better with Luis in it? The answer, I realised, is a resounding 'yes'. And so, when I wake up on New Year's Day, I'm back in those strong brown arms, under his psychedelic duvet, his solid, muscular body pressed against mine. 'Happy New Year,' I think to myself.

It's a Sunday afternoon in late summer and I'm sitting on car deck six waiting to disembark the ferry at Le Havre, after another work trip to London. My phone beeps with a text from Sarah: 'Biffy really missing you. Now sitting by the door waiting 4 U to return. The little fella seems to know U R back today. He sends hugs and a big lick. Sarah XX.' Just the thought of my black hairy pal with his black button nose and eager little face, is like a warm hug, a wave of pure, undiluted love and joy.

I see that Luis has also called several times, while I was mid channel with no signal, and this has a similar effect. Not even the man beeping his horn behind me can spoil the euphoria I feel at the thought of being reunited with him in a few hours' and 400 kilometres' time.

The car in front of me revs its engine and I follow it off the ferry, arriving back in France, to the extravagant August heat. The sun is high in the sky, which is a pure, wedding-garter blue. This time, I sail through Le Havre to the motorway, with no wrong turns or unintentional diversions.

For once, I know exactly where I am going and I am going there as fast as I can. I pay the toll to cross Le Pont de Tancarville and then drive south as fast as possible towards the big bold sun – to a land of smiling sunflowers, hay bales, rhapsodic blue sky, pink sunsets and wild poppies. There is an open road ahead of me – on a Sunday afternoon I have the autoroute to myself – and joy at the other end.

I've done this journey from Le Havre to Villiers many times in the four years that I've lived here – sometimes sad, sometimes excited and occasionally with a flash of optimism, or, most often, with a curious mix of all of these feelings. But never have I travelled so lightly, with such a feeling of pure happiness – and a sense that my life cannot get much better than this.

I drive at an exhilarating (barely legal) speed until I reach the services at L'Air de la Dentelle d'Alençon. I rush in, buy a Diet Coke for the purposes of staying alert, and head straight back to the car, not wanting to waste a single minute. With impeccable timing, just as I'm opening the car door, my phone bursts into life with a blast of salsa music – the special ringtone that I associate with one particular person. 'Where are you darling?' demands the gruff, masculine voice at the other end, sounding very impatient.

'I'll be with you very soon *chéri*,' I say.

'But where are you?' he demands.

'Still an hour and a half north of Tours,' I say. 'But not long now.'

'OK, *chérie*,' he says, mollified. 'Hurry up! I'm waiting for you.'

I jump back in my car and drive, as fast as I can, back to my village where everything I want and love is waiting. I have done this journey, from the ferry port to Villiers, many times but this time it is different. Finally, someone is waiting for me.

TOUT SWEET
Hanging Up My High Heels for a New Life in France

Karen Wheeler

ISBN: 978-1-55278-846-2   Paperback $18.95

Also available as an ebook

In her mid thirties, fashion editor Karen has it all: a handsome boyfriend, a fab flat in west London and an array of gorgeous shoes. But when Eric leaves, she hangs up her Manolos and waves goodbye to her glamorous city lifestyle to go it alone in a run-down house in rural Poitou-Charentes, central western France.

Acquiring a host of new friends and unsuitable suitors, she learns that true happiness can be found in the simplest of things – a bike ride through the countryside on a summer evening, or a kir or three in a neighbour's courtyard.

Perfect summer reading for anyone who dreams of chucking away their BlackBerry in favour of real blackberrying and downshifting to France.

'an hilarious account of a fashion guru who swaps Prada for paintbrushes and Pineau in rural France'

MAIL ON SUNDAY Travel

Have you enjoyed this book? If so, why not write a review on your favourite website?

Thanks very much for buying this McArthur & Company book.

www.mcarthur-co.com